THE ROAD TO
ROARINGWATER

Christopher Somerville was a teacher for many years before becoming a full-time writer and broadcaster. He contributes the 'Walk of the Month' feature for the *Saturday Telegraph*, and writes regularly for the Travel section of the *Sunday Times*, as well as presenting country walks on Anglia TV. He is married, and lives in Bristol with his family.

D1049067

By the same author

Walking Old Railways
Walking West Country Railways
Twelve Literary Walks
South Sea Stories
50 Best River Walks of Britain
Coastal Walks in England and Wales
Britain Beside the Sea
English Harbours and Coastal Villages (*with John Bethell*)
The Other British Isles
The Bedside Rambler (*editor*)
Welsh Borders
The Great British Countryside

THE ROAD TO ROARINGWATER

*A Walk Down the West
of Ireland*

Christopher Somerville

HarperCollins*Publishers*

HarperCollins*Publishers*
77–85 Fulham Palace Road,
Hammersmith, London W6 8JB

This paperback edition 1994
1 3 5 7 9 8 6 4 2

First published in Great Britain by
HarperCollins*Publishers* 1993

Copyright © Christopher Somerville 1993

The Author asserts the moral right to
be identified as the author of this work

ISBN 0 00 638102 2

Set in Ehrhardt by
Rowland Phototypesetting Ltd
Bury St Edmunds, Suffolk

Printed in Great Britain by
HarperCollinsManufacturing Glasgow

All rights reserved. No part of this publication may be
reproduced, stored in a retrieval system, or transmitted,
in any form or by any means, electronic, mechanical,
photocopying, recording or otherwise, without the prior
permission of the publishers.

This book is sold subject to the condition that it shall not,
by way of trade or otherwise, be lent, re-sold, hired out or
otherwise circulated without the publisher's prior consent
in any form of binding or cover other than that in which it
is published and without a similar condition including this
condition being imposed on the subsequent purchaser.

For all who walk
Ireland's countryside,
play her music
and sing her songs

CONTENTS

ILLUSTRATIONS

ACKNOWLEDGEMENTS

I planned and carried out this long walk through Ireland with the help and guidance of many kind people.

I'd especially like to thank Mark Rowlette of Bord Fáilte's London office, and Bob Cashman of Aer Lingus, for their invaluable help.

Cathal McConnell provided me with introductions to some of Ireland's great singers and music-makers; and I shamelessly used his well-respected name to establish my credentials with session musicians in bars and back kitchens from Banba's Crown to Baltimore. Father Liam Slattery of Clifton Cathedral put me in touch with his friend Father Michael Liston of Cratloe, Limerick, for which I'm very grateful. Michael and Biddy Somerville took time and trouble to acquaint me with the history of the Somervilles of Castletownshend, West Cork. I'd also like to thank John Brunner for suggesting the title of this book.

Among those who helped me along the way in Ireland, I'm delighted to express my thanks to Mr and Mrs Maurice Doyle of Malin Head; the staff of Hargadon's bar in Sligo; Nicholas Prins, administrator of the Gore-Booth family's affairs at Lissadell; Stanley and Eilish Diamond of Skreen; Michael Monaghan, who gave me a cup of tea and a sandwich in the wastes of the Bellacorick bog; Ernie Sweeney of Castlebar; Oliver Geraghty, who braved the Nephin Beg with me; Joe and Pauline McDermott of Skerdagh Outdoor Activities Centre, Newport; Frank and Phil Chambers of Newport; Pat Egan, Ulcan Masterson, Johnny Curtis, Matt and Geraldine Molloy and the other members of Westport's musical community; Didi Korner and Anne Kelly, who allowed me to share the magic of Island More; Theresa and Tom Conroy of Dunmánus, Glencoh; Kevin Gill of Inishmore, and Roger and Angela Faherty of Inishmaan in the Aran Islands.

I'm equally grateful to Eamonn Brophy, Mick and Colm of Taafe's bar in Galway city; the Kavanagh family of Cloonnabinnia; Tim Robinson and his 'Folding Landscapes' (truly reliable and informative companions in the wilderness); Maeve Fitzgerald, Teresa McGann and Gussie Russell of Doolin; John and Anne Sims, hospitable host and hostess of Island View near Lisdoonvarna; Tony Holden and Brigid Mullins of Kilfenora, who told me about Mullaghmore; Sean Spellissy, bookseller and writer of Ennis; Nuala Enright of Sixmile-bridge, who showed me how to play bingo; Donie and Geraldine Sullivan of Ardagh, and Geraldine's parents, for a spontaneous mid-day party; Maureen Curtin, Tom Finn (mastermind of the Dingle Way) and Paul de Grae, Dee Sullivan, Kevin, Kate and the other musicians of Paddy Mac's and Bailey's bars in Tralee; Pól and Marie O'Colmáin, Paul Duffy and Mary O'Flaherty, occasional dwellers on the Great Blasket, and Seán O'Catháin who was born and reared there; Jon Magna, my good friend, who came over to share a few days of the walk; Jack Buckley, Éimer, Leonard, Frances and Mary of Cork Mountaineering Club; Christy O'Leary, piper of Kenmare; Rose-Marie Salter-Townshend of Castletownshend; and, last but not least, the O'Driscolls of Cape Clear Island – Concubhar, Eleanor, Aisling, Croiona, Verona and Concubhar Og – who helped me cele-brate the end of the road to Roaringwater.

For permission to reproduce quoted material my thanks are due to the Gallery Press, Dublin, for 'A Farewell to English' by Michael Hartnett; Wolfhound Press, Dublin, for *Skerrett* by Liam O'Flaherty; Tim Enright and Chatto & Windus for *Twenty Years A-Growing* by Maurice O'Sullivan; the Educational Company of Ireland for *Peig* by Peig Sayers, published by the Talbot Press; and the Curtis Brown Group Ltd for *Some Experiences of an Irish RM* by Edith Œnone Somerville and Martin Ross.

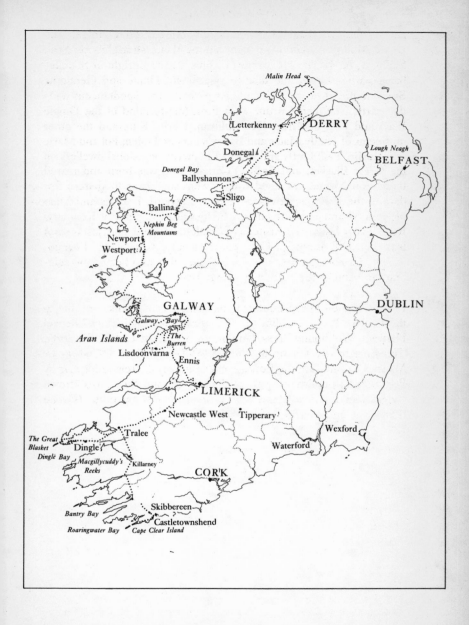

Malin Head

Letterkenny DERRY

Donegal Lough Neagh

BELFAST

Donegal Bay
Ballyshannon

Ballina Sligo

Nephin Beg
Mountains

Newport
Westport

GALWAY

Galway Bay

Aran Islands The
Burren

Lisdoonvarna Ennis

DUBLIN

LIMERICK

Newcastle West Tipperary

Wexford

Tralee

The Great
Blasket Dingle Waterford

Dingle Bay

Macgillycuddy's
Reeks Killarney

CORK

Skibbereen

Bantry Bay Castletownshend

Roaringwater Bay Cape Clear Island

WHERE'RE YE GOING?

The three little girls on pink bicycles were in a hurry to get where they were going. They had caught up with me as I hobbled down into Buncrana town after a long day among the Donegal hills and bogs, appearing as if by magic at my elbow, wobbling along in line astern like a flock of ducklings. Three pairs of china-blue eyes looked up at my pack and down at my peat-stained boots. Three wide mouths hung open in three freckled faces. I limped along the pavement, nursing my blisters and looking forward to a pint of Guinness at the first available pub, while my infant outriders back-pedalled energetically to stay abreast.

Suddenly the leader found her tongue. 'Where're ye goin'?' she demanded with a face-splitting grin. I hesitated. To County Cork, should I say? From top to bottom of Ireland? Thirty miles gone, and seven hundred more to go? At the moment it looked as if I might not even make it as far as that longed-for bar. I looked down at the inquisitive little face beside me, and opted for the short answer. 'Into Buncrana,' I said. 'And where are *you* going?'

She found room for a couple more inches of cheeky grin. 'To me auntie's, silly!' she piped triumphantly, and led her cohorts off in fits of giggles.

It was the question that everyone asked, sooner or later. The old man leaning on his gate, the solitary turf-cutter in the wilderness of a bog, the chance acquaintance chatting at the bar. 'Where're ye going?' Car drivers shouted it out of their windows as they drove past. Women popped their heads over washing lines to ask. Men stopped me in the street to find out. The pack lurching between my shoulder-blades, the hiking boots and the map were signs and symbols, filling in my stranger's outline with the colours of the free man freely travelling the roads and hills of Ireland. An agreeable, if not wholly justified, image: the unfettered wanderer with infinite time to spend, choosing new horizons as the mood took him. And as Ireland began to get its hooks into me, to drain me of hurry and worry, to fill me with the warmth of its hospitality and its uniquely relaxed tempo, I learned to travel hopefully and not to fret too much about the arriving.

Where was I going? From the northernmost point of Ireland, Malin Head, down to the southernmost headland, on the tip of Cape Clear Island at the mouth of Roaringwater Bay – yes, that broad itinerary always underpinned the journey. I aimed to shape a southward course from County Donegal and its borderlands with Northern Ireland into the Yeats country of the Sligo hills, out west among the vast peat bogs of Mayo and down through the Connemara mountains to the isolated Aran Islands in Galway Bay, in search of a traditional way of life that I had heard was on the brink of passing into history. From there I'd take a great loop through County Clare, tramping the limestone uplands of the Burren where Arctic and Mediterranean flowers grew side by side, looking for the pubs where old and young musicians still played Irish music for their own pleasure.

At Limerick city I planned to make a temporary break in the long chain of the journey and leapfrog fifty miles forward to explore the Dingle Peninsula in the soft rains of high summer, and see for myself the effects of the crowds of foreign tourists who at that time of year would be joining the holidaymaking Irish in their annual invasion of this out-of-the-way, Gaelic-speaking corner of the country. Then I would hop back again to Limerick to pick up the journey where I had left it and set out on the final stage of the road to Roaringwater – down lonely back roads through County Limerick and County Kerry, turning south by way of Killarney's celebrated lakes and mountains into the south-west toe of Ireland.

Why was I going? Because of a long-standing love of Irish traditional music and Irish literature. Because a country I had never set foot in had given me some of my best and warmest friends. To discover if, as I suspected from what those friends told me, the west of Ireland still sheltered pockets of resistance to twentieth-century life and its steam-rollering advance through the courtesy and hospitality of remote communities. To test my vague but undeniable fears of what twenty years of the current Troubles and centuries of disastrous history might bring, in the way of prejudice, dislike or outright confrontation, to an Englishman wandering through Ireland. To put those fears into perspective by hearing and seeing for myself, there on the ground. And, with a steadily rising excitement the nearer I came to starting the adventure, to plan and carry out a seven-hundred-mile journey on foot, by far the longest I had ever attempted, through unknown and difficult country: an irresistible personal challenge.

I soon realised that the journey as I had first dreamed it – a single, mighty, non-stop walk from start to finish – was not going to be a practical possibility. Fathers of four children have other calls on their time and energy, not to mention their bank balances. So I took the journey in sections of roughly a hundred miles, sometimes longer, flying back to England between stages to visit my family and let the impressions sift down and settle. Blisters healed during these breaks; strength returned; commitment sharpened.

Even so, my will often wavered. Car drivers would frequently slow as they passed me, winding down their windows to offer a lift. Once or twice, when the road was boring beyond endurance, or when the beguiler looked full of fun or fibs, I jumped in and rode for a mile or two. Once or twice, stuck on a lonely road at dusk in the rain, I let a bus carry me the fag-end of the day's journey. These sins of omission might perhaps have accounted for thirty or forty miles of the seven hundred. There were times, lying on a mountain top with my chin in my hands, sitting in a jam-packed room at midnight listening to a fiddle player at full tilt, wandering among the empty miles of a peat bog that stretched from one skyline to the other, when the purpose that drove me down those seven hundred miles misted over and shredded away. At such times I was glad to see it fade.

Walking down the length of Ireland, I learned to trust in the kindness of strangers and to expect nothing but the unexpected. Nothing was as I had imagined before setting out, and perhaps that was the best lesson of all. In short, I learned to slow down and open up, to do in Ireland what the Irish do. But I was still wrapped in perfect ignorance when, with winter rudely refusing to move over and make way for spring, I found myself on a freezing, boisterous morning marooned on Malin Head.

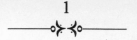
THE HILLS OF DONEGAL
Malin Head to Sligo

'Good luck,' said Maurice Doyle with a grin, shaking my hand under the gaunt old signalling tower on Banba's Crown. 'May the road rise to meet you.' He ducked back into his car out of the blasting April wind and drove off with a cheery wave, leaving me shivering on the northernmost tip of Ireland.

Malin Head looked as bleak as could be. The wind, roaring in from the north-east, was whipping the dark blue sea below the cliffs into racing ranks of whitecaps. It gusted round the ruins of wartime look-out huts and howled through the blank windows of the tower. Inland, the Inishowen Peninsula ran away southwards in wrinkles of brown and green, heather and grass bending low before the gale. A treeless, wind-scoured landscape, scattered with whitewashed farmhouses sited in hollows and in the lee of rocky outcrops out of the worst of the weather. The road snaked down from Banba's Crown and away out of sight in the direction of Malin Head village where the Doyles had put me up the previous night. Beyond rose the hills of Donegal, their pale blue domes humped under long streamers of cloud. And beyond again, invisible but vaguely outlined in my imagination, seven hundred miles of the loneliest and wildest land – Ireland from top to bottom, pregnant with possibilities, with adventure, with unheard stories and unsealed friendships. Just now, though, those miles lay heavily inside me, a cold lump of apprehension and unease.

Shouldering my pack, I noticed a tiny plastic doll's shoe lying in the grass beside the hut ruins. I picked it up and stowed it away in my anorak pocket with an obscure feeling of good omen. Then I turned my back on the whitened sea and set my boot to the first step of the road.

From Malin Head the blunt-browed peninsula of Inishowen broadens southwards, its flanks washed by Lough Swilly on the west and Lough Foyle, running up from Derry city (or Londonderry, depending on where your loyalties lie) in Northern Ireland, on the east. Lumpy with mountains in the centre, narrowing to a tiny waist where the two sea loughs converge thirty miles to the south, it's one of the remotest parts of the remote county of Donegal. Here, in spite of the advent of electricity and the motor car, life is still a struggle for the farmers who piece together a living from their tiny holdings among the bog, heather and rocks. For every snug, thatched house with peat smoke drifting from the chimney there is a tumbledown ruin, often in the same farmyard, proof of the harshness of country life that drives most Inishowen youngsters away to the cities or overseas to England or America as soon as they can get out. There's no romantic softness here to attract city escapers, no easing of the hard bond between people and land. The very first man I met was digging over his field by hand, driving a heavy, wide-bladed spade in with his boot and turning over an acre of black peat soil into furrows for his early potatoes by muscle power and the sweat of his brow. He had dug nearly half the field already that morning, and was in no mood to stop for a chat. 'How are ye doing?' he called, the Donegal greeting to friend or stranger. 'Oh, I'm fine – how are you?' I called back over the wall, but he was already hard at work on the next spadeful, head down and leg thrusting, absorbed in labour. It was a symbol that was to recur again and again on my journey down the west of Ireland – the solitary man in the empty landscape, basic labour against a back-drop of stark beauty, adding a guilty spice to my own freedom.

Primroses were struggling out into the spring sunshine along the road, glowing sherbet yellow in the dun brown of the winter heather, and the gorse was freckled over with buttery petals. Lark song rose, along with my spirits, as the road climbed over the shoulder of Knock-amany Bens to a breath-stopping view down on to the broad sands of Lagg Beach. Half a mile wide and two miles long, the beach ran away south towards the hills along the shore of Trawbreaga Bay, empty and shining, a perfect carpet of flat, white sand, shallowing so gradually into the green water that breakers were creaming in immense arcs a good mile out to sea. Behind this virgin beach minia-ture mountains of sand dunes were piled hundreds of feet high under dull green blankets of rough grass, their seaward angles scooped bare by windblow. I clambered down the hillside to the beach and trudged those two miles in delight, kicking up sand and humming 'The Hills of Donegal' against the battering of the wind. There were no ice cream wrappers, no radios or shouting people to mar the bare perfection of Lagg Beach. It was only that evening, in a bar in Carndonagh, that the realities of life a few miles from the border with Northern Ireland came into focus, when I heard of the cache of arms belonging to the IRA that had been discovered on the sands the previous year.

Now, though, Lagg sands lay in Eden-like emptiness as I rounded the point and made for the shore road down to Malin village. The waters of Trawbreaga Bay swept seaward as I walked on against their flow, sending the plovers screeching up from their pebble nests on the shingle banks. Curlews were pulling worms up from the sandbanks below the old arched bridge at Malin village, where I, too, looked about for some refreshment. The village was grouped charmingly round a triangular green studded with trees, with a gracious square-built hall off to one side and a tall, pinnacled church tower as a centrepiece. Snugly settled among its trees under the heather-covered hills, it recalled some lochside village in the Scottish highlands – not surprisingly, since it was laid out by Scots on land confiscated by that most Scottish of English kings, James I. Malin village was the first piece in the complicated jigsaw of Irish history whose overall picture was to become gradually clearer the further I walked along the road to Roaringwater. As the weeks and months unrolled and the landscapes shifted and changed, I learned to read the shapes of the towns and villages, the look of abandoned fields and what lay behind the faces of those who unfolded parts of the story to me in deep conversation or chance remark. The story of what had happened in the past to shape the Ireland of the present grew from casual jottings in a notebook to become a living and demanding thing. But not a hint of any of this disturbed the unruffled surface of my cluelessness on this first day out from Malin Head.

Back in 1541, when King Henry VIII of England proclaimed himself King of Ireland, he did so in the knowledge that the power of the English Crown had been steadily on the wane there for at least three centuries. In 1169 the Normans had been the first invaders from across the Irish Sea, invited over by Dermot MacMurrough, King of Leinster, to help him in his quarrel with the High King of All Ireland, Rory O'Connor. MacMurrough had abducted the High King's wife, and Rory O'Connor had seized the opportunity to banish his troublesome rival. At first the Normans made a great success of their invasion, grabbing land and building castles in an unstoppable surge across the country. England's shrewd Henry II quickly forced the submission of the Irish kings in 1171, and guarded his back by making a series of alliances with selected Irish chieftains to keep overall control in his hands rather than in those of his powerful and over-independent barons. But, with the help of Scottish supporters, the Irish fought back in a series of recaptures and victories over the following two centuries. By the time the Tudors were established on the throne of England the occupying forces were penned in a strip of coastline around Dublin known as 'The Pale', and English influence in Ireland was a very lame, if not yet quite a dead duck.

Against this background the Tudors moved to re-establish the authority of the Crown, rightly seeing Ireland as a cauldron of Catholic disaffection and a potential jumping-off point for an invasion of England. The Reformation had scarcely touched Ireland, and there were plenty of Irishmen with less than no love for the English and all they stood for. Henry VIII and Elizabeth I made sure that the sting was drawn from the Irish threat by confiscating estates and land, denying Catholic families all power and position, and imposing punitive penalties and taxes on them. There were rebellions – four major ones during Queen Elizabeth's reign – culminating in the rising of 1601 headed by the Earl of Tyrone, Hugh O'Neill, and stiffened by 4500 Spanish soldiers who landed in Ireland to join the rebels. All previous uprisings had been crushed, and this one was put down so vigorously by Lord Mountjoy, the English commander, that Irish insurgence came to a full stop. O'Neill fled the country, and by 1610 Ulster in the north-east was already in the hands of the English Crown and being 'planted' with Protestants loyal to England, along with Scots brought over for the purpose. The plantations continued all through the seventeenth century. Oliver Cromwell was especially assiduous in putting down rebellion, moving in his Ironsides in 1649 to end ten years of civil war with spectacular brutality, and packing most owners of land in the north and east of Ireland off to the rocky wastes of Connacht in the west. A new ruling class of English and Scottish Protestants took over the Irish properties and built their own settlements across the stolen country. Small wonder that new villages such as Malin, for all their neat precision of design, stuck out like blunt Scots thumbs from the empty hands of Ireland's landscape.

The flavour of this afternoon in Malin village was American-Irish. Near the bridge McClean's bar, as dark and somnolent as an Irish bar should be, was attached to McClean's grocery shop. In one corner of the bar Hollywood actors at their most wooden were playing out a laborious tale of murder and madness on the television screen, ignored by the young girl lounging in a pool of sunlight on the window seat idly picking her fingernails. Her boredom, given vent through a succession of cavernous yawns, was palpable.

The old man who ran the shop and bar came through to serve a customer. 'Back from Chicago, then?' he said as he waited for the Guinness to settle in the glass. 'Aye,' returned the man on the bar stool, 'and off back in six weeks' time.'

Walking out and across the bridge on the road to Carndonagh, I wondered how many of the men and women I had seen that morning forking over their peat fields and throwing buckets of scraps to the hens had been across the Atlantic for Christmas or Easter, visiting sons or sisters. For every young Donegal man or woman who heads away from the empty homelands to jobs and excitement in London or Birmingham, there is another flying off in the opposite direction to the imagined honeypots of the New World. These strong ties between Ireland and America – forged in suffering during the nine-teenth-century famine and eviction years, and continuing in high hopes in these more affluent times – were to become a dominant theme as I travelled on into Ireland's depopulated west.

The Donegal schools were making a late start the following morn-ing. I walked out of Carndonagh at a quarter to ten in the company of scores of teenage schoolchildren, larking, fighting, swearing, pushing each other into the road as they scuffled their way down to the day's lessons. Half of that exuberant bunch might have been destined in a couple of years' time to take the boat for England or the plane for New York, but just now they were full of the untrammelled joys of spring. 'McGuinness! McGuinness!' they jeered at a solemn boy sitting on the school wall gazing into the dark eyes of his girl. McGuinness, swinging one crumpled-trousered leg against the bare leg of his companion, was not to be lured into confrontation. I left the noisy gang taunting the young lovers, and took to the Buncrana road across the bog, with the larks for company.

Any traveller through Ireland sees plenty of bog, and this was a fine introduction to that characteristic landscape. Brown and grey, the peat wastes rose gradually on each side of the road, stretching off to the feet of rocky hills. Gorse clumps made bright splashes of colour in the drab blanket, along with green ribbons of grassy tracks leading out to the turf banks where blue-and-white plastic sacks stood in rows, full of cut turf. Chatting to the solitary turf-cutters I met in these vast bogs, I soon learned to drop the Scottish 'peat' in favour of the Irish 'turf'. Turf on this side of the Irish Sea is not the green and springy grass of the downlands of England, but the chocolate-brown underlying peat that burns in fireplaces all over Ireland.

I turned off the road and made my way up one of those winding bog roads towards a distant figure out in the wilderness, bent over his turf bank, an ant-size morsel of life labouring away under the 2000-foot crown of Slieve Snacht, the highest peak in Inishowen. A pair of ravens was tumbling with grating barks over his head, but he worked on with never an upward glance, digging a narrow-bladed spade into the side of his bank and slicing off the foot-long turfs with monotonous accuracy. A long, sickle-shaped mound of turfs stood on the edge of the bank, each peat brick full of whitened chips of wood. This landscape had once been covered with trees, and their bleached, splintery bones stuck up out of the bog as far as the eye could see. Massive trunks four and five feet thick lay where they had been dug out and thrown aside, bog timber perhaps thousands of years old. Bog, tree stumps, mountain and labouring man made up a picture unchanged through millennia. The turf-cutter gave me a wide grin, displaying rabbit teeth crookedly fixed in a bank of red gum, but had no word of greeting or conversation. We stood together for a few minutes, during which I became aware of the two squint eyes in his round moon face, behind which no words or thoughts were stirring. 'Well, goodbye,' I said to the blank eyes, and left him to his work. On the road a mile below I looked back and saw his tiny figure under the slope of Slieve Snacht, bending and straightening among the turf banks.

The road swooped on before me, up and down the swell of the boglands and round the flanks of hills, between two dully glinting reservoirs and up to a pass where I looked down on to the grey gleam of Lough Swilly and the tumbled hills of western Donegal rising beyond. In the sombre beauty of this uncompromising landscape the litter along the roadside struck an especially miserable note, calling to mind the waste-disposal customs of the Scottish islands where discarded 'carry-out' bottles and cans line every road, no matter how remote. Along the Buncrana road everything chuckable had been chucked out of passing car windows – plastic bottles, lager cans, cigarette packets, a music cassette still in its box, paper handkerchiefs, ice cream cartons, a telephone directory. There was a sourly symbolic warning for Donegal Catholics of the Lord's sense of humour: an empty packet of Durex Nu-form Extra Safe condoms entwined with a pair of knickers in a sedge clump, and a few yards further on a bottle of baby talc and a plastic nappy.

From this linear rubbish tip I walked down into the soft, pastoral country of the Crana River valley. The mountain ranges drew away, and fertile green fields watered by clear streams lay each side of the road in place of the sterile bog and its oily pools. Newborn lambs knelt on black knees, butting at the udders under the matted fleeces of their mothers. Primroses bloomed and birds sang in the hedgebanks between the tiny fields. I swung along in fine style, whistling jigs and looking forward over the widening silver coils of Lough Swilly, all the way down to Buncrana.

Two rivers come down from the hills at Buncrana – the Crana ('river of the trees') and the Owenkillew ('river of the woods') – to empty into Lough Swilly, the Lake of Shadows. Buncrana itself, designated 'a rather jaded seaside resort' in my guidebook, has another and more lyrical name: 'Parthas Eireann', Ireland's Paradise. More practically, it has become the Town of Jobs since the American textile company Fruit of the Loom set up its big factory here in the 1980s to produce sweatshirts and T-shirts. At that time half the youngsters of the Buncrana area, with no prospect of work at home, were emigrating to England and the United States. Fruit of the Loom gave them the opportunity to stay in their native town and earn good money. On my way along the seafront I met young girls coming in twos and threes from the enormous red-striped factory, lighting up fags and gossiping, glad to be shot of another day at the sewing machines. In the White Strand Motel, where I flopped exhausted into an armchair and ordered a restorative pint of Guinness, the barman was full of news of a giant reservoir soon to be built under Slieve Snacht, supplying two million gallons of water a day for Fruit of the Loom's operations at Buncrana. As we chatted and the shadows lengthened across Lough Swilly, the barman began to talk of the changes he had seen in his forty years.

'My grandparents, now,' he said, absently wiping a cloth across the bar top, 'they lived way up by Slieve Snacht at a little place they call Illies. My grandfather built the house himself with his own hands – this would be about 1900. He took the stones for the walls out of the fields and the roof timbers from the bog. The only things he had to have made for him were the windows and the door. They didn't have much, the old pair, but they lived well. I used to go up and stay with them, and I remember the milk, the eggs and bread, the vegetables, all produced by themselves. And all their neighbours in Illies were just the same. Today there's almost no land in cultivation up there. People might put in their potatoes and get their turf for the fire off the land, but that's all there is in it.

'When I came back home from England I was all for going up to live at Illies, but my wife wouldn't hear of it. And now I think she was right – the children wouldn't have stood it. No television, no video games, no entertainment laid on, and very lonely. But still, there's something tells me we're going all wrong. My grandparents raised nine healthy children out of that house, after all, and none of them any the worse for the lack of those things.'

For the walker, Irish maps are only one step short of a disaster. At a scale of two miles to the inch they show none of the footpaths and hill tracks which the Ordnance Survey sheets of Great Britain so clearly fix in place. It was small comfort to me that a splendid new series of 1:50,000 maps was about to be published by the Irish Ordnance Survey as I set out on my walk. The course of the long-abandoned Londonderry & Lough Swilly Railway, which I had hoped to follow down to Letterkenny the next day, was not even hinted at on my map. On the ground it proved to be entirely overgrown, a deceptive siren that lured me on from one impassable broken bridge to the next. I quested around in a marshy wilderness along the shores of the lough all day in a rising gale, cursing Irish mapmakers and field drainers with increasing vehemence. But my flounderings had one happy result: they led me over the slobs on to Inch Island.

As a description of what lay between the two embankments built by the railway company to link the mainland and Inch Island, 'slobs' can't be bettered. Marshes, wetlands, boggy ground – none of these quite catches the sloppy, slimy feeling of the Irish term. The six miles of low-lying ground between Lough Swilly and Derry were all slobs before drainage schemes and the coming of the railway in the 1850s dried them out; a wide corridor of wet marsh where wildfowl congregated in their hundreds of thousands and the secrets of the few firm trackways through the morass were known only to locals. The railway embankments shut the tides out from the slobs, trapping a remnant between Inch Island and the shore: two thousand acres of purple-brown freshwater wetlands fringed with stiff grey grasses where swans sail and great flocks of wigeon ride on the sheltered water. Stumbling down to the edge of the slobs from yet another fruitless search for the Letterkenny railway line, I walked beneath a heron hanging with frantically flapping wings above the screaming telephone wires on the embankment. He was still there in the same place, heaving unavailingly against the solid barrier of the wind, when I reached Inch Island and was blown like a feather, pack and all, along the margin of the slobs.

Inch Island lay swept by the wind, anchored by the thin arms of the embankments; a few quiet acres with that true island feeling of having dropped connections with the outside world. The lanes of Inch made a gently rising and falling circuit among whitewashed farms under the brown crest of Inch Top, the island's peak. I idled along between banks of stitchwort and speedwell, hailed by passing islanders with the universal Donegal greeting, 'How're ye doin'? How are ye?' – the equivalent of the Yorkshireman's 'How do?' or the Midlander's 'All right?', requiring only a nod or grunt by way of answer. The chirpy postmistress in the island's one shop, an Inch Islander to her fingertips and through many generations, had more to say. Anxious to defend the good name of Donegal, she deplored the violence over the border in Northern Ireland. 'So you plucked up your courage and came over,' she commented as she sold me a chocolate bar. 'And you've seen that we're not all mad over here?'

Insanity seemed to have seized the writer of the local walkers' guide to the area, as I discovered back on the mainland when I sought clarification of the map's unhelpful blankness. 'You can cross to the Letterkenny line,' he assured me when I halted on the brink of a broken bridge over a river. Yes, but how? Only by swimming the muddy water, or by flying. I slogged a mile upstream to a bridge unmarked on either map or guide, then gave it up in despair and aimed for something I needed neither map nor guide to make out – the dark block of the ancient hilltop fortification of Grianán Aileach, a landmark nearly three thousand years old.

From down by the lough the fort looked like a flat-topped pillbox hat perched on the crown of the hill. Up in the wind at eight hundred feet it stood in magnificent strength, a massive ring of stone three times the height of a man, its interior rising in three tiers to a narrow rampart over which the gale did its best to push me. The Irish Tourist Board, Bord Fáilte, had a photograph of two lovers smiling sweetly in broad sunshine on the rim of the fort, with a panorama of Lough Swilly and the whole of Inishowen sweeping away below. But this was another sort of day entirely. The wind flayed the old stones, heralding a milky storm of rain that blotted out the hills as I looked out from the rampart. Life up here must have been a wet and chilly affair for the O'Neill tribe who made Grianán Aileach their stronghold for many centuries before the Normans came to Ireland. Niall of the Nine Hostages was their greatest chief, High King of All

Ireland in the fifth century and a ferocious raider into Britain and Europe; his nickname was given to him in recognition of his prowess in war. His descendants split the clan, which divided into separate O'Neill and O'Donnell factions. The O'Donnells stayed on to rule Donegal, while the O'Neills went south and kept the grudge burning by claiming sovereignty over their ancestral land. The quarrel lasted for a thousand years, until the clan leaders Red Hugh O'Donnell and Hugh O'Neill, Earl of Tyrone, made common cause against James I in the hopeless rebellion of 1601. Their stronghold on Lough Swilly had been a ruin for hundreds of years by then, sacked and sacked again in the violent course of Irish history. Scene of many bloody battles, it was also a holy place, blessed by St Patrick when he came to preach there in AD 450. The fort was probably built around 1700 BC, with a strength in its solid circular shape that lasted the best part of two thousand years, until Murtagh O'Brien, King of Munster, laid it low in 1101. 'He ordered his soldiers to take away a stone for every sack of provisions they carried,' says *The Donegal Guide*, adding mildly: 'the place may have declined after this'. Grianán Aileach, the Temple of the Sun, was a sad jumble of broken walls by the 1870s, when Dr Walter Bernard of Derry decided to rebuild it to its original eighteen-foot height. The counties of Donegal, Derry, Antrim, Fermanagh and Tyrone are spread at the feet of the Temple of the Sun, but only Donegal and Derry were visible through the blur of rain as I paced a head-down circuit of its walls. The rain advanced, sweeping Inch Island behind its grey skirts. I put my back to the wind and bowled down the hill and along the lanes to Letterkenny.

Somewhere in the hills above the town towards the end of that long, damp day I came across an elderly couple driving their six cows and four calves through the puddles of the lane to their farmyard gate in the half-light of evening. Chickens were clucking around the yard, and a pig was rooting in the doorless entrance of a tumbledown two-storey farmhouse, long abandoned. The old couple's modern bungalow stood alongside, a neat white block in the muddy jumble of the farmyard. They stopped at the gate for a word. 'How are ye? How're ye doing? Off on a hike, are ye? And ye've picked the evening for it!'

I asked about their farm – whether they made a good living out of it. It was a sore point with the old man. 'There's no more money out of the government these days, and we don't get the pension. We're landowners, ye see,' he said sardonically, indicating with a sweep of his gnarled hand their dozen acres of stony Donegal hillside. What about their children? 'Oh, they're away from this. One boy's away doing sound for the big bands in America, and the other's in a recording studio down in Dublin. And the girl's a radiographer. Sure they wouldn't want to stay on the farm. It'll all go when we do.' The two wrinkled old faces looked worried and tired. I had touched a raw nerve: children raised and gone to make a more prosperous way in the world, and now the end in sight of generations of toil on that hard-bitten little farmstead. Limping down towards the lights of Letterkenny, I thought of what the barman at Buncrana had said, and wondered how long it would be before the old couple, along with their chickens and cows, their pigs and potatoes, were gone for ever from the hillside.

'Cold evening,' said the receptionist at Gallagher's Hotel as the door swung shut behind me. Gallagher's was a haven of warmth, of soft lights glowing on wooden panels. I sat down on the bed in my room and took stock of the effects of the first three days. Fifty miles walked. Feet? OK, though left heel blistered. Legs? Aching. Pack? Ref. Christian in *Pilgrim's Progress*. Spirits? Strangely low. None of the elation that normally accompanied the start of a walking adventure, and a depressing lack of energy. I eyed my pack, propped up against the chair. Thirty-five pounds of dead, dragging weight, crushing me hard to the ground at every step. Was it the culprit? I thought over its contents. Clothes, books, writing materials; washing things; maps and guides; camera; a pair of shoes. All seemingly indispensable. Then the survival gear – sleeping bag, survival bag, mint cake, spare laces, knife, whistle. How much of that could I jettison to lighten the load? Could I risk the lonely hills and bogs without it, trusting to luck and the kindness of dwellers in the wilderness? Why the hell was I feeling so low? I couldn't decide. Worse than that – I could hardly take off my boots. Lethargy folded its arms around me, as seductive and deadening as any drug, easing the pillow up to meet my descending head.

Next morning, looking in the mirror at two glazed red eyes and a streaming nose, I had my answer. The wind and rain on the hills had hatched something nasty in my bloodstream, given extra bite by the unseasonable cold. All Letterkenny seemed to be suffering the same malaise. In St Eunan's Cathedral the old men kneeling in the back pews coughed and snuffled over their prayers. The soaring Gothic chamber of the church, gloomy enough already in its grey and yellow paint, rang mournfully to the handkerchief explosions that punctuated their Hail Marys and Glory Be's. On the far side of the Cathedral square, peat smoke plumed horizontally in the wind from the tin chimneys of a line of travellers' caravans drawn up under a gorsy cliff. The tinker women shuffled in slippers from one caravan to the next, while their men in grimy vests picked over piles of rusty motor parts behind the vans and shouted at shivering dogs. It was a depressing picture, even allowing for the bug making merry in my system. 'Drop me a penny?' suggested a crop-haired, snot-nosed boy, appearing at my elbow. Scars on his scalp gaped through the stubble. His mother, peeping through the window of a chrome-smothered caravan, let the lace curtain fall resignedly as he trotted back to her penniless. Sweet charity would have to come from someone else today. I headed back to the warmth of Gallagher's Hotel, abandoning all thoughts of pushing on south until tomorrow.

Next day the bug had flown, and I made a dozen miles over the hills to Stranorlar with new springs in my heels. This was deep, wild country of low mountains and wide valleys, narrow packhorse bridges over fast-running rivers and miles of lonely road along which lay small farms. Their fields ran down the slopes, the higher ones pasture-land from which the stones had been laboriously scraped into great heaps by bygone generations, those down near the rivers tufted with sedge and sodden with water. I marched along, seeing no one, into Stranorlar, where a group of children were gazing entranced at a rusty old tank engine parked by the roadside on a low-loader. 'My father drove that engine on the Donegal Railway,' remarked an old man at his house door, seeing me smile with pleasure at the sight. 'She was called *Drumboe*. Many's the time me and my uncles would be on the road down to Donegal town, and my father coming the other way in the engine would lean out the cab waving and shouting, "There they are, the boys!" My uncles would be maybe eighty years old, but they were still "the boys" to him, d'ye see?'

In Stranorlar I had some hard thinking to do. The map, for what it was worth, showed minor roads and hill tracks crossing twenty miles of the loneliest country imaginable in a straightish line south-west towards Ballyshannon on the coast, where I planned to spend the following night. From Ballyshannon I would head south-west out of Donegal and into County Sligo and Yeats country. What I now noticed, and should have seen before, was a thin dotted line bulging out to enclose six or seven miles of the hill route: the border with Northern Ireland. One promise I had made to myself – and my family – before setting out on the journey, was to stay well clear of Northern Ireland and the possible risks to life and limb for a lone Englishman on the wrong side of the border. I might have been easier in my mind about that short dip in and out of the Province but for recent events that were the talk of Donegal as I walked through it. The latest incident had taken place only two days before I set off from Malin Head: the shooting dead of a young man at Castlederg, a village just a few miles across the border from Stranorlar. Now there were reports of firebombs on a Belfast to Dublin bus. I'd already noticed an unpleasant tension in the border towns and villages of Donegal. I called in at the Garda station and asked advice from the policemen there. From them I got a clearer picture of that remote country south of the town – a maze of back roads closed to traffic; empty miles of wilderness where Army helicopters might suddenly appear and land beside a solitary walker to pull him in for a round of questioning; isolated farms and fields where things might be happening which it would be bad to stumble across. 'But sure, you'll be fine. You'll see nobody, ten to one. That's right out in the wilderness,' said the young Garda reassuringly as his finger traced paths and roads he had never heard of down the map. I was not so sure.

The county of Donegal runs side by side with Northern Ireland from top to bottom. It's one of the ironies of the whole tragedy that from Malin Head on that first morning I found myself looking south, from the very top of Southern Ireland, at the northernmost point of Northern Ireland.

Nothing fits in the terrible jigsaw – not the geography, the politics or the human divisions. Now, in 1991, seventy years after the creation of the border, two separate sets of Troubles later, the news was still of tit-for-tat murders between Protestant and Catholic paramilitary organisations. Resentment between small sections of those communities burns with terrible, consuming heat; between much larger sections with a low but never-dying flame. And beneath the internecine strife still smoulders, in some hearts on both sides of the border, a residual dislike of the 'Brits', specifically the English. 'We're used to it,' the locals say of the soldiers, the searches, the guns and barbed wire that greet any trip across the border to the shops of Derry city or Strabane. But however polite the soldiers, and however necessary their presence, they symbolise repression to many people. Coming into Derry on my first evening on my way by bus to Malin Head, I had passed through the steel-jacketed, slit-windowed border cross-ings with their 'pigs' – armoured personnel carriers – parked snout to tail in squat menace along the road; had seen a young soldier in full battledress dramatically posed on one knee in a daffodil bed, aiming his snub-nosed automatic rifle down the road while a col-league opened the bonnet and boot of a car stopped at traffic lights. My skin had crawled with disbelief, in spite of two decades of tele-vision pictures of just this scene. Soldier and car driver were smiling pleasantly at one another, but what was going on behind the two masks? And how, come to that, could I know what effect my toffee-nosed English accent would have in bars and boarding houses, the nearer I approached the border? 'Ah, sure, you'll have no problem at all as a tourist,' soothed the Bord Fáilte representatives when I dis-closed my reluctance to fly to Belfast and take a bus across the province to Derry. 'What you hear is all terribly exaggerated by the media. There's no problem about being English at all.' Yet in sleepy Carndonagh I had been warned by an elderly farmer with one or three Guinnesses too many inside him, 'Don't you go crossing the border. You're English – just you keep out of that place. They're a pack of bloody murderers over there.'

Half reassured by what the Stranorlar Garda had said, I arranged for a taxi to drop me next morning at a point near enough to the border for me to slip unobtrusively across on foot. But the face of the landlady at my bed-and-breakfast place, white with shock and disapproval when I told her my plans, sent me back to the taxi driver. I found that he, too, had had a change of heart. 'No, I wouldn't go there if I was you. In God's good name, I wouldn't,' he said at once. 'You wouldn't know just who might be about on those back roads. It's a case of maybe finding yourself in the wrong place at the wrong time. That's a bad country about there, especially at the moment.' I told him that in that case I'd take the main road down towards Donegal town through the Barnesmore Gap, staying clear of trouble, and he grinned broadly in relief and poured me a cup of tea. His wife relaxed the anxious smile she had been holding, probably ever since hearing of his intended destination, and put on a tape of fiddle music – Aly Bain, the Shetland fiddler, playing his heart out at a concert. The tension dissolved. 'Do you know him, now? Ah, he's the great man!' and away we went over the tea cups in a spiral of reminiscence and tall musical stories. Up in the Scottish isles a couple of years before, the mention of Aly's name had opened all doors and all bottles to me, and here in another corner of the Celtic world my path was being smoothed again by acquaintance with that fiery little genius. We toasted him in tea, and I left the house whistling the Shetland air from the tape, with a load off my mind.

Spring's attempts to give winter a shove in the back were still making little progress as I tramped the track of the Donegal Railway through the Barnesmore Gap. This is one of the great scenic treasures of Ireland, a narrow pass four hundred feet above sea level where the road, the Lowerymore River and the old railway line squeeze south-west together under towering ridges that sweep up magnificently – Barnesmore on the south at almost fifteen hundred feet, and Croaghconnellagh looming more than two hundred feet higher to the north. There's a splendid Donegal Railway poster showing a night train roaring at full speed through the Gap, glowing like a meteor under the dark peaks. The railway was closed in 1959, leaving a winding trackbed to grow green and gorsy, and I followed it through successive bands of warm sunshine and showers of freezing sleet for mile after mile until a side lane enticed me down from the embankment and back into the lonely border landscape.

The Donegal Railway saw its share of excitement during those earlier Troubles of the 1920s, just after the creation of Northern Ireland. Running through wild hills where policemen were few and far between – nothing much has changed hereabouts in that regard – the railway was always under threat of attack. Trains were stopped, hijacked, derailed; railway employees were assaulted and passengers terrified on many occasions. In one famous incident a train was held up between Donegal and Ballyshannon by a Republican gang. But they had reckoned without the courage and resourcefulness of the General Manager of the Donegal Railway, Henry Forbes, who happened to be a passenger that day. As the train jerked to a halt Forbes drew the pistol he was prudently carrying, dropped on to the line out of sight of the hijackers, crept forward under cover of the train until he was level with the engine, and put the gang to flight with a burst of shots. He then chased them across a cornfield, managing to overtake and capture one of the men who had stumbled and fallen. The train was restarted, with the prisoner cowering under the General Manager's pistol. Not a policeman could be found at Donegal town, so Forbes continued to guard the man all the way up through the Barnesmore Gap to Stranorlar, where the forces of justice took him into custody.

There were no signposts along the side road I followed, but with the map held under my nose like a short-sighted priest at his breviary I made my way from one turning to the next, from bridge to bridge and farm to farm, through more lonely hill country. Some of those side roads, little more than muddy tracks, led off towards unpatrolled border crossings five miles away over the hills. Mindful of the concerned and kindly warnings I had received back at Stranorlar about what might or might not be going on behind the farmhouse curtains or in the tumbledown barns, I took no photographs and made no notes; just moved along as quickly and quietly as possible, swearing under my breath at the farm dogs that came snarling to the ends of their lanes. I didn't want to be seen pointing my Dazer at them: it might be mistaken for something a good deal deadlier.

The Dazer is an altogether splendid invention, a little box of tricks about the size of a spectacle case that fits neatly into the hand. You point it at any advancing cur and press a button, which causes the device to emit an ultrasonic beam of sound inaudible to the human ear but deafening to dogs. I have only the maker's word for this, but the effect is startling. Dogs curl up, run off or stop dead in their tracks. I had tried it on the first dog to go for my ankles, at the first farm gate I passed after setting off from Malin Head. To my discomfiture, the little light on top had refused to come on. The bloody thing must be broken, I thought as I resorted to the untechnological use of foul language and raised boot. In Carndonagh I showed the Dazer to the young man in the electrical shop. Could he do anything by way of repairs? Smiling patiently, he changed the battery. The red light glowed again. I tried it out on an inoffensive spaniel in the street. It bolted for home, whimpering. In the border country of County Donegal the Dazer would have saved me a lot of bother with the farm dogs, but I felt it would be better kept out of sight in my pocket.

There were old-fashioned beehive haycocks in the farmyards, and wafts of pungent turf smoke drifted across the lanes from the farmhouse chimneys. Among the primrose banks and catkins the miles wheeled slowly by. I passed through Bridgetown and Ballintra, tiny villages now bypassed by the broad highway of the N15 and free for the first time in many years from the pounding lorries and summer streams of tourist cars. Now, in the deathly silence of an April Sunday, they seemed free of all life as well. A couple of boys scuffling on the pavement in Ballintra stopped to gape as I went by, but they gave me no cheery 'How're ye doin'? How are ye?' It was a relief to come off the long road after twenty miles of silent trudging, into the plush foyer of Dorrian's Imperial Hotel in Ballyshannon, down on the south-western toe tip of County Donegal.

Ballyshannon has its place of honour in the misty uncertainty of Irish mythological history. Here, according to legend, the patriarch Parthelanus landed from Asia Minor to begin the first invasion of Ireland. Parthelanus was ninth in line of descent from Japhet, son of Noah, which would put his arrival at about the time of Abraham – perhaps 2000 BC. He is said to have set up his house on the tiny slip of rock called Inis Sainer that lies in the mouth of Ballyshannon harbour, where the River Erne snakes its way between great sandbanks to the sea in Donegal Bay. Parthelanus named the islet Sainer after a favourite hound belonging to his wife Dealgnait – a remorseful commemoration. The great man had dashed the dog's brains out on the flagstones in a fit of fury when he suspected Dealgnait of carrying on with a servant.

After a long bath and another inspection of the ever-deepening blister on my heel – the Donegal roads had done it no good at all – I wandered down to the harbour and stood looking out over Inis Sainer, picturing Parthelanus in his jealous rage. Herons were picking over the piles of seaweed on the shore. The sand dunes rose in grassy peaks across the harbour, whose winding channel shone in blinding silver sinuations under boiling black storm clouds over Donegal Bay. The bay's waters can be dangerous. They have claimed the lives of many fishermen, including the three commemorated by a monument that faces out to sea. The three men are shown transformed into joyously leaping dolphins – a beautiful and moving notion.

Walking back to the hotel I made an idle detour up to the church above the river and found myself staring at a graveslab with a familiar name. William Allingham, who had enjoyed a good measure of fame as a poet in Victorian times, died in London in 1889, aged sixty-five and full of honours. But he was born at Ballyshannon in a humble house in The Mall, a lane leading down to the harbour, and lies in the churchyard under a simple slab. Allingham wrote many better poems than the one he is remembered for, 'Up the Airy Mountain'. I had disliked that jingle on first contact with it at school, abhorring the tweeness of the 'wee folk, trooping all together' on Allingham's wretched mountainside. But somehow it had become the focus of a great bedtime game with all four of my children. 'Up the airy mountain, down the rushy glen, we daren't go a-hunting, for fear of little men,' I would chant, jigging the children on my knee. Then, in an unauthorised extension to the rhyme: 'The choo-choo train goes . . . UP!' (jerking the chortling infant upwards) 'and the choo-choo train goes . . .' (breathless pause, rounded eyes, fixed smile and bated breath – and that was just me) '. . . DOWN!' The victim would fall floorwards between my suddenly opened knees, to hang rigid with delight an inch from the carpet. Standing there at William Allingham's grave I gave him inward thanks for turning so many bedtime bad moods to laughter, and headed back through the rainy twilight to the hotel, missing the children with a sharp pang.

In the morning I walked out west along Ballyshannon harbour, not sorry to be turning my back on the tensions of the border country. The individual Donegal people I had met had all been pleasant to the stranger, and the Stranorlar taxi driver and his wife had shown me real hospitality. But there had been barriers, unspoken but clear, and a general feeling of something withheld. Greetings along the road had become more perfunctory, hands raised less often from steering wheels in salutation, the nearer the border had come to my line of travel. As soon as I walked out of Donegal and into the top corner of County Leitrim – and, within a couple of miles, out of Leitrim and across into County Sligo – the tension disappeared. A lorry driver, chugging lazily past, leaned out of his cab to shout, 'Aren't ye the happy man?' That's just what I was that bright, blowy morning, striding towards the great cliffs of the Benbulben range of hills that stood up ahead. With the sun on their green backs and their faces shadowed purple, they made a formidable barrier to the south, a rock rampart forcing the roads out and away along a great flat apron of coastline.

Exciting country, that lifted both eyes and heart out of the sloughs of the north.

I got as close to the feet of the hills as I could, climbing through the little resort village of Kinlough at the seaward end of Lough Melvin and on up side tracks across boggy wastes where curlews were calling and little groups of cows grazed among the clumps of sedge. Now the mountain wall, sweeping up from the plain, resolved itself into separate features of dome, cleft and sharp peak. Dead ahead rose the 1700-foot wedge of Ben Wisken, shooting up in a green arc to plunge dramatically over in a vertical black cliff. I trudged towards the peak, mesmerised by its knife-blade clarity against the clouds building over Sligo Bay. What was marked on the map as a road turned out to be a 'boreen', a narrow lane between stone walls, so little used by motor traffic that grass grew unchecked in its central strip. The banks under the stone walls were choked with spring flowers – primroses, violets, celandines, anemones, daisies – a brighter and more crowded spatter of colour than I had seen for many years in any English lane. I followed the boreen until an old man at his gate stopped me for a chat. 'I'm eighty years old, now,' he told me, rasping stubbly jaws ruminatively between finger and thumb as he gazed up at the hills behind his farm, 'but do you know, I used to walk to Sligo town regularly over that ould mountain. Up into that hollow, over the top with me and down to the road.'

'How long would you take to do that?' I asked. He gave me a wink, hinting at the nature of the pleasures that had called him over the hills to Sligo. 'Ah,' he said, ramming his stick in among the primroses, 'I was like a dog in those days. Like a dog! An hour and a half – I'm telling ye the truth! I could thravel then! Well, good luck to ye,' and he stumped away back to his house.

Turning the flank of Ben Wisken I saw ahead the flat-topped table of Benbulben, in whose shadow the poet William Butler Yeats lies buried. With the possible exception of James Joyce and Dublin, no Irishman is so identified with a part of Ireland as is Yeats with these mountain bluffs and valleys of north-eastern Sligo. Here, on the edge of what Bord Fáilte promotes as 'Yeats Country', I stopped in the flowery boreen to look down over fifteen miles of flat coastal country – turf bog, sedge marsh and pastures dotted with farms – and away back along a blue strip of Donegal Bay to the Donegal hills in the distance. Barnesmore and Croaghconnellagh were two tiny humps,

guarding the invisible Gap. Standing in the lane I thought my way
back through the burdened border land to Stranorlar, to Letterkenny
and the lonely peninsula of Inishowen. With Sligo still a few foot-
burning miles away, and the trend of my journey now set firmly to
the west, it was a good place to look north and say goodbye to the
hills of Donegal.

2

THE WILD NORTH-WEST
Sligo to Westport

Hargadon's bar in Sligo town at two o'clock on a sunny afternoon. A young couple with a baby sit at one end of the marble counter, sipping coffee. On the middle of the counter lean two elderly men with a whiskey apiece in front of them, their sticks propped against the dark wood panelling of the bar. I perch on a stool at the other end, my back against the wall, pack on the stone floor, sore feet idly swinging in the first soft shoes for a week. The baby babbles contentedly, but no one else has a word to say. Outside in O'Connell Street the sun beats down in thick spring warmth, but in Hargadon's a holy gloom lies on the panelling, the polished tables in the little half-glazed snuggeries and the sagging ranks of ancient apothecaries' medicine drawers across the room from the counter. On the walls hang mirrors embellished with the names of long-vanished brands of drink, and old tobacco advertisements featuring clean-cut ramblers in 1930s shorts and short-back-and-sides haircuts, filling their pipes on heathery hilltops. It's an unwritten but rigidly observed law that all Irish bars must have darkened windows to spare their customers the pain of the reality of the outside world, but the cool dimness of Hargadon's surpasses all. Here is found the Holy Grail of Irish drinkers, heavenly peace and quiet, the absence of all that jars or discomfits.

Pat the barman appears, wrinkling his brow in anxious concern for my empty glass. 'Would you like a look at the paper?' he murmurs, handing over a copy of the *Irish Times* as he sets my refill of Guinness on top of the beer-pump case to settle in its own good time. It takes five minutes for the creamy waves to course down inside the glass and darken to the finished black of the drinkable pint, but I'm in no hurry. Pat moves away to see to the other customers, returning to let a little more stout into my glass and fill it to the brim. I put my aching feet to the stone flags and limp over to the lamp-lit sanctuary of a panelled booth, glass in one hand and *Irish Times* under my arm. Here I lounge and read of a vote passed yesterday by a conference of the National Federation of Christian Brothers Schools Parent Councils, agreeing to maintain their stance against the sale of condoms to young persons. I note that the Archbishop of Cashel and Emily has urged parents and teachers to promote in children the Christian virtue of chastity. Then I cease reading, lay the paper on the bench beside me and give myself up to complete laziness. The creamy-topped pint in front of me has hardly been sipped, but that's not really the purpose of a long afternoon in Hargadon's. If you can't find contentment in that silence, and that cool brown half-light, you must be hard to please indeed.

Hargadon's, despite the silence, is known as a talking pub – a place with no piped music, where you go if you like a good long rattle. There are dangers in settling down in a talking pub such as Hargadon's, however. Some of the talk may not be altogether entertaining; and if you are trapped in one of those walled-in snuggeries, as I was when the bearded American slid in beside me, it can be hard to escape. 'Cultural energiser for the area' – was that the job description he gave himself? At the end of his monologue, a solid hour's worth, it was impossible to remember anything in detail. Something about exploring the creative relationship between ancient man and the Sligo landscape: a great deal more on his plans to mount a summer solstice celebration with flashing mirrors and torches on the hilltops around the town, with futuristic music booming from the valleys. Somehow he had persuaded the Irish government to part with a large grant of money to help him energise Sligo and its populace. He was only slightly taken aback to find that I had heard of none of the writers on the art/landscape interface that he quoted, and not in the least deterred by the complete silence I kept and could find no way of breaking. On and on he went, forbidding me to go where I was planning to go, laying out a new and dynamic route for me linking points of cosmic energy all over Ireland. Halfway through the ordeal, denied all opportunity to speak, I burst out in a spasm of uncontrollable nervous laughter. The energiser gave me the briefest of startled glances and went right on with his solo performance. I clenched my fists beneath the table and stuck it out until he went away to drain someone else's patience.

Sligo town was not entirely sunk in lethargy. Outside the record shop the high school boys at the end of their lunch break thronged in their skin-tight trousers and pencil-slim ties. Along the lines of old-fashioned tailors' shops and grocers the pavements were busy with Sligo folk about their business. 'No, I won't tell ye the way to the bank – I'll take ye there meself,' said the man on the street corner, 'and could ye spare me a pound, could ye?'

Sligo is an eighteenth-century town in feel and appearance, with its shabby but still elegant houses and shops packed tight along the streets. It's a courteous town, too. 'How are ye?' say passers-by as their eyes meet yours. In the library I asked for Robert Lloyd Praeger's classic Irish travel book, *The Way That I Went*, a stirring mish-mash of botany, geology, legend and anecdote that I had sought in vain in the Sligo bookshops. Overhearing my request, an old man at the counter held up a copy. 'I was about to take it out,' he smiled, 'but sure you're welcome to it. I'll call back for it tomorrow. Not at all – you're very welcome, now.'

Informality is the keynote in Sligo, in public as well as in private. At dinner time in the restaurant of the Clarence Hotel the young barman/waiter/man-of-all-work sat with his back to the guests at a table by the kitchen door, stolidly munching his way through a great plate of chicken and tomato sauce washed down with cups of strong tea. At breakfast next morning there was another hotel employee hunched in the same chair, crunching through a mound of toast. On another evening in Sligo's Chinese restaurant I watched the teenage waitress make a leisurely round of the tables, stopping to exchange local gossip with each diner in turn. 'So they've moved, have they? Above in Wine Street now? And the tall feller – him with the yeller car – I hear he's lost his lovely girlfriend, the poor man.'

Down along the quay by the river, abandoned warehouses raised rotting stone walls lined with barred, broken windows. In these back quarters of Sligo I caught the feeling of a place little changed by the years. But the modern world has inexorably set its mark on the town. Right beside the imposing old town hall a monstrous multi-storey car park, as ugly as it was badly-needed, was creeping skywards layer by layer. And by the bridge the mills that once put money in the purses of the Pollexfen family have given way to the up-to-date Silver Swan Hotel.

It was with the Pollexfens that William Butler Yeats spent the childhood holidays that fixed Sligo and its mountains and coast as a lasting influence – perhaps the most important one – on the rest of his life. His father, John Butler Yeats, was a prodigal and hard-up artist, and Mrs Yeats came again and again with her children to stay in Sligo when times were tough at home in Dublin or London. She had been born a Pollexfen, and both she and the children found security in the familiar town. William roamed far and wide over the countryside around Sligo as a boy in the 1870s and 1880s. The long, cliff-encircled back of Benbulben to the north of the town was the focus of many an excursion, remembered in such later poems as 'Towards Break of Day':

> I thought: 'There is a waterfall
> Upon Ben Bulben side
> That all my childhood counted dear;
> Were I to travel far and wide
> I could not find a thing so dear.'
> My memories had magnified
> So many times childish delight.

In 'The Tower', written when he was in his sixties, he dreams back to boyhood in Sligo,

> . . . When with rod and fly,
> Or the humbler worm, I climbed Ben Bulben's back
> And had the livelong summer day to spend.

In early obscurity and later fame, Yeats had Sligo in his blood-stream. These days he is in many ways the lifeblood of the town in return. There's a bronze statue of him by the bridge, striding on spindly legs, cloak blowing, hair and bow-tie flopping, round spectacles perched on arrogantly tilted nose. His clothes, at first glance seemingly patterned in a horribly loud check, turn out on closer inspection to be inscribed all over with lines from his poetry. Scholars, poets, lovers of Yeats, Americans in search of their roots, students in search of inspiration, all flock in summer to the little town under the hills to try and see what Yeats saw. They drive up the narrow roads into 'Yeats Country' for a view from the tops. And they cluster round the poet's grave in Drumcliff churchyard under Benbulben where he was brought to be buried in 1948, nine years after his death in France. Yeats wrote his own epitaph four months before he died, in the poem 'Under Ben Bulben':

> Under bare Ben Bulben's head
> In Drumcliff churchyard Yeats is laid.
> An ancestor was rector there
> Long years ago, a church stands near,
> By the road an ancient cross.
> No marble, no conventional phrase;
> On limestone quarried near the spot
> By his command these words are cut:
>
> *Cast a cold eye*
> *On life, on death.*
> *Horseman, pass by!*

Sligo people don't on the whole display a passionate interest in Yeats. Familiarity has bred, not contempt, but an easy and rather dismissive familiarity. He's an efficient money-spinner for the town, and 'a grand old fellow, sure he was,' as more than one person told me. I heard a good story about the grave-worship in Drumcliff: 'A couple of fellers I know was cutting the grass in that graveyard, and what should they see but a great coachload of Yanks in the road. Quick as a flash they knocked a slit in the top of their lunch tin and put it down on the grave like a church collection box. And then they went for a little walk. When they came back the old box was half full of money. That paid for a few drinks, and no one the wiser.'

Yeats's family connections with the district, and his growing reputation as a young poet in the 1880s and 1890s, made him welcome in many houses in and around Sligo. One of the most liberal and sympathetic of the Anglo-Irish families, the Gore-Booths, had lived at Lissadell, a few miles from Drumcliff on the shore of Drumcliff Bay, since 1604 – well before the great 'plantations' of Cromwellian days. Yeats first came to Lissadell in 1894, a dreamy and fervently nationalistic poet just about to turn thirty, and made friends with Constance and Eva, the daughters of Sir Henry and Lady Gore-Booth. The rich and influential long-term English settlers known collectively as the Ascendancy were not usually as supportive of the Irish desire for Home Rule and a resurgence of Gaelic culture as were the Gore-Booths. Eva was a poet herself, and became a notable champion of the rights of working women, while her sister, Constance, threw herself body and soul behind the nationalist cause. In 1900 she married Count Casimir Markiewicz, a Polish nobleman and painter she had met while an art student in Paris, but the marriage did not last long. Constance's daughter Maeve was left at the age of six to be brought up by her grandmother at Lissadell, while Constance herself continued a fiery path culminating in a sentence of death for her active part in the Easter Rising of 1916 in Dublin. She was pardoned, but served a term in prison. Soon she was back in jail again for making inflammatory speeches in support of Sinn Fein, the political movement that in 1919 was to form an alternative – and bitterly anti-British – government of Ireland. During this second sentence Yeats was to write the poem 'On a Political Prisoner' for her, though scarcely in her honour. He had undergone his own spiritual pilgrimage from airy Celtic mysticism and nostalgia, through burning nationalism and out again the other side. The executions of fifteen leaders of the Easter Rising in the months following the abortive rebellion had shocked him back into a more cautious nationalism, but he regretted the effects of such angry politics on so many of his erstwhile friends. In his poem, Yeats remembered Constance Gore-Booth, the young horsewoman, as she was in the years at Lissadell:

> When long ago I saw her ride,
> Under Ben Bulben to the meet,
> The beauty of her country-side
> With all youth's lonely wildness stirred,
> She seemed to have grown clean and sweet
> Like any rock-bred, sea-borne bird . . .

I was looking forward to visiting Lissadell, attracted by that mellifluous name and by Yeats's evocative description of

> The light of evening, Lissadell,
> Great windows open to the south,
> Two girls in silk kimonos, both
> Beautiful, one a gazelle.

An elderly nephew and niece of Constance and Eva Gore-Booth still lived in the big house, I was told in Sligo, and they usually opened both house and grounds to visitors in the summer. This early in the year Lissadell was still closed, but a short phone call was all it took to put me in the front seat of a roaring old Land-Rover driven by the family's administrator, Nicholas Prins. As we clattered out of Sligo, Nicholas gave me a potted history of the Gore-Booth fortunes since Yeats's time – a gentle and melancholy decline. Sir Jocelyn Gore-Booth, the brother of Constance and Eva, had had eight children; his heir had been a ward of court since his twenties due to mental illness, two other sons had been killed in the Second World War, the girls had remained unmarried and for the past forty years the estate had been indifferently run by the Irish High Court, which had taken over its administration. The great house itself, built in 1832 by Sir Robert Gore-Booth, had slowly decayed as rain, wind and neglect nibbled away at its fabric. Now the estate was once more in the hands of the family, and Nicholas was working piece by piece, as time and money allowed, to get the affairs of Lissadell running smoothly again.

We jolted to a stop in the old dairy yard where crumbling cattle sheds surrounded a nettle-choked midden. Cast-iron milking stalls, the latest thing in dairy technology when they were introduced nearly a century ago, rusted in their sheds, and wooden chairs and cupboards rotted in the damp rooms of the cowherd's house. Beyond the yard stood other estate workers' cottages, smothered with ivy up to their tottering chimney stacks. 'We're renting out the dairy yard to a shellfish company,' said Nicholas, opening a worm-eaten door on a line of steel tanks. 'The cottages we're hoping to convert into holiday accommodation. Most of the farm land on the estate is rented out, and we're doing some commercial felling in the woods. But you can see the work involved.' He gestured at the ivied cottages and the overgrown woodland behind them. 'It's a question of as and when. I run my own farm, so I can only give a certain amount of time to this. But I enjoy doing it.' His courteous smile held a hint of steel. 'The Ascendancy families are all written off these days as finished and done for. The government would love to buy up Lissadell and turn it into a Yeats Centre, but it would be very satisfying if the family could go it alone. I'm happy to help them try to do that.'

The dark grey block of Lissadell house faced out on to long grass and overgrown shrubs, a cold and drab picture. The full effect of decades of penny-pinching came home as we wandered through the stately rooms. Fine pictures, gathered in the 1830s from all corners of Europe, hung round the walls of the ballroom under tarnished gold chandeliers. Their colours lay hidden beneath the dark stains of the years. Dust clung thickly round the echoing stairwell which rose from the entrance hall to bedrooms where rainwater ran down the walls, loosening the ancient embossed wallpaper that hung down in curling strips. Shelf upon shelf of books stood mouldering in the billiard room: books of Irish history, of *belles lettres*, books on polar exploration collected by Sir Henry Gore-Booth, father of Yeats's friends and a famous polar adventurer of his day. Nicholas Prins stooped to a cupboard and pulled out a yellowing bundle of letters written to Sir Robert Gore-Booth by his friend Lord Palmerston, the British prime minister. Down in the gloom of the basement the kitchens, store rooms and cellars lay cold and empty. 'I always think of Lissadell as a great ship,' Nicholas remarked as we surveyed a kitchen range vast enough to serve a fleet. 'It ran on the same basic ingredients – mountains of coal and mountains of labour.'

We climbed up ladders and through the dust-laden attic beams, out on to the slate roof of Lissadell. Dark ranks of conifers, planted by the High Court administrators during their long tenure of the estate, boxed in the house like a blank-faced army. But over their massed tops the view that Yeats knew could be seen: long-backed Benbulben to the north, Drumcliff Bay on the seaward flanks of the estate, Knocknarea beyond with the flat-topped tomb of Queen Maeve, the legendary warrior-queen of Connacht, on its summit. The gloom of Lissadell lifted as I gazed at the surrounding mountaintops. Now I could appreciate how superbly the house had been sited, and just what an inspiring view it had commanded before the conifers had closed in. But these roofs, sloping inward to badly placed gutters, had a fatal design flaw. It hadn't mattered when there had been a score of maintenance workers to keep the gutters clear, but now neglect had let the rain down inside the walls to eat away at the very bones of the house.

Two of Sir Jocelyn Gore-Booth's children, frail and elderly these days, still live at Lissadell. Back in the hall, Angus Gore-Booth hovered diffidently in the doorway for the ghost of a handshake before slipping away. His sister Aideen stayed bravely at her station to shake more hands. Forty ladies from Waterford had arrived by coach for a pre-season special tour. Nicholas Prins took charge, sweeping them off in a quietly murmuring group to view the dining room where Count Markiewicz had painted portraits of the family and their servants on the walls in waggish mood one long-ago evening. Waiting for the Land-Rover ride back to Sligo, I wandered off into the shrubberies where the rhododendrons, tangled together in overgrown thickets, soon shut away the big old house and its imprisoning hosts of conifers.

My last night in Sligo was a lively one, an evening of thunderous cajun and country music in TD's pub. A bunch of tubby middle-aged men had forsaken their families to whip up a tremendous mood on the pub's tiny stage, laying into their guitars with fret-melting enthusiasm, while in their midst a young demon fiddler sawed away, flicking his sly cat's eyes sideways at the girls. There was a sober point to the evening's jollity: the raising of as much money as possible towards the £50,000 needed to send a young Sligo boy with cerebral palsy across to England for residential treatment. 'If you could take a look in that little lad's eyes you'd empty every penny in your pockets,' said one of the guitarists as he brought round a collecting bucket. Money rained into the buckets, and music poured out with the Guinness until the early hours. Next morning, yawning prodigiously, I left Sligo with regret. Shabby, friendly and relaxed, it had been the perfect place to shake off the last of the border blues.

On the road down to Ballysodare the map led me astray once more. A woman with a rosary wrapped round one hand stopped to put me on the right track, but before doing so she unburdened herself about the Troubles. 'Sure it's terrible what they're doing to each other up in the North, murdering each other. You wouldn't do to an animal what they're doing to human beings. There's no sign of peace in it at all.' The rosary beads rattled through her fingers. She had been reading in her morning paper of yet another killing, a car bomb in Armagh that had blown a Protestant businessman to pieces as he waited at traffic lights. 'It would be such a beautiful island if only people would live in peace with each other. These talks, now – they can't even agree on a place to hold them. Did you ever hear of anything so stupid?'

The talks – the Brooke initiative, as the newspapers had styled them – had dominated the headlines for the past couple of weeks. After many months of subtle moves behind the scenes, the Northern Ireland Secretary, Peter Brooke, had succeeded in getting both Loyalist and Republican leaders to agree to sit down together at the same table and discuss the future of the Province. No one had dreamed that a British politician could have made so much progress, but Brooke was proving to be a sympathetic and long-sighted man with a better grasp of the realities of the situation than his predecessors in the uncoveted post. All the parties had convened at Stormont Castle in Belfast. But now familiar noises were making themselves heard. The Irish government would have to be involved, as all sides had agreed. But the Unionists would not hear of going to Dublin for that stage of the talks unless the Irish government would agree to renounce its claims on the Province, which Dublin would not countenance. Well-worn tracks, round which the aimless greyhounds of stubbornness and intransigence were starting yet another circuit. Desperate compromises were being sought. How about the Scilly Isles? Somewhere on the Continent? A submarine? An exasperated Peter

Brooke was preparing to issue an ultimatum, with strict time limits for deciding on a venue. The fog seemed to be closing in once more, and all those bright hopes were in danger of being dashed. Meanwhile, the car bomb in Armagh and the agitated rattling of the rosary in the sunny Sligo lane.

With a sigh and a shrug, the woman pulled herself back to the matter in hand. 'Oh yes, the road to Ballysodare. Well, you take that lane there, now, and you'll come to St Bridget's Well. That's where they used to say Mass when it was outlawed, back in the old days. Then you go round by the end of Lough Gill and you'll find the road there. Goodbye, now, and God bless.'

There was no danger of missing the holy well. A great statue of Jesus on the cross stood high on a shady bank among trees above the stone wall that enclosed the gently stirring water, along with a blue-shawled Mary, a stand for votive candles and marble tablets inscribed with prayers to St Bridget. It was the lunch-break hour, and local people were paying quick visits to the shrine. A young man in jeans and a fashionable windcheater was dipping a jug in the well as I came down the path. He drank, then stood in prayer in front of the candles. A man and his teenage daughter parked their car and came up to the well for a quiet five minutes. An old couple followed them, arm in arm. A spare half hour in the middle of the day – so pop up to St Bridget's Well and say a few prayers. It was all as natural as breathing, and it eased the bitterness of the morning's news from Belfast and Armagh.

Down by Lough Gill the road was lined with horsetails among the primroses and violets. The boggy ground was thick with carr woodland of alder and willow, and long beds of reeds ran out into the flat waters of the lake. Knobbled hills of bare limestone made a frame for the water. A tiny old man, spotting me a long way off, got off his bike as I greeted him to give me his life story in the well-turned phrases of a poet. 'I was a young man up in Newcastle upon Tyne. Sure, they're an innocent type of race up there. I had a lovely girl in that sweet town, but what I didn't have was so much money as would buy her a birthday present. But I brought her a kiss, and maybe a little bit more, for they're partial to such things in those parts. And who isn't?' I said I couldn't imagine anyone who wasn't, and he grinned delightedly. 'Now, you have it! You have it right! It's a lovely world, sure it is, with the colours of the clouds and the blue sky, and the colour of the children going to school, and the colours of the cars on the white roads, and the cows in these fields. And if you'd like to camp in any of our fields here, you're as welcome as the flowers in spring.' Walking on, I began to wonder if I had just been treated to my first slice of full-strength Irish blarney.

At Ballysodare, the 'town of the waterfall of the oak tree', the river ran under a bridge and crashed down towards the sea over a series of weirs. The mills they once powered stood forlorn and derelict along the banks, windows smashed and high walls green with moss. There were older ruins along the bay, where green hummocks overgrown with hawthorn hid the stones of a monastery founded in the seventh century. The community's church was a collapsing shell of masonry entirely swallowed by ivy, a rounded Romanesque doorway its only recognisable feature. In the jungly graveyard I unshipped my pack and wandered unburdened around the headstones – John McLoughlin (1894) and his wife Catherine (1896), whose son had come all the way over from Pawtucket, Rhode Island to bury them; Annie, John and Florry Byrne, all dead in infancy at the turn of the century, lying together under a tablet 'Erected by their Father'. The ruins of the church, graveyard and mills were silent under the afternoon sunshine, but back at Ballysodare bridge there was plenty of noise from the youngsters just released from school. Smoking, swearing, spending their bus money in the shop and then trying to hitch lifts, they sparked crude life into the sleepy day.

'So you're visiting? Did you know that W.B. Yeats used to stay here?' demanded a man in the village street, stopping me with a hand on my arm. 'The Pollexfens owned all these mills. Yeats used to exercise his horses in the fields round by the old church. That's news to you, now.'

'Do you like his poetry?' I asked. He chuckled and slapped his palms together in amusement. 'We suffered him in school!'

At Ballysodare the coastline stops meandering southward and turns for a long seventy-mile run to the west. County Sligo gives way to County Mayo here in Ireland's loneliest and least-visited corner. Clean beaches, rocky headlands and wide bays line the coast, free of all modern seaside development. Two great and ancient mountain ranges, the Ox Mountains and the Nephin Beg, rise from a hinterland of vast blanket bogs – eternally waterlogged, ever-expanding wastes of peat and pool – around whose edges the little towns and villages lie widely scattered along roads that see scarcely any traffic outside the couple of summertime tourist months, and not much then. This was one of the hardest-hit areas in the Great Famine of 1845–9, when people died in thousands from disease and starvation in their turf huts and on the roads to the handful of workhouses, and as much as half the population fled to Britain or America. Youngsters are leaving today, too, unable to find work on the tiny farms and unwilling to miss out on all the glories revealed to them on their television screens. The fishing, the walking, the beaches and mountains are superb, but tourism is still only in its infancy here. You can feel more truly alone in the Nephin Beg, more out of touch with the modern world in the bogs of Mayo or on the back roads out towards the Mullet Peninsula in the extreme north-west corner of the area, than almost anywhere else in the whole island. The Nephin Beg in particular, 150 square miles of roadless mountains sprawling down through the west of Mayo, gave me pause for thought. Somehow I had to find my way round or over them, on a path marked on the half-inch map – but I had learned to put little or no faith in the map when it came to roadless country. 'Wind-swept and desolate and inaccessible', commented Robert Lloyd Praeger in *The Way That I Went*. The Nephin Beg were going to put me to the test, I could see. But for the moment, striding out of Ballysodare on another bitterly cold morning – the wind seemed to have got itself stuck in the north this spring – it was the Ox Mountains that stood in my way.

I chose a north-facing corner of the hills, which probably explains how I came to be scrambling down a rockface halfway through the afternoon with fingers so white and frozen they could hardly grip the tufts of heather. I was chilled right through to the bone and beyond, whistled off those knobby ridges by a wind with a wintry cutting edge. The plan had been to hurry along from peak to peak for five airy miles, but they had turned out to be a damn sight too airy. Early on I had enjoyed a classic view over Yeats country from the 900-foot summit of Doomore, with all the poet's favourite heights assembled – Knocknarea in the foreground, Slieve League misted by cloud across Sligo Bay, the ship's prow of Benbulben standing out small but sharp ten miles away – and at my feet the Ballysodare River winding out to sea through its sandbanks in a succession of silvery bows and curves. Inland the Ox Mountains swooped away towards

Mayo in long brown shoulders. Their rocks, the oldest in Sligo, had been buckled and squeezed over five hundred million years into fantastic patterns of loop and swirl, with layers of hard white quartzite baked between the folds. The heather grew along the ridges in knee-high tufts, concealing cracks in the underlying peat down which my boots would plunge every couple of minutes into soft, gulping bog. There were no boot marks other than my own on the ground: scarcely even a sheep track. I crunched and high-stepped along, sliding and stumbling, until the rising wind almost succeeded in pushing me over one of the quartzite cliffs. It was time to take my deep-frozen hands out of their pocket haven and warm them up with some palm-skinning slides down the crags.

Down below, in the graveyard at the hamlet of Skreen, I took it easy for a while among the monuments. Some local stonemason had possessed more than his share of skill, to judge by the carvings on the table tombs decaying in the tangle of undergrowth. The same confident hand had worked the smooth grey limestone of several monuments into puff-cheeked seraphim glowering from garlands of fruit and flowers, and had carved beautifully shaped letters in the inscriptions. The best work by far had been commissioned in 1826 by the son of one Alexander Black, a local farmer who had died in 1810, aged sixty-three. Mr Black was shown at his familiar daily labour, ploughing a field; but surely he would never have risked such Sunday-go-to-Mass finery in the mire of a half-ploughed field. In top hat, immaculate stock, tail coat with a multitude of buttons, waistcoat, knee breeches, stockings and fancy shoes, he strode behind his plough after a pair of fine-faced horses that would have better suited a racetrack. The tools of his calling hung in mid-air above the plough – flail, hay rake and fork, shovel and spade. There was nothing rough or rustic in the mason's display of mingled craftsmanship and artistry.

By one of those happy coincidences not to be planned or foreseen, my bed-and-breakfast host that night turned out to be the great-grandson of that master carver. Stanley Diamond's ancestors had come over to Ireland at some time in the distant past – from Palestine, he thought – and the mason's skill had been passed from one generation to the next in an unbroken line. Stanley himself was a mason, though his work was mostly restricted these days to what brought the steady money in: carving plain inscriptions (no seraphim or top hats) on headstones.

His wife Eilish greeted me with rhubarb pie and oceans of hot tea. Stanley, coming home with a day's stone dirt still on his hands and clothes, took ten minutes to wash himself and then settled with his stockinged feet up on the sofa to entertain me with talk of his time working in Northern Ireland, when he would find himself 'invited' to contribute to Loyalist collections at meetings inflamed by the Rev. Ian Paisley – and a couple of hours later Republican activists would knock at the door of his lodgings with their own collecting buckets. Eilish capped that story with one of her own about the punishment meted out to a Protestant woman of her acquaintance who had recounted it in anguish: 'Sure, they couldn't have done worse! They made me kneel down and say the Hail Mary!' In the morning, the Diamonds' two little girls came to the door to say goodbye. Like all Irish children they had been learning their native language in school, and were bursting to use it on me. 'Slán leat!' they squeaked in high glee, and waved until I was out of sight.

Now the coastline bulged northwards before turning down into the wide waters of Killala Bay where Sligo slips into Mayo. I walked for miles into the wind along Dunmoran Strand, where flocks of knot and other small shore birds swirled above the tangles of ribbon weed, this way and that, like one many-winged bird. A couple of ruined farmhouses stood on the low cliffs above the rush of glass-grey waves on untrodden sand. Round the curve of the coast at Enniscrone on the edge of Killala Bay was another tremendous beach with not a soul on it. The low clouds overhead shone with silver light reflected up from enormous sheets of flat, wet sand. You could have put ten thousand people on that great crescent of sand and still found elbow room.

It was too early in the year for the modest crowds that came to Enniscrone in summer. Too cold, as well. 'It's not natural, this cold weather in May,' grumbled the shopkeeper as he made me up a couple of sandwiches. 'We're used to getting a good bit of hot just now. I haven't even heard the cuckoo.' The man beside me tapped his forefinger authoritatively on the counter. 'You say that, now, John,' he said, 'but I'll tell you what I heard yesterday, and no shadow of a doubt about it – the corncrake. Down by the river there, where they haven't cut for silage yet.'

I kept a sharp ear out walking down the River Moy that evening, but the corncrakes were keeping their heads and voices down. The drab brown birds with the harsh, two-tone call have been harried almost out of existence by modern agricultural methods. The meadows in which they nest and hide are no longer left to grow long and lush. The grass is mown off short early in the season nowadays, and the cows are grazed on chemically enriched grass or on artificial feed. The corncrakes, with no hiding place left on mainland Britain, have declined dramatically in numbers. They cling on to existence somehow, on Hebridean islands and out here in remote parts of Ireland where old farming ways persist. It was good to know that the hush of Enniscrone evenings was still being pierced by those grating cries in the long grass.

The famous Black Pig of Enniscrone was easier to spot than the corncrakes. He stood by the road halfway down the village's main street, concrete snout lowered to the grass, little blank eyes under scowling brows, front legs stiff with rage, a picture of porcine truculence. But the fury of his expression was all bluster. His black-painted flanks had been worn shiny by children riding on his back. Compared with his mythological forebear, this was a mild-mannered pet of a pig. The original Black Pig, in whichever version of the legend it features, would have crunched him to pieces in short order, concrete and all. The pig of the old tales crops up all over Ireland, mostly in the form of a destroyer of people and crops in the manner of dragons in British legends, leaving ditches in the ground where he stops to root, and springs of water where he urinates. A hero – sometimes St Patrick – chases him from county to county before catching and killing him. The most complete Black Pig legend is a sad and terrible story of long drawn-out revenge, violence and magic, beautifully structured and intricate, with no hint of a happy ending. One of the earliest of Irish legends, it draws heavily on Greek mythology, particularly the legend of Jason and the Argonauts.

The de Danaan were a mystical race of magic-workers who had conquered Ireland's previous primitive inhabitants, the Firbolgs. Soon afterwards a quarrel had arisen between two chiefs of the de Danaan, Cian and Tuireann. Cian was riding across a plain when by bad luck he came across the three sons of Tuireann – Brian, Uar and Uraca. With the help of his druidical wand he changed himself into a black pig, but Brian was not fooled. He speared the pig, and when Cian resumed his human shape to beg for mercy the three brothers stoned him to death.

Cian's son, Lugh, was a mighty and subtle-minded warrior, and when he learned of his father's murder and saw his mangled corpse, he determined to exact a prolonged revenge on the murderers. At a meeting of the de Danaan he extracted a confession from the brothers, and got them to agree to pay him an eric fine – blood money, in other words. The terms laid down by Lugh meant almost certain death for the young men. They were to bring him three apples from the Garden of the Hesperides at the end of the world; the skin of a magical pig belonging to the King of Greece which could heal any wound; the fiery, all-conquering spear of the King of Persia; the immortal horses and wind-swift chariot of the King of Sicily; seven pigs belonging to the King of the Golden Pillars; an invincible dog owned by the King of Iora; and a cooking spit from the submarine island of Fiancara. Lastly they were to give three shouts from the Hill of Mokeen, the home of a friend of the murdered Cian who had given a solemn vow to keep his hill free of shouts. All the treasures, needless to say, were thoroughly guarded night and day by any number of fierce parties.

The three sons of Tuireann set off with heavy hearts. However, thanks mainly to the no-nonsense attitude of Brian, they made tremendous headway. One after another the treasures fell into their hands, usually after the slaughter of entire kingly courts. The brothers hacked and stabbed their way round the Mediterranean in fine style, stopping only to recover from the wounds received in each encounter. Brian even donned a glass diving helmet to fetch the cooking spit from the bottom of the sea. But the Hill of Mokeen was their undoing. They laid its guardian and his three sons low, but received such terrible wounds in the fight that only the magic apples from the Garden of the Hesperides or the healing pigskin could save them. But they had already delivered these portions of the eric fine to Lugh, and he was not about to deny himself his revenge. Coldly he refused the dying brothers their cure. Brian, Uar and Uraca drew their last breaths together, followed shortly afterwards by their heartbroken father, Tuireann, and their sister Eithne.

The Moy is a beautiful river. It funnels north from Ballina to a suddenly widening estuary among the piled dunes and sandbanks by

Enniscrone. This is salmon-fishing water, shallow and fast-running, where incoming fish are taken on flies and with nets. There were groups of hopeful boys lashing the water from the green banks of the Moy as I crackled my way over the cockle and tellin shells of the estuary and slogged down the Quay Road above the river, looking forward to a bath and a bite in Ballina. Back on Dunmoran Strand I had taken my last look at the outlines of Knocknarea and Benbulben, reference points in the landscape for the past week. Now I could see the Nephin Beg mountains in the distance, pale blue undulations running into the south-west fifteen miles off. At Castleconnor the ruins of a castle built in the 1520s by the O'Dowd chief of the area stood up in a tower of shattered stonework beside the river; and here I crossed from Sligo into Mayo, from the richness of a coastal land of trees and good pasture back to the harshness of bog, lough and stony mountain, a slow transition that unfolded over the next couple of days. Set against the hard facts of poverty, unemployment and emigration, there is a bitter tang to Mayo's wild beauty. But now, turning a bend of the Moy to find the bridge and spire of Ballina set over the river, framed by willows and backed by the tall cone of Nephin Mountain like the prettiest of paintings, all was sweet. The picture had a darker side, however. Irishmen were hanged from Ballina Bridge by the British in 1798. There had always been trouble enough in Connacht.

Ireland's four ancient provinces of Connacht, Ulster, Munster and Leinster were long established by the time St Patrick came from his long sojourn in Europe to convert the Irish in AD 432. Each province had its own king and interconnected, inter-warring chieftains, all loosely bound by Celtic law and Celtic culture. In isolated homesteads and small groups of dwellings the people lived under the all-pervasive influence of their ruling families, linked to the past by myth and tradition and bound to the present by subsistence farming, cattle-raiding and tribal warfare. The de Danaan may have been among the first of Ireland's invaders, but they were by no means the last. The Celts came – perhaps Indo-Germanic peoples from central Europe in around 500 BC, perhaps a far older race of warmer-blooded Greeks who pre-dated even the de Danaan themselves. The Belgae arrived from Gaul in the century before the birth of Christ, by way of southern Britain; the Vikings brought their customary fire, sword, rape and plunder just before the turn of the ninth century AD. All these groups settled down to intermarry and add their tithe of individual culture to the mix. By the time the mighty King of Munster, Brian Boru, became High King of All Ireland early in the eleventh century, Christianity had brought further powerful strands to the web: strands of learning, of literacy and enriched artistry, operating side by side with a druidic, Celtic tradition. It was a messy jumble of cultures, but a fruitful one. Then came the Norman invasion, a shockwave that gradually became absorbed – more or less – in its turn. What set the fuse of resentment and unrest burning in the west of Ireland were the brutalities of the Tudor suppressions; and, especially, the upheavals of the seventeenth century, when Oliver Cromwell forced landowning Irish families out of their fertile lands in the east and drove them across the River Shannon in poverty and despair, 'to Hell or Connacht'.

It was a simple idea, and in the short term an effective one. The province of Connacht embraced all the land west and north of the Shannon – Mayo, Sligo and Galway – the rockiest, barest and poorest land in Ireland. The landowners from the east, their power and independence broken, had to make the best they could of this stone-hard country, while new settlers from across the Irish Sea inherited the lands of milk and honey they had vacated. Added to the suppression of Catholicism and the denial of human and political rights already established in Tudor times, this policy left a terrible legacy of anger and growing patriotism in Connacht, and sowed the seeds of all the anguish that was to follow.

The Irish language and Irish culture were the standards around which the dispossessed peoples of Connacht gathered from now on. In 1595 the rebel leader Hugh O'Donnell had conducted a somewhat forthright linguistic survey among English settlers in the province between the ages of fifteen and sixty. If they could not speak Irish, they were slaughtered. After the Cromwellian 'solution', Connacht became a hotbed of rebellion, inflamed at the turn of the eighteenth century by the introduction of the bitterly resented Penal Laws. Catholics and Nonconformists were bracketed together under this new suppression, which excluded them from activity in politics, law, the armed services and all other public life. They were forbidden to hold property, to possess arms or horses worth more than £5, to vote in elections. And, hardest cross of all to bear in this country, their bishops were placed under bans and their Masses forbidden. In Connacht, as all over Ireland, the faithful took to the hillsides, the holy wells, the lonely valleys and hidden caves to celebrate Mass and to talk of revenge and rebellion.

The various 'risings' between the sixteenth and nineteenth centuries all met with the same fate – defeat. The consequences for ordinary people of the failure of all these uprisings were summed up by the poet and courtier Edmund Spenser – no lover of the Irish – in his description of the aftermath of the Desmond rebellion of 1579–83 in Munster, which was put down with such savagery that the victims were reduced to a state nearer death than life:

> Out of every corner of the woods and glens they came creeping forth upon their hands, for their legs would not bear them; they looked like anatomies of death; they spoke like ghosts crying out of their graves; they did eat the dead carrions, happy where they could find them; yea, and one another soon after, inasmuch as the very carcasses they spared not to scrape out of their graves.

The adventure of Killala Bay in 1798 followed much the same pattern, although it had seemed to have bright prospects at the outset. A Republican party, the United Irishmen, had been formed in 1791 to press for Home Rule, and they were to be supported in an armed rising against the English by eleven hundred soldiers from France under the command of a French Republican General, the fiery Joseph Humbert. The Frenchmen landed safely in Killala Bay in August 1798, and for a few weeks things went well. Humbert raced thirty miles south with his men and a force of United Irishmen to Castlebar, where they thrashed six thousand English soldiers who ran away so vigorously that the rout became known as the 'Races of Castlebar'. But Humbert's ships, his only means of escape if things went wrong, had slipped away from Killala Bay and sailed for France in order to avoid confrontation with the British Navy. The rebels and their French allies were harried, pushed back and soon defeated, and the leaders of the United Irishmen ended their rising at a rope's end on the bridge at Ballina.

It was a self-perpetuating cycle. Each defeat spawned a fresh rebellion, each rebellion crumbled to another defeat and bloody retribution. The greater the repression, the fiercer the flames that sprang up from the ashes of defeat. Denied all their rights and prospects, forced back into primitive ways of life, with no hope of betterment, the Catholic Irish of the west became objects of mingled pity and contempt to their English landlords and to the educated Irishmen of the east. The stereotype figure of the ignorant Paddy in tattered clothes at the door of his hut in the bogs of Connacht, gullible and improvident, began to feature in English cartoons. The stage was being set, piece by piece, for the nineteenth-century tragedies of eviction and famine which still scar the landscape of Connacht, and which are not forgotten by its people.

In the lounge bar of the Imperial Hotel in Ballina that night, the Lions' Club was playing charades. The place was packed with Ballina folk, out for a good time and ready to cheer anything that moved. 'Books, plays, fillums or just about anything for your subjects,' roared the young chairman at the top of his superlatively loud voice. The teams sat on stools, stiff and nervous at first. 'Film,' gestured the young woman from the Bank of Ireland team. She stuck up two fingers – 'Two words,' murmured her team-mates, faces screwed up in concentration. 'First word.' She stretched one hand over her head. 'Tall ... mountain ... tree ... up ... high! High!' shouted the players. 'Second word!' The girl pointed to her watch. 'Time ... clock ... hands,' floundered the team. She shook her head in agony as the seconds ticked by: pointed to her ears. 'Sounds like!' She fed herself with an imaginary spoon. 'Moon ... June ... soon ... tune ...' They just couldn't get it.

'Time's up!' roared the chairman. 'The fillum is – *High Noon*!' The crowd jeered and catcalled. The Bank of Ireland flopped limply on their stools, giggling. They were out of the contest, but no one cared a hoot, least of all themselves. At two in the morning I was woken by a cacophony of non-harmony singing down in the hotel's lobby – 'Thinking of THINGS!!! – like a walk in the PARK!!!' sang the revellers, keeping time with a fusillade of handclaps. They know how to enjoy themselves in Ballina.

'So where're ye going?' asked the receptionist the following morning as I hoisted the pack in the lobby.

'Over to Bangor Erris,' I said.

'Ah, out in the bogs. The wide open spaces, yes? Well, good luck to ye, so.'

*

The great blanket bog of north-west Mayo starts unceremoniously a couple of miles out of Crossmolina. At one moment you're walking through rolling green dairy farmland, surrounded by trees and neat white houses, a landscape taken well in hand by its people. Then you top a rise in the road and look west into an utterly different, wild and lonely country. At this point you stand on the outermost edge of a vast saucer of blanket bog, a disc of desolate, almost uninhabited peat moor that extends nearly a hundred square miles. A semi-circle of hard, bare mountains hems it in: the Nephin Beg to the south and west, and to the north the peaks of Slieve Fyagh, Benmore and Maumakeogh. In all this great open space there is not a single settlement larger than a hamlet. People live in solitary houses, or in twos and threes along the road that creeps over the centre of the plain. Farms are small, and in spite of modern machinery they demand as much in the way of hard labour and pared-back economy as the bog farms of a hundred years ago. These farmers are fighters, wrestling a living from their harsh brown landscape. But Mayo's blanket bog is not really farming country at all. Mostly it is empty ground, silent and forbidding of human influence, where a mile or so off the road you can sit on the heathery edge of an abandoned turf bank and hear nothing but wind and lark song. Neither is it tourist country. Such visitors as Mayo has – fishermen for the most part – drive on across the bog on their way to somewhere else. The mountains that wall in the bog are high and continuous enough to dominate any other landscape, but here their blue ridges only emphasise the enormous emptiness. The bog grips the mind and holds the eyes. It induces a state of mind as near a heavenly trance as a solitary walker can hope to approach.

That, however, is when the sun shines. In the kind of weather hanging over Mayo that morning the bog looked unutterably dreary and bleak as I trudged along the road into its fringes. The wind blew straight out of the west into my face, laden with water fresh from three thousand miles of Atlantic transpiration. What wasn't falling on me was wrapped in grey shrouds around the mountains, or driving horizontally across the dull brown waste in swirls of mist. Nephin Mountain had vanished in smoking cloud. The dark trees of the forestry plantations roared, showering drops across the road. At long intervals heavy lorries swished by, trailing plumes of spray that smacked into and through my rain gear. The farms dotted along the roadside were soaking up water from the sodden ground, their walls darkening with damp patches. A teenage girl in gumboots, her T-shirt plastered to her plump person, plodged through the puddles of a farmyard to greet me at the gate with 'Good morning! And it's a wet one!' Observant, that girl. In the dour little shop at Eskeragh I slunk in out of the rain and bought a bottle of pop as an excuse. There was no hiss as the cap came off. The chemical-tasting fluid inside, purportedly connected with lemons and limes, was as flat as a pancake. I looked at the sell-by date. Six months ago. Bloody morning: bloody bog.

As usual, it was an act of human kindness that tipped the balance back. Dully watching the dull, misted landscape roll by as I slogged along, I noticed a patch of grey in the brown. More than a patch: a giant gash in the body of the bog, pimpled with yellow machines. I turned off the road and squelched between rain-spotted drainage ditches to get a closer look. The nearer I came, the more extensive the damage appeared: a square mile of ripped and battered bogland, stripped naked to its chocolate-brown flesh of solid peat. At the edge of the diggings there was a tiny hut, and in front of the hut a stocky man with his hand outstretched. 'Michael Monaghan,' he announced as he crushed my fingers. 'You'll come in and have a cup of tea.' It was not a question.

We sat inside the hut while Michael's kettle boiled. The tea, of industrial heat and strength, was plonked down on the table in a couple of cracked old mugs. Michael opened his lunch box and pushed his sandwiches in my direction. 'Rough and ready,' he said, 'but you're welcome to it. Go on!' His warmth was irresistible. I swallowed my polite protestations ('But that's your lunch!') and took two. Michael beamed, and began to tell me about the turf business.

The firm he worked for was engaged in cutting turf to feed the electricity generating station at Bellacorick, just up the road. I had already seen the giant cooling tower, looming from miles away through a pall of rain and its own clouds of steam. Bellacorick power station supplies electricity to all north-west Mayo, and was built right in the middle of its fuel supply – the bog. Michael's machines were standing idle this day, a Saturday, but during the week they would be busy stripping the bog of its grass and heather, rooting out the stumps of bog oak, milling the top few inches of peat into fine powder and scraping it into ridges, to be scooped up and loaded into lorries ready for the furnaces at Bellacorick. A length of rusty narrow-gauge railway ran round the rim of the workings, with an antiquated diesel locomotive parked at one end. The scraping, rooting and digging machines, however, were the latest thing in turf-cutting technology, equipped with fearsome toothed grinders and spiders'-webs of struts. They had grubbed up nine hundred acres of bog in this area, and there were thousands more being worked in the vicinity. The great bog, after three or four thousand years of minimal exploitation for domestic fires by spade and muscle-power, was being nibbled away with ever-increasing speed and efficiency. Two or three square miles had already been destroyed, along with their plants, wildlife habitat and sullen, irreplaceable beauty. On the other side of the coin, I would be filling a bath that night with hot water and, with any luck, sitting in a brightly-lit pub drinking a glass of Guinness poured from an electric pump – all courtesy of Bellacorick power station and its turf fuel.

We chatted away a lazy hour in the little hut by the workings – fishing, turf-cutting, details of our families. By the time Michael had given me a lift back to the road on the step of his tractor the rain had stopped and sunshine was pouring like honey across the bog. I waved goodbye to my hospitable instant friend, and dallied for another few minutes over the stumps of extracted bog oak that lined the drainage ditches. The centuries of interment in peat had warped the wood into fantastic shapes, writhing and rippling like the muscles in an anatomist's model, bleached by sunlight with streaks of silver, caramel brown and ochre. Wood carvers were paying good money for these prime materials, Michael had told me. I couldn't imagine how human artistry could improve on such natural extravagances.

The sliced-off cone of the Bellacorick cooling tower loomed larger and larger in the landscape as I walked west along the road. Now its attendant pylons, power lines and poles could be seen making stark black webs above the bog. Downwind of the power station the spicy smell of sun-warmed heather and peat began to be invaded by the sour fumes coiling lazily out and down from the tower and its associated tall chimneys. I was glad to duck into the little bar in the shadow of the tower, where the English FA Cup Final was showing on the TV.

The blue-overalled power station employees and the locals in the bar were not really interested in the football. What captured their attention was the sight of the Prince and Princess of Wales shuffling along to take their seats before the kick-off. 'Oh, there's Di, now,' said someone. 'Sure, she's looking well.' There seemed to be genuine delight in his voice. The camera swung from the fashionably-suited Princess to the sober-suited Prince. 'Ah, there's Charlie, now,' said someone else. A ruminative pause followed. You could sense a tremendous punchline building. 'Sure, he's looking well, too.' A murmur of assent ran along the line of blue-serge backs at the bar: 'He is, he is. He is, so.' I found it hard to believe. The Royal Family would not have drawn such a respectful reaction in any ordinary English pub on Cup Final day. Here in southern Ireland I had been half-expecting the viewers to throw things at the screen. Not a bit of it. They were quietly pleased with Charles and Di, and didn't mind sharing their pleasure. On the pitch Spurs had a key player carried off injured, missed a penalty and finally beat Nottingham Forest 2–1. But the soccer was only a sideshow to the few snippets of Royalty flashed to Bellacorick in the course of the match.

The power station, however dominant in its immediate surroundings, was only a pimple on the face of the blanket bog. All that afternoon as I tramped on westward the bog stretched away – but a bog transformed by sunshine. It smelt rich and warm; its peat glowed red, brown and water-blue, its vegetation sparkled in tender green. The Nephin Beg mountains threw off their misty shawl and showed deep corries scooped into their shoulders. Fishermen began to appear, standing waist-deep in the quick-flowing Owenmore River as they cast and cast again in hopes of a trout. I followed the river through its deepening, twisting valleys, burrowing into the neck of the Nephin Beg and finally setting my back to the great twenty-mile stretch of bog as it met the lower lands towards the coast at Bangor Erris, where I stopped for the night, in the bleakly beautiful heart of Erris.

Within the boundaries of Connacht, Ireland's poorest province, the old barony of Erris had always been a byword for poverty and bare pickings. Erris encompassed most of the worst land in County Mayo, bog and mountain shut away in the north-western corner by the Nephin Beg mountains and their outliers. Peninsulas cut the coastline of Erris into tatters, making it hard for boats to put in safely. It took a good deal of effort and determination to get into or out of Erris. Until the road across the bog from Crossmolina to Bangor Erris was metalled in 1924, the only land communications with the district were by the roughest of paths over hill or bog, most of them no better than trackways and drove roads. Travellers in the eighteenth and nineteenth centuries said their prayers at Crossmolina or Newport before setting out into Erris, where civilisation all but disappeared. Reports of life in Erris in the 1830s give a picture of rock-bottom poverty; of ten and fifteen people living in single-roomed cabins, some measuring only ten feet by seven feet, cut into the bog itself with walls of peat and roofs of heathery sods. These damp, smoke-filled caves were entered by crawling on all fours. People dressed in rags, and were almost all illiterate. There were ten schools in the quarter of a million acres of Erris, most of them 'hedge schools' held in one of the pupils' cabins where the unlicensed, usually self-educated teacher would do his best for those children who could afford his fee of a penny or so. With very rare exceptions the people were Catholics, but fewer than one in four attended Mass: the churches were too scattered, the roads too bad, the rags they wore too shaming. But the sexual mores of Erris were strict, with or without the guidelines of the Church. Illegitimacy made an outcast of both mother and child. Instead, people married young – as soon as they could get a scrap of land from their parents – and had enormous families.

Twenty-six thousand people were living like this, or not much better, when the census of 1841 was taken in Erris. They farmed what arable land there was in such hard country – two-thirds of Erris was unworkable moor and mountain – by heaping up ridges of seaweed, old roof thatch, sand, and human and animal excrement into what were ironically named 'lazybeds', a method of farming that would drain the energy from the strongest worker. In the lazybeds grew the potatoes on which everyone depended. For the poverty-stricken subsistence-level people of Erris, as for the rapidly increasing population of the whole of Ireland, it was a lucky thing indeed that their staple food was such a hardy and dependable crop.

At the start of 1845 the population of Ireland was about 9 million. It had doubled and redoubled during the preceding century, the fastest rate of growth in Europe, for reasons that were rooted in the country's poverty. In much of Ireland, and especially in the poorest western districts, there was no paid work at all. The acquisition and use of money were outside the experience of many Irish communities, such as those in Erris, which had no contact with industry or commerce. Life in these remote places was a simple matter of continuing to exist. When you are too poor to have any prospects of bettering your condition, there is no incentive to delay finding a partner. Married at sixteen or seventeen, fixed to your half-acre of lazybed by the need to scrape up rent for your landlord in the form of a few sheaves of barley or oats, entirely ignorant of the world outside your immediate area, you could easily produce fifteen or twenty children in as many years. Most would be likely to survive, too, given the excellent nutritional qualities of the potato. The potato was the rock on which this primitive way of life was founded. Once that rock began to crumble, the whole structure came crashing down in ruins.

The Great Famine of 1845–9 made a mark more indelible than any other single event in Irish history. Everyone in Ireland has something to say about the Famine. In every discussion touching on landscape, on depopulation and emigration, the Famine is the constant benchmark in time: 'back before the Famine' or 'since the Famine'. Its effects were far more disastrous than those of the Scottish Highland clearances which were taking place at around the same time, though the same mass emigration to England and America flowed from it. There were instances enough of indifferent or callous behaviour on the part of landowners, both Irish and British, at the time of the Famine, and more than enough of blundering incompetence and hard-heartedness by the British governments who were supposed to relieve the sufferings of their dependent neighbour. But what happened in those years, when the potatoes rotted and blackened in the ground and a whole population sickened and starved, was a tragedy beyond the influence of any individual or any government. All the pieces of the disaster were in place decades before it happened – the overpopulation, the poverty, the bad land, the lack of any security of tenure among the peasant people, the near or complete absence of public amenities such as hospitals, roads or relief centres. And, above all, the complete dependence of Irish men, women and children on the potato. When the *Phytophthora infestans* fungus arrived in Ireland in the late summer of 1845, from America by way of Europe and Britain, the pieces fell together.

In that first terrible October, as the people opened their lazybeds to gather the winter's food and found only stinking black slime inside, there was hope of relief from Britain. And, after some initial havering while the government tried to withhold it so as not to interfere with the private enterprise of the food traders, relief of a sort did arrive. Indian corn was allowed on to the market; food depots were opened at the principal ports; local committees were set up to co-ordinate the distribution of food; programmes of relief works were started; the various Poor Law Unions were required to set up fever hospitals in connection with their workhouses. For a while it looked as if Ireland might be able to get through the difficulty. But the problems of distributing relief on such a scale to a people unused to dealing with the outside world, in a country with little effective centralised organisation and a poor infrastructure, began to mount up. It was no use, for example, to pay those who flocked to the relief works of areas such as Erris in money, or to sell them corn from the depots. Money was not their accustomed medium; and the price of the corn could not be set low enough for the victims to afford, for fear of ruining the country's merchants. Within a year, as the scale of the disaster and the extent of the relief needed became apparent, the British government realised that it might as well be pouring its funds into a bottomless pit. The food depots were ordered to be closed, and the number of relief works increased. Hundreds of miles of roads that would seldom be used and canals that never saw a drop of water were built throughout Ireland as a result; but the workers found little or no food to buy with the few shillings they earned.

Yet beef, milk and corn were all being produced in Ireland, and the starving people watched them leaving the ports week after week. The landlords, English and Irish alike, had to have their rent paid one way or another, and these were the means. However poor an individual might be, however humble his bog cabin and patch of ground, he dared not fail to ensure his tenure. To consume the produce of his ground in lieu of the rotten potatoes was to invite eviction and a desperate existence of homelessness and begging. It's easy, looking back on the misery of the Great Famine, to lump all the landlords of the time together as cold-hearted oppressors; there were certainly plenty of these, clinging on to their own privileges and rights at the expense of the livelihoods and all too often the very lives of their tenants. But there were others who did their utmost to relieve

65

the starving people in their charge. The young Marquess of Sligo, for example, forswore his rents, sold most of his possessions and abandoned every one of the pleasures of his social position – the hunting, the entertaining and lavish spending – in his attempts to lighten the burden of his tenants. The landlords themselves, indeed, were not invulnerable, many being only one step up in influence and ease of living from the peasants who paid them rent. When in 1846 the entire potato crop failed for the second year running, and the British government cut off its grant money in favour of a rate to be levied on all 'persons of property', many landowners could not pay it without increasing their already uncollectable rents. Early in 1847 the supply of cheap corn was stopped, too; instead there were to be soup kitchens, funded from a further increase in the rate demanded from the landlords. So the evictions continued, the estates went bankrupt and the starving people wandered away to fend for themselves.

There was only one year during the Great Famine, 1847, in which the potato crop escaped the blight, and so few potatoes had been planted the previous year that the disaster was hardly checked. Disease became rife, with typhus and relapsing fever (both spread by lice from body to body) raging through the settlements where people huddled together for warmth and companionship in cabins without any form of sanitation. The workhouse hospitals and the dispensaries were crammed with sick and dying people, overflowing into tents set up by the government. Accounts of those places by visitors during the Famine years tell of children so wasted and yellow that they looked and smelt like living corpses; of fever victims turned away to crawl off and die out among the bogs or on the mountain slopes.

From June 1847, under the newly-passed Irish Poor Law Extension Act, responsibility for famine relief was thrown entirely on to the various district Unions, which administered Ireland's small number of workhouses. The relief was to be distributed only to inmates of workhouses and funded entirely by the impoverished landlords. In October of that year the soup kitchens were closed. The British government felt it had done enough, and that after all the Irish should solve their own problems. No matter what the difficulties, the rents would just have to be collected, by fair means or foul, as the Chancellor of the Exchequer, Charles Wood, made clear in November 1847 in a letter to the Lord Lieutenant of Ireland, the Earl of Clarendon.

Arrest, remand, do anything you can; send horse, foot and dragoons, all the world will applaud you, and I should not be at all squeamish as to what I did, to the verge of the law, and a little beyond.

This new, hard-nosed approach proved impossible to implement. In Erris, to take one of the most desperate regions, rents had been difficult to collect at the best of times among the roadless hills and bogs. The nearest Union was centred on Ballina, forty miles to the east, and Ballina had responsibility for 120,000 people scattered over half a million acres. The district of Erris, way out in the back of beyond and unable to pay its dues, was felt to be outside the Union's remit. And so, when two hundred starving Erris people turned up at Ballina workhouse on 12 June 1847, after a journey whose agonies can hardly be imagined, they were sent back empty-handed.

In 1849, the fourth year of the Famine, after yet another complete failure of the potato crop, cholera came to join typhus in ravaging the weakened, destitute Irish peasants – those that were left. For now the overpopulated landscape was overpopulated no more. Disease and death by starvation had made away with much of that human surplus. Hundreds of thousands more had fled the land, packing on to the emigrant ships, some with a few pounds in their pockets from their landlords, many with no more possessions than they could carry. They went to America, to Canada, to England, thankful to be quitting their devastated country and at the same time torn with all the Celt's anguish at leaving the homeland. They took their troubles with them, too, dying of fever in the hellishly crowded ships or in the holding camps on islands off the American coast while they waited to be admitted. Most preferred to go to the United States, with its jobs and its freedom from British influence, but many took the cheaper ticket (subsidised by a government keen to supply its colony with new workers) to British North America, as Canada and the other lands north of the U.S. were then known.

The figures for 1847 tell a grim tale. In that year over a hundred thousand emigrants left for British North America. Seventeen thousand died on the Atlantic crossings, twenty thousand in Canada and another thousand in New Brunswick – one in three of those who set out. And the survivors were not generally welcomed with open arms. Diseased, destitute, illiterate, ignorant and unskilled, they made a sad show beside the fresh-faced German immigrants who stood to attention on the decks of their ships, singing hymns in harmony as they sailed up the St Lawrence. It was the slums and the worst jobs for poor Paddy, and generations of prejudice and suspicion before he began to appear on the upper rungs of the social and financial ladder. In this bitter ground the seeds of anti-British feeling among the American Irish were first sown, with the establishment of the Fenian Brotherhood in the 1850s. The harvest is being reaped today by the Republican organisations of Northern Ireland, with their funds handsomely swollen by sympathisers in New York, Chicago and Detroit.

By 1850 the worst of the Great Famine was over, though there would be further failures of the potato crop in the coming years. The catastrophe had left a ruined land, great tracts of it empty, its cabins crumbling and lazybeds reverting to bog. Their outlines are to be seen everywhere you go, and especially in the west. The best of Ireland's young people were gone, too, scattered across the world to start again and sink or swim by their own efforts. Now Irish men and women married late rather than early – those lucky enough to find a partner in the depopulated land. In Erris they had a better chance than most. The district had lost seven thousand of its twenty-six thousand people during the Famine, but thereafter the population level stayed remarkably static. The explanation is a straightforward one: the people of Erris were quite simply too poor to buy even the cheapest tickets on the emigrant ships. Some of the landlords were destitute; the others began to recover and to put their rents up. New owners came in, spreading more English influence. The Irish language went into what may yet prove a terminal decline. The floodgates of emigration were opened, and have remained open ever since: in today's Erris, half the school leavers are gone within a couple of years. And, perhaps more far-reaching than any of these consequences, the flames of nationalism were fanned anew.

In 1848 the nationalists of the Young Ireland movement, poorly armed and with only a fraction of the forces they had hoped to raise, were crushed in a brief engagement with the police at Ballingarry in County Limerick. But the unrest would not die down. Landlords and their agents were murdered. The 1850s saw the birth of the Irish Republican Brotherhood, forerunner of the IRA, with strong links across the Atlantic to the Fenians of America. Under their charismatic leader James Stevens the Irish Fenians were inspired to rise in 1865 and 1867: barracks were attacked and parties of police and soldiers engaged, but both insurrections were quickly defeated and the Fenian leaders transported. A decade later Michael Davitt, the one-armed son of an evicted Mayo farmer, founded the Land League, an essentially non-violent organisation that used refusal to work, boycotting, social ostracism and the pressure of mass meetings and vehement argument to further its aim of securing Ireland's land for Ireland's people. The desire of Irish tenants to have and hold their own land led to massive support for the Land League, obliging the government to pass a Land Act in 1881 that guaranteed fair rents and security of tenure to all tenants. The desire to be rid of the British altogether would lead to the Home Rule movement, to the Easter Rising of 1916 and ultimately to the founding of the Irish Republic and the separation from Ulster. It would point the way to the dead young man in Castlederg, and the car bomb in Armagh; to the anxious faces of the Stranorlar taxi driver and his wife, and the Sligo woman picking away at her comforting rosary beads. The bullets and bombs were primed back then during the Great Famine, its chaos and maladministration; and further back, too, when the Saxon drove the Celt across the Shannon into poverty and dependence.

The population of the Irish Republic today is around 3 million – one-third of its pre-Famine peak. About 2½ million people disappeared from Ireland during the Great Famine – somewhere between a quarter and a third of the population. Records were sketchy enough before 1845, and by the end of the disaster were in complete disarray, so the proportion of those who emigrated and those who died will never be known. But a reasonable guess would put the number of deaths during the Great Famine at around one million.

In the comfortable sitting room of a smart modern house in Bangor Erris, relaxing in a deep armchair after the thirty-mile hike from Ballina, I found myself looking at starving faces in a soup queue, dying children and wailing mothers in a tented hospital encampment, long lines of hopeless people trudging away from their homelands. It was the television news, and this was Ethiopia in 1991. A strange moment.

*

The Fianna were a band of chosen warriors under the leadership of the legendary third-century hero Fionn MacCumhaill. It was no easy matter to gain membership of that select brotherhood. To be received into the Fianna a warrior had to pass certain tests. He had to be a man of matchless integrity, honesty and valour. He had to be a complete and polished poet. He must ward off the spears of nine warriors, thrown at close quarters and all at the same instant, while buried up to his waist in the ground and armed with no more than a shield and a short hazel stick. He had to evade pursuit and wounding by the Fianna, all running after him at full tilt through the woods, without having a hair of his braided locks disturbed by the passing branches and without cracking any stick underfoot. While running at top speed the candidate must also duck below a stick held level with his knee, leap over one at head height, and pick a thorn out of his foot with his fingernail. In his novel *At-Swim-Two-Birds* the great Irish comic writer Flann O'Brien adds a hilarious list of supplementary requirements: 'With the eye-lids to him stitched to the fringe of his eye-bags, he must be run by Finn's people through the bogs and the marsh-swamps of Erin with two odorous prickle-backed hogs ham-tied and asleep in the seat of his hempen drawers.' After my day among the wild wastes of the Nephin Beg with Oliver Geraghty of Newport, I think the Fianna may have found their man.

Oliver is in his early twenties. He is a rock-climber and a white-water canoeist. He is a hill walker, a mountain runner and a marathon cyclist. He can take a party of novices camping in the wilderness, navigate them across bog and mountainside in the dark and bring them safely back to civilisation. For that matter, he can lead an Englishman safely through the Nephin Beg on a misty day. He doesn't drink or smoke. He's fun to be with, and as reliable as a rock. Whether he can pick a stone out of his trainer treads while running flat out, or carry sleeping hogs in the seat of his drawers, I didn't discover. Oliver told me little about his accomplishments in a direct way; I discovered them in passing conversation. He was content to introduce himself as a plumber and part-time outdoor activities helper. He would be a remarkable young man in any setting. Here in remote north-west Mayo there are not too many like Oliver Geraghty, staying home to contribute so actively to their depopulated community.

I had fixed myself up with a companion for the thirty-mile trek through the Nephin Beg by way of a chain of phone calls to members of the small but steadily growing number of hill walkers in the west of Ireland. Walking around in the countryside for pleasure is not really an Irish custom. Probably there has been a bit too much of it in the daily life of rural communities; forty miles a day gathering sheep on the hill, three miles to the nearest pub, a thousand times up and down a field after the plough. Whatever it is, the solitary walker gets a lot of funny looks. But things are changing, particularly since the Castlebar International Walks have got under way in recent years. Each June walkers come from all over the world to tramp the roads and hills during a week of walks round Castlebar, a few miles inland from Newport. Irish people themselves are beginning to look to the hills, and their network of old drove roads and trackways, with fresh eyes. There are plenty of walkers in the hills of Wicklow and around Dublin these days; but out here in County Mayo such activities are still in their infancy.

The old mountain track through the Nephin Beg between Bangor Erris and Newport, however – twenty-eight miles of walking as rough and wild as you could wish for – is becoming something of a celebrity among hill walks. A group of friends in Newport decided over a few drinks one night in 1987 to walk the track. Nineteen people turned up for the ordeal, and drank their way through three barrels of free beer at the almighty party that followed. There were forty people next year, over a hundred the year after that. In 1991 they were limiting entries to 150, and turning down hundreds of late applications. The participants walk the Bangor Trail from Bangor Erris to Newport all day, and whoop it up most of the night. Oliver Geraghty sticks to the 7-Up at the party, but he's an indispensable part of the day, shepherding laggards and covering twice as much ground as the average walker. He knows the Bangor Trail back to front, in fair and foul weather. Now my chain of phone calls had brought him up to Bangor Erris early on Sunday morning, to see me safely over the remotest mountain walk in Ireland.

On the map the Nephin Beg Mountains fill a triangle of perhaps eighty square miles, its head pointing north to touch Bangor Erris and its broad base running east and west along the upper shore of Clew Bay and on inland towards Lough Conn and Crossmolina, where Nephin Mountain stands a little apart from the main range. There's an inner triangle of high tops over two thousand feet – Nephin Beg itself, Glennamong and Birreencorragh. The dotted line of the Bangor Trail snakes down the map, keeping to the flanks of Nephin Beg Mountain at first, then squeezing through a narrow pass under Glennamong to reach lower ground at Lough Feeagh, where a road leads down to Newport. The mountain section of the trail is about eighteen miles long, with few, if any, escape routes if the mist comes down or exhaustion sets in. Some parts have been all but eroded away by mountain bikers, and in places the trail simply disappears. It's a long, tough walk, even for an experienced walker skilled in the use of map and compass. Getting lost among the Nephin Beg would be no joke, either for the victim or for those who set out to find him. With Oliver Geraghty at my side, though, I faced the hills with confidence.

It was one of those days of tantalising mist hiding all the views. The Nephin Beg had pulled the covers over themselves once more, and only their feet stuck out of the bottom. We climbed away from Bangor Erris, up into the mist on the winding trail. A complete hush closed in. Grey curtains of vapour opened up for a moment or two, showing brown slopes rising into cloud, then swept shut again. The trail was a quaggy mess underfoot, the stones that had once paved it all jumbled into awkward lumps, its narrow channel on the mountainside invaded by wet bog a foot or two deep in places. I went in up to my knee before Bangor Erris was out of sight. Oliver kept to the hillside just above the track, leaping athletically from clump to clump of heather, and soon I was clumsily following suit. There was not a hope in hell of keeping clean and dry on the Bangor Trail. Within an hour we were both clad in leggings of peat and dripping with mist and sweat. As we gained height the green bog of the trail gave way to rough chunks of rock spattered with white crystals of quartzite. The summit of Nephin Beg Mountain gleams white with quartzite, the guidebooks had informed me. If so, it was gleaming unseen this day.

From the first pass we came to there was a view below mist level down into a long valley where the Tarsoghaunmore River meandered in a succession of extravagant loops. Down on its banks stood the ruins of a stone-built cottage, where drovers on the trail would have stopped for a bite and a chat while their beasts rested and drank at the river. 'The old track was the only way to bring the cattle from Newport up to the market in Bangor Erris,' said Oliver, stripping off in the roofless kitchen of the cottage and donning a thermal vest against the cold. 'The drovers were known at every house along the way, and there'd always be something to eat on the table. They were welcome, bringing the news and a new face to the door.'

We took off our boots and socks and stepped into the ice-cold water of the Tarsoghaunmore River. One day there may be a footbridge here for walkers on the trail, but for the present it's a case of slip and splash, wince and curse. On the far bank the path vanished, but Oliver led purposefully away up a narrow valley and on to the flanks of Nephin Beg Mountain. Blood sugar levels were topped up by a steady supply of chocolate bars from Oliver's rucksack; morale was kept up, too, by his stories of expeditions into the mountains with groups of schoolchildren from the Skerdagh Outdoor Activities Centre near Newport. The little white skull of a lamb lay in the grass by the trail, causing him to chuckle. 'That's a bog dog skull, you know. A cross between a wild dog and a sheep. Very savage, the bog dogs – at least, that's what I tell the kids when we take them out here on a night's bivouac. I have them sleeping in a circle, with their feet to the centre and their heads to the outside. "That way the bog dogs won't bother you," I tell them. One boy was so scared he was sure he'd seen one, and two of the lads away up the mountain howling at him. I heard him telling some Germans in the Youth Hostel all about the bog dogs he'd seen. It was his big adventure, you know?'

At the heart of the Nephin Beg the trail sweeps round the side of a great valley three miles across, its floor gleaming with small lakes and filled with quaking bog that would suck down anyone foolhardy enough to try a crossing. But people had lived and farmed here in the Scardaun Valley, both before and after the Great Famine. The green outlines of their lazybed strips and circular sheepfolds lay as if printed on the brown face of the bog. On the hillside by the trail the shells of their houses still stood by waterfalls and spring wells, looking out over the waste to the surrounding mountains. We stopped to drink the cold, peaty water and sit for a while, five miles at least from any inhabited house or tarred road, speculating on the hardships of life at Scardaun in the old days.

That evening, snug in a hospitable house in Newport, I was to read an account of a journey along the Bangor Trail made just before the Famine. The Reverend Caesar Otway published his book *Sketches in Erris and Tyrawley* in 1839, recounting his adventures along 'the old and only pass into Erris'. The track was pretty bad in those days as well. 'No mortal made carriage could ever have exercised wheel upon its track,' writes Mr Otway. 'Who would venture on its unpleasant ways but the smuggler or the outlaw?' He mentions the Scardaun bog, which had almost swallowed the togher or path across it. 'As the ponies looked at it they drew back and snorted.' They had good reason to be wary. The only way that the inhabitants of Scardaun could get their own horses across the bog was by tying ropes round their heads and tugging them along the togher quickly enough to prevent them sinking.

Otway and his companion stopped for the night somewhere near Scardaun – perhaps at the very house by whose ruins Oliver and I had sat talking. The cabin in which they slept had no door; instead, there were 'two low orifices, one in front and one opposite to it. As the wind blew one or other was built up with sods, the other closed with creels to keep the cattle out.' The floor was covered with rushes. They dined on potatoes, eggs and butter, and drank poteen, the high-octane home-distilled whiskey that could either warm and elate or blind and kill you, depending on the skill of the maker. At bedtime the whole family stripped naked and lay down on the rushes under rough blankets, in a carefully arranged order. The eldest daughter (the most likely to attract – or invite – the attentions of strangers) went next to the wall, with her sisters ranged beside her in descending order of age. In the middle lay mother, then father, and then the sons. The guests lay on the outside, as far away as possible from the womenfolk. Strangers might be offered hospitality in Erris under Celtic custom, but to trust them was another matter.

We got up from our damp seats by the derelict cottage and climbed on, round the valley and over the shoulder of Nephin Beg Mountain, heads down, keeping a sharp lookout for the bright green patches that hid the soft, sucking bog. The trail led under Glennamong ('Glennamoo, we call it. Strangers always get that wrong,' said Oliver) and wound down out of the hills into a great tract of conifer plantation. Here, eighteen miles out from Bangor Erris, the walking wounded on the annual Trail Walk collapse into a minibus and are driven down to Newport. I had fully expected to be likewise exhausted by this stage, but walking with a cheerful companion had been like having a spare pair of legs. We strode on over Sheep Pass and down the forest tracks to Srahmore Lodge, where a bearded man with a grin of welcome on his face was just getting out of a van. Joe McDermott had come up from Newport to walk the last seven miles with us.

Joe is a badger of a man, with a bush of dark beard streaked grey above which two strikingly blue eyes look out at the world. Mountains, water, rock faces and ancient tombs and forts are the things closest to the hearts of Joe and his wife Pauline. They sold the semi-circular house they had built in Dublin and came west to Mayo, to find some challenge in life. 'I was a history teacher in the city,' Joe explained as we marched with new energy across the hills above Lough Feeagh, 'and I found myself one day giving a lesson on the painting of the Sistine Chapel while looking out of the classroom window at a round tower, a piece of Irish history right there under my nose. And I thought: "What the hell am I doing here? What's going on?" So we sold the house and moved out here to Mayo.'

The McDermotts found a derelict schoolhouse near Skerdagh, a couple of miles out of Newport, and by hard labour and undimmed conviction they converted it into an outdoor activities centre. Apart from a starting grant from Bord Fáilte, the whole enterprise has had to fund itself. Joe, Pauline and Oliver take school parties rock climbing and canoeing; they give handicapped people a day to remember out on the hills; they get whey-faced executives from the city to splash through streams and camp out under the stars. There's a good dash of culture in with the hearty red-faced stuff, too, for those who want it – expeditions to the court tombs and stone forts of pre-Christian Ireland, lectures on the flora and fauna of the area; trips to the gigantic prehistoric site at Céide Fields on the north Mayo coast where five thousand acres of tombs, fields and enclosures have been unearthed from the bog that buried them. And in the evenings, back in Newport, the Skerdagh people take whichever group they have been with to the pub.

All these outdoor pursuits, especially the hill walking, are to a certain extent un-Irish activities. People are not yet convinced of the pleasures of exposing themselves to the elements. The local sheep farmers, however, far from treating the McDermotts with suspicion, are pleased with the respect they show the mountains and the enthusiasm they engender among children and adults alike for this still largely unvisited area. Finding Oliver Geraghty on their doorstep was a piece of good fortune for the McDermotts. The three of them have shaken a good deal of healthy life into Mayo. I found being with them as brisk and refreshing as a boots-off crossing of the Tarsoghaunmore River.

The long day's march came to an end just before nightfall at Oliver's house on the outskirts of Newport. We drove down into the town and parted, with a promise to meet up in the pub later on. There was freshly caught wild Atlantic salmon on the table at De Bille House in Newport that night, and an evening of yarning to follow. Frank Chambers was my host, a veteran of the Bangor Trail and the chief link in that telephone chain that had put Oliver Geraghty at my side in the mountains.

You can't get anything done in Newport without involving Frank. He owns one of the busiest bars in the town. He runs an auctioneering business. He is the County Councillor for the Westport district of Mayo, and in the west of Ireland that means a degree of involvement in local affairs that would make any English councillor's hair stand on end. Frank is one of the fifteen members of the national executive of Fianna Fáil, the ruling political party. One day he'll be in Dublin discussing national policy on environmental pollution or the EC, the next he'll be back in Newport deciding whether Mick O'Reilly should be allowed to build an extension on his house. Newport is a pretty little town which has become run-down and unkempt in recent years, and its renovation is one of the biggest calls on Frank's energy. He never stops thinking and working. At well after midnight I found him on the pavement outside his pub, having presented some award and made a speech at a function earlier in the evening. Everyone who passed had a word for him – a whisper in the ear, a confidential mutter. He bowed his trimly bearded head to this mouth and that, murmuring judiciously: 'Whisht, now! Whisht! No, no . . . well, we'll see what we can do . . . Yes, OK, right you are . . . Whisht, now, don't say that, Tommy! . . . Yes, all right . . . good night to you, now.' It was a priestly performance, bending an ear to the confessions and complications of the little town, dutifully on call while he must have been longing for his bed.

Lying in my own bed in Frank's house in the early hours, drowsily flicking through my notebooks, I found a passage I had copied back in Sligo library from Robert Lloyd Praeger's *The Way That I Went*. It summed up my own reaction to the moody isolation of the Nephin Beg Mountains:

> I confess I find such a place not lonely or depressing, but
> inspiriting. You are thrown at the same time back upon

yourself and forward against the mystery and majesty of nature, and you may feel dimly something of your own littleness . . . Go up to the hills, as the sages and saints have done since the beginning of the world, and you will need to be a very worldly worldling if you fail to catch some inarticulate vision of the strange equation in which you stand on one side and the universe on the other.

I had indeed felt something of my own littleness, and was thankful for the good companionship that had made the journey through the Nephin Beg so painless. My legs were tired enough after twenty-eight miles. How did Oliver Geraghty's grandfather feel, I wondered, at the end of the epic days he was accustomed to spend in those hills? That hardy man would get up at sunrise and drive his cattle from his farm, four miles south of Newport, over the 'old and only pass' to market at Bangor Erris. After selling the beasts and buying new ones, he would turn round and walk back with them through the mountains to reach his farm the same day. Sixty-four miles in hobnailed boots, without counting the innumerable side tracks and uphill dashes after straying cattle.

I left Newport the next day and came down to Westport, and in those ten miles the summer arrived. A warm mid-May sun began to shine in a blue sky, dissolving the mists that had cloaked bog and mountain. In Westport the shopkeepers stood in shirtsleeves at the doors of their dark little shops, chatting amicably with passers-by. The waters of the Carrowbeg River at the bottom of the town sparkled under their hump-back bridges, and elderly men stood chaffing each other under the trees along the Mall. A gaggle of nuns going into the church beamed at me from under their veils. There was a good warm feeling to Westport, throughout the three days I idled there, for which the sunshine was only partly responsible.

Westport is one of those towns you never want to leave. Something in the air here attracts all manner of people from all manner of places. German organic farmers, Irish musicians, English writers, Scandinavian craftspersons: they drift in, sniff the air and stay for a month or a lifetime. Unlike other such towns in Cornwall or West Wales, the people of Westport don't seem to mind these 'blow-ins' at all. 'They add a bit of colour to the place,' say the shopkeepers and pub owners. 'And they attract the tourists in summer.' Westport social life is so relaxed as to be practically horizontal. You just go into the first bar you see, sit down and say hello to the nearest person. Conversation is guaranteed.

The pub is the great focal point of social life in Ireland, much more so than in England. The Guinness is certainly good (they say it's the water drawn from the River Liffey, and you might believe them until you take a look at Dublin's murky waterway); but the pubs would probably go on bulging with people if the Liffey ran dry tomorrow. They go to the pub for 'the crack', that untranslatable commodity that's a mixture of fun, chat, high spirits, music and conviviality. There's enough beauty and drama in the landscape to fill any photograph album, but it's in the pubs that you'll find good crack. The best advice on walking routes, the tallest stories and the kindest offers of food, bed and friendship that came my way all emanated from chance meetings in the pub.

Westport's pubs are full of good crack. In Westport I learned to lay my English inhibitions aside at the pub door, and walk in expecting to be drawn into talk, laughter and whatever musical sessions were going on. Westport runs on music, as far as I could tell. There are any number of young musicians in the town, most of them startlingly good, all of them busy each night getting sessions going in the pubs. Musicians' etiquette in England demands that you wait to be asked to join in, and if you are not as skilled as those already playing you'd be better off keeping out of it. In Ireland, etiquette is probably the name of the horse that won the 2.35 at Leopardstown. You pull up a stool (if you can get close enough), whip out your instrument and saw, strum or tootle away.

On my first night in Westport I walked in on a session in the Arches Hotel. Pat Egan on guitar, Ulcan Masterson blowing the whistle and Johnny Curtis hammering his bouzouki were well into the jigs and reels, but they waved me up beside them as soon as they caught sight of the harmonica in my hand. My harmonica-playing skills are not much better than basic, but no one cared a rap. It took a while that night to clamber over the barrier of restraint and honk away quietly in a corner. But next evening in Hoban's bar I waded in with the best of them. If I needed an excuse, it was there at my elbow – a line of pints of Guinness that had been built up by unseen hands. It was my birthday, and someone had passed the word round. There was a bed waiting for me above Molloy's bar if I wanted it. Pat Egan would meet me for a cup of coffee at midday the following day. He'd be delighted to have me to stay, if that's what suited me. Would a maladroit harmonica-blower from Ireland, a complete stranger, have been treated like this in an English country town?

In England the first reaction to the sight of a stranger tends to be caution, if not outright suspicion. He might be up to no good; he might not fit in; there could be the risk of rebuff when making contact. The Irish view of the stranger, I was learning as I went along, is usually the reverse. The possibilities are what counts. This man might have a story, or some news, or a tune we haven't heard. Whoever he is, he's bound to be worth a few words at least.

Westport's friendly atmosphere is helped by the layout of the place. It was a planned town, designed by the Georgian architect James Wyatt for the Marquess of Sligo. The sloping grid of streets is packed with little shops and pubs, and along the Mall by the river is the town's strolling parade. Westport House, the mansion built on the hill outside the town in the 1730s, was the scene of an event during the Great Famine that wrung the heart of young Lord Sligo. On 31 August 1846 he came out of his door to face a starving crowd, and saw them sink to their knees and beg him for relief. Westport folk still talk affectionately of Lord Sligo, who sold most of his possessions to feed his tenants: 'Yes, he was a good man, good to the people of Westport back in the Famine. There was a soup kitchen up there at the top of the town, you know. That's why we call this street Hungry Hill.' They put up a statue to another 'good man in the Famine', George Glendinning, a rich banker and son of the Rector of Westport, who poured out his money in relief schemes and handouts. Others pulled the statue down in 1922 – Glendinning was British. The plinth in the Octagon, halfway up the town, stood empty for decades. Recently the people of Westport raised money among themselves and put an enormous column on the plinth, with a statue of St Patrick perched on top. 'I don't like him,' said a girl I'd seen in a café the previous day, offering me a Polo mint and keeping me company up the street towards the statue. 'They've made him too young. It's not the St Patrick I know from the book pictures – great long beard and a bald head on him, you know?'

*

79

In the long winter months Westport is still much as it always was. You can take a good hour to walk up the street, Johnny Curtis told me, stopping for a chat with this acquaintance and that. Everyone knows everyone else. In the last five or six years, though, Westport has become a popular place in summer. Coachloads of tourists no longer sweep through on their way from Galway to Sligo. They stop, book in and stay a few days. Where cars used to go up and down the roads in a general mêlée, they now race round a one-way system. The musicians are certain of playing seven nights a week, but nine out of ten in their audience will be Americans, Swedes, Germans, Dutch, French, British. The place is uncomfortably crowded between June and September. There are still dark old pubs where the locals can go to get away from the tourists, shops where those behind the counter have plenty of time for a chat. But no one knows how much longer it can go on that way.

Two days after my birthday I caught the bus to Galway and the airport. It was a wrench to leave the music and the crack, but I needed time at home with the family, back in my own version of the real world. It would be June when I came back from England to take up the journey at Westport again. Maybe by then the clouds would finally be off Croagh Patrick, the holy mountain. I was keen to climb up there, one of the highest points in Ireland, for a long look over the next stage of the adventure – south-west into the rugged lands of Connemara.

3

THROUGH CONNEMARA
Croagh Patrick to the Aran Islands

'I'm done,' gasped the stout American girl as she subsided in red-faced exhaustion on a rock at the side of the Pilgrim Path. She lit a cigarette and waved me past, accepting defeat with a wry smile. Five hundred feet of climbing had brought the burgers home to roost. 'Great view from here, anyway,' she called after me, settling herself to puff her fag and gaze out over the scatter of green islands down in Clew Bay.

Further up the steep path, however, the elderly German couple were still going great guns. Their bare calves bunched and slackened rhythmically as they stabbed their alpenstocks in among the boulders, surging up the side of Croagh Patrick like a pair of squat little tanks. By the time I'd sweated up to the saddle of flat ground at a thousand feet they were scurrying up the last, killing section of the climb, dislodging quartzite slabs and laughing merrily. I envied them their energy. It was all I could do to make forward and upward progress in the wilderness of tumbled, sliding rock that littered the flanks of Croagh Patrick's majestic cone. The path had disappeared completely. The rock slide reared away at one in three, rising overhead and filling half the sky, wobbling and skidding under my boots. I had no alpenstock to push on, but with hands forcing knees downwards I followed the trail of sweat drops spattered on the stones from the Germans' brows and slowly, laboriously, crawled my way up to collapse against the wall of the chapel on the summit of the mountain. The climb had taken every ounce of energy in my body. How some of the pilgrims on Garland Sunday in July manage it in bare feet I can't imagine. Others climb in stiletto heels. Back in AD 441 St Patrick probably did it in sandals.

The saint's ascent of the holy mountain is fairly well documented, along with a great deal of more or less improbable legend. As a youth, Patrick had been captured by Irish sea raiders from his home country of Wales, and had spent six years in Ireland as a shepherd in a state of reasonably comfortable slavery before the inner voice that spoke to him throughout his life sent him over the sea again, probably to the Continent, for some twenty-five years. Little is known about his movements during this period. But in AD 432 he was back in Ireland as a bishop, with the daunting responsibility of kindling Christianity among the almost entirely heathen and exceedingly warlike natives. Patrick seems to have been a far-sighted man, for all his self-confessed lack of education. He was aware of the structure of Ireland's druidical religion, and was willing to incorporate many of its festivals, practices and holy places (including Croagh Patrick, which was sacred to the Irish as Cruachan Aigil, the mountain of the eagle) in his new order of things. Legend has it that he fasted forty days and nights on the summit of the mountain while conducting a spirited bargaining session with God, using an angel as go-between. Patrick negotiated assurances that Ireland would be spared the final horrors of Armageddon, that all the Irish would be saved, and that at Judgement Day he would be allowed the role of judge over all the men of Erin. The Lord baulked at this last demand, but gave in when the saint threatened a lifelong sit-in on the peak. For good measure, Patrick also hurled his bell through a menacing cloud of black demon birds, and banished all the snakes from Ireland. This strong-minded saint would have made mincemeat of the gold-mining company whose designs on the heart of the holy mountain had been thwarted a month or two before I climbed Croagh Patrick.

After sitting for a while outside the chapel, getting my breath back and revelling in the view (the mountains of Connemara heaped along the southern horizon, the flat lands of Mayo stretching off into the east, the saucer of Clew Bay below with the Nephin Beg standing nobly on guard beyond), I slid and scrambled back down the Pilgrim Path to fetch up in Campbell's bar at the foot of the mountain. Here the barman filled me in on the gold-mining story. There had been a tremendous furore when traces of workable gold were discovered on Croagh Patrick in 1988. A mining company with strong Finnish connections had prospected the seams and put in an application to work them over five years or so. Local people knew little or nothing of what that might mean in terms of spoil heaps, mining traffic and pollution of watercourses and Clew Bay; but they quickly learned. Their protests were soon swelled by complaints from environmentalists and religious groups from all over the world. Buddhists, Hindus and others wrote to the Irish government to register their dismay at the threat to Ireland's holy mountain. The annual pilgrimage up Croagh Patrick to attend Mass on the summit had taken place on Garland Sunday, the last Sunday in July, for well over eight hundred years, but pilgrims had been climbing the mountain since shortly after St Patrick's inaugural ascent. The mining company had failed to reckon with the emotional clout of those fifteen centuries of tradition. The Catholic Church stood by at first, preserving a dignified silence. But then the company began to claim that this absence of comment implied consent. Late in 1990 Archbishop Cassidy of Tuam stepped in to defend his patch.

The pilgrimage had become a subject of controversy in recent years, with huge crowds starting the climb by torchlight shortly after midnight – a wonderful sight, with the side of the mountain glowing in a snaking line of lights, but a dangerous trend all the same. Some pilgrims, too well fortified in the pubs, were injuring themselves on the dark slopes, and others were arriving at the chapel on the top in no fit state for prayer or penitence. The Church authorities had issued a ban on the night pilgrimage, not increasing their popularity thereby. But now everyone made common cause in the face of the mining threat. In vain the company promised to hide the spoil heaps within the workings inside the mountain. They were up against the power of national and international opinion. The government declared Croagh Patrick inviolable ground, and the venture was stopped in its tracks shortly before I came to Ireland. A number of measures have been incorporated into Mayo's county development plan to forestall any future assaults on the golden heart of the mountain. Time will tell whether they can hold off such potentially lucrative development in the face of the emigration and unemployment that continue to haunt this western side of Ireland.

From Campbell's bar I hitched a lift back into Westport, and there I made ready for the next stage of the journey, the long road south through the mountainous heart of Connemara. For most visitors this is the quintessential west of Ireland, the harsh land of rock, bog and hill where romance and fearful history are intertwined. Before setting out into bleak and beautiful Connemara, however, there was one more treat on the already full menu of Mayo. On the summit of Croagh Patrick I had looked down on the little green drumlin islands of Clew Bay (one for each day of the year, local people say), grassed-over mounds of clay and rubble dragged down from the hills and dumped in the bay by melting glaciers at the end of the last Ice Age. From the mountain top the drumlins looked like swimming sea monsters, baring yellow teeth of clay at the Atlantic waves attacking them from the west. A handful of hardy folk still cling to one or two of the islands, fishing and farming, maintaining links with the mainland by a slender lifeline of small boats. Pat Egan, the Westport guitar player, discovering that I was keen to get out to one of the Clew Bay islands, had fixed me up a visit to his friends Didi Korner and Anne Kelly, the lone inhabitants of Island More. Yes, said Didi over a cup of tea in Westport, I was more than welcome to come out and spend the night with them on Island More. There was nothing fancy in it, though. Your man Pat would have been telling me that.

After twenty years, Ireland has thoroughly invaded Didi's speech, as well as his soul. A tall, spare man, grey of beard and unhurried of demeanour, he first came to the Westport area in the early 1970s on holiday from his native Hamburg. He came back to Ireland at every opportunity after that, year after year, biking all over the country, and found nowhere to compare with Westport as a place to settle and put down roots. He was a social worker in a club for wild motorcycle boys in Hamburg, so he had reason enough to fall in love with Westport and its relaxed, accepting atmosphere.

It took him ten years to find the right place, but when the advertisement appeared in *Exchange & Mart* magazine – 'Island More: house, boat, acre of garden, shellfish income' – Didi knew he could leave Germany behind for good. He bought the island house from the Englishman who had renovated it, moved in and began a life of fishing and organic gardening. The other Clew Bay islanders came over to Island More for a cup of tea, sniffed him over and decided he would do. There he was, occupant of a few hundred acres of grass and heather five miles out from Westport quay, with oyster beds to dredge and a run-down garden to work back into shape, a modest market for his shellfish and vegetables on his doorstep, a good roof over his head and a sheltering hill at his back. And there he remains, self-sufficient and self-contained, sharing the hard work and the unbroken peace of the island with Anne, fully intending to make old bones on Island More. On his trips into Westport he dives enthusiastically into local life, the pub gossip, the music and the crack. I heard plenty of grumbling against German 'blow-ins' buying up tracts of land in the west of Ireland, fencing off their property and making no effort to communicate with local people or to understand their way of life. But everyone in Westport had a good word for Didi.

The car in which Didi and Anne drove me to Rosmoney quay was an MOT inspector's nightmare, but it went. From the jetty we rowed out to a tiny fishing boat and puttered off through the maze of waterways between Clew Bay's islands. Croagh Patrick stood tall and dark over the bay, dominating the green-backed drumlins scattered at its feet, its conical head brushing the clouds. 'That's Inishlyre,' Didi said as we passed a low-lying island with a couple of houses tucked down on a pebbly bay. 'There's three families in it, fishing and farming. The old man still works as a pilot – Clew Bay has some bad waters.'

We anchored off Island More's stony strand, and splashed from the rowing boat up the beach and through the garden gate. If there is a more productive garden in the west of Ireland, I'd like to see it.

The patient spade-work of Didi and Anne had filled the acre of ground between the wind-break hedges with a well-controlled riot of vegetables and fruit – lettuce, cabbage, broccoli and cauliflowers; asparagus and artichokes; parsnips, swedes and beetroot; shallots, onions and garlic; a mass of herbs; apples, plums, beans, sprouts. In the conservatory at the side of the house tomatoes hung in a jungle of leaves, and dried field mushrooms were threaded on strings among the rafters. 'This garden has never seen a drop of artificial fertiliser,' said Didi with quiet pride. 'We sell mainly to the sailing school on Collan More island just across the water there, and a little to the quality restaurants ashore. We make enough to keep going, as well as the fishing, you know.'

I had brought a bottle of Jameson's Irish whiskey and a hunk of goat cheese along with me, and there was no nonsense about saving the present till the guest had departed. Well warmed, Didi and I set off on a leisurely ramble around his little kingdom. Upwards of a hundred people had lived on Island More in the last century, raising cattle and crops, fishing the bay and the inshore waters. By 1950 they were all gone to softer beds and easier livelihoods on the mainland, though a few of the last inhabitants still retain ownership of small portions of the island and keep a couple of houses in good repair for the occasional visit. We scrambled over the grassy humps of old field boundaries, strolled the sloping meadows over orchids, birds'-foot trefoil and clover, stood for many minutes on the western cliffs looking out into the sunset over the crouching back of Clare Island ten miles offshore. A little window of prismatic colour, like a chip of rainbow, hung against the clouds over the Atlantic. The shingle spits of the Clew Bay islets shone like silver in the fading light, patterned on the water of the bay in a subtle and beautiful geometry. Down in the deserted village on the shore the island cows sheltered in the ruined rooms where many of their now land-bound owners were conceived, born and reared. Didi kicked the thick carpet of dung in one of the houses and grinned: 'This is where I get my fertiliser.'

Across the narrow waist of the island an abandoned pier drooped its disintegrating stone finger into the bay, and here Didi settled himself on a stone to roll a cigarette while I sat and gazed my fill at water, islet and mountains. Walking back along the shore to the house in companionable silence, Didi stopped and held up a warning hand. I peered ahead through the half-light and saw what I had long dreamed of seeing – a big sea otter, bounding across the stones ten yards away, his dark body undulating. He slipped into the water with hardly a ripple and vanished. 'Gone fishing,' said Didi.

How can one capture in words what can't be caught or pinned down to time and place, even to a time and place as serene as Island More on this still, sunlit evening? Among a lifetime's walks only a handful lie unclouded in the memory, to be drawn out at will as if from a library and walked and savoured again in their entirety. Island More is one of these.

Back at the house Anne had set out a meal that gave the evening its finishing touch. At half-past ten, in the soft light of a paraffin lamp (no electricity on Island More), we pulled up our chairs and set to on fresh vegetables straight out of the garden and a heap of oysters straight out of the sea. I had eaten one oyster in my life up to this moment, and had barely been able to force that thick ball of raw mucus down my heaving throat. But these oysters had been baked, and went down considerably more than a treat with the help of Didi's hard-biting home-brewed beer. The talk turned to the future of islands such as these: whether they could go on supporting populations in the face of all that the modern mainland world had to offer. Didi had pointed out one of the Clew Bay islets, Dorinish, and told me the story of how John Lennon had bought it in the free-spending heyday of the Beatles. Lennon himself had hardly set foot on his purchase, but he had let it be known that any beautiful people who wished to be beautiful there were welcome. A straggling procession of hippies had brought their drugs and their dreams to Dorinish, most of them sticking it out for a few months in tarpaulin-covered holes in the ground before retreating from the weather, the loneliness and the sheer impracticality of living on fresh air. One couple had hung on for a year or two with their four children, building themselves a hut of sorts. Islands have a way of impressing reality on their inhabitants, particularly incomers with visions of the free and simple life. Living as Anne and Didi do, trading with the outside world and playing their part in its social activities, cutting their unassuming coat in accordance with their threadbare (if excellent quality) cloth, island life of this unromantic sort can be made to work. They would like to get into the tourist trade in a modest way, taking small parties of visitors round the islands by boat and landing them on Island More for a good lunch. No bed-and-breakfast enterprise, though; no camping or tourist information centre; nothing that could alter the balance they have worked so hard to establish. 'I want to grow old on this island,' Didi said as he puffed another roll-up into a glow in the darkened room, 'and I certainly intend to. There's times when the fishing is dangerous, but we go out every day in spite of the weather, because we need to. We can be cut off for a couple of weeks by the gales in winter. But we can manage.' He waved his hand out at the night, where the spiny leaves of the artichoke plants outside the window nodded in the wind, outlined in reflected lamplight. 'We have what we need, and that's enough for us.'

Next morning it blustered and spat. The clouds rolled down from the mountain tops and lined up along the slopes. Back in Westport I said goodbye to Didi, and made twenty miles over stony moor and under misty mountain in a long day's march south and west. Rocky outcrops began to push through the skin of the bog, and the hills rose higher in grey spines of naked quartzite. The road ran through ever narrower valleys where pink clumps of rhododendrons lined the hedges and round, thatched turf stacks stood in the fields. There was a feeling of entering an entirely different country, harder and wilder than the open green lowlands around Clew Bay, further from the grip of modern civilisation. By the bridges and roadside hamlets were monuments to volunteers killed while serving with the IRA; but these were not the bombers and knee-cappers of present-day Belfast and Derry. 'Erected to the memory of the West Mayo Brigade IRA,' was inscribed on the base of a Celtic cross at Carrowkennedy, 'who fought here against British forces on the 2nd June 1921.' Leaning on the wall of the cemetery at Leenane at the end of the day, I read the gravestone of Patrick Wallace, who had had the words 'Old IRA' added to his inscription. He had died full of years in 1985, proud to let future generations know of the part he played as a young man in that long-ago war of independence as a volunteer in a very different Irish Republican Army.

Bord Fáilte designates Galway city as the tourist's 'Gateway to Connemara', but the south-going walker passes through that gateway on the Mayo/Galway border at Leenane. The little village, a single row of shops, pubs and houses, curves around a bay of the narrow, glacier-gouged fjord of Killary Harbour. The inlet runs almost ten miles inland from the Atlantic, a superb natural deep-water anchorage and haven two or three hundred yards wide, a slit of sea-water under mountains that tower straight out of the fjord to two thousand feet and more. To the north stand Ben Gorm and Mweelrea, and opposite them the craggy ranges of the Maumturk Mountains swing away south-east through the central highlands of Connemara together with their neighbouring peaks of the Twelve Bens. Composed of sand from prehistoric seabeds baked into shining white quartzite, these remote hills beckon the wanderer at the same time as they threaten him. In sunshine they are overwhelmingly beautiful; in rain and cloud they become bare knuckles raised against all comers. The outlines of lazybeds are scratched all over their lower slopes, showing where human effort in hard times past forced a scanty existence out of this adamantine landscape. Even to the well-fed, well-equipped walker with all modern conveniences tucked into his rucksack and the certainty of a motor road leading to a comfortable bed not too far away, these mountains reveal the steely truth beneath the romantic image of Connemara.

Now that modern tourism has opened up the mountains and ragged sea coasts of western Galway, many peripheral areas are keen to creep under the cloak of the region that goes by the name of Connemara. But Connemara has a central place in an Irish culture that has nothing to do with tourism. Before railways and good roads penetrated the slab of country bounded in the north by Killary Harbour, in the east by Lough Corrib and on the west and south by the Atlantic, dwellers in the anglicised east of Ireland were making pilgrimages into Connemara to tap into their traditional language and heritage. Painters, writers, musicians, historians and folklorists, together with Dublin teachers and office workers, bumped west along the mountain tracks and coastal cart roads to stay in thatched cabins with Connemara families and get back to their roots. In the late nineteenth century there was a tourist boom as better communications led to the expansion of holiday towns, such as Clifden way out in the west. These days the railway goes no further west than Galway city, but the visitors pour down to the wild and beautiful Connemara coastline in ever lengthening crocodiles of cars. Connemara is one of the areas of Ireland no tourist wants to miss; and Irish families from the east send their children out here to spend time in the summer schools learning to use their schoolroom Irish among people who speak it as a first language.

Irish is not at all a practical language for communication with the wider world, and city youngsters stuck out in the wilds of Connemara for weeks on end can be rather less than wholehearted about the whole thing. But there's no denying the strength of the language's revival. The Limerick poet Michael Hartnett explained his decision to give up writing in English in his poem 'A Farewell to English', condemning poets and writers who cram every kind of cultural influence into their work:

Chef Yeats, that master of the use of herbs
could raise mere stew to a glorious height,
pinch of saga, soupçon of philosophy
carefully stirred in to get the flavour right,
and cook a poem around the basic verbs.
Our commis-chefs attend and learn the trade,
bemoan the scraps of Gaelic that they know:
add to a simple Anglo-Saxon stock
Cuchulainn's marrow-bones to marinate,
a dash of O'Rathaille simmered slow,
a glass of University hic-haec-hoc:
sniff and stand back and proudly offer you
the celebrated Anglo-Irish stew.*

There are many Gaeltacht areas in Connemara, Irish-speaking regions where government grants make it a little easier to build a house and find a job in this unproductive land. Only a little easier, however. Connemara's stunning beauty goes hand in hand with unemployment, emigration and poverty today as it has always done. Tourist money spreads a thick enough jam in the pretty towns along the coast, but back in the bogs and hills that make up the central area of Connemara most people are hard put to it to find a scraping of butter for the plain bread of everyday life.

From Leenane an old hill road climbs round the western flanks of the Maumturk Mountains and runs south along the Inagh Valley, a stony path that will one day be waymarked and signposted as the Western Way. For the present, though, there are no aids to direction-finding once you have put Killary Harbour behind you. After a mile or two I found myself adrift in an empty ocean of brown bog and

* The Gallery Press, Dublin 1978

rocky hillside, utterly barren and desolate: an uplifting experience, to be dependent on a narrow strip of trackway and my own wits and map-and-compass skills. The old road led me into many a bog and mire, but I moved along at a good speed with the larks for a marching band. The early discomforts of Donegal with pack and boots seemed to have been walked away in the intervening couple of hundred miles. There were no real difficulties about wayfinding, either. With the Maumturks at my left elbow and the sharp heads of the Twelve Bens leaning ever nearer on my right, all I had to do was watch out for the forestry. Like all conifer plantations, the forests along the Inagh Valley were riddled with misleading firebreaks that shot off from junctions in fours and fives, each one just like the others, none signposted. But at the point of maximum confusion the trees fell away to reveal the track running straight and true across another immensity of bog, where a solitary cabin with a rusty tin roof and a tiny thatched out-house stood untenanted. On the far side of the valley swooped the pale grey crags and valleys of the Twelve Bens, two and a half thousand feet in the sky. Not far from the lonely hut, close under the flank of Letterbreckaun Mountain, the remnants of a little whiskey still – stone fireplace and grass-grown mashing hollow – were half-hidden in the side of a cattle pen. The fiery poteen distilled there by the men of Letterbreckaun must have been one of their few pleasures and avenues of escape from this primitive landscape, so open to the view and so enclosing to the ambitious mind. The ruins of their houses and field walls lay on the lower slopes of the mountain, below the long hummocks of their lazybeds. There was no way of telling how long ago the last of the Letterbreckaun villagers had piled their possessions on to carts and jolted away for the final time down the rocky road I stood on.

That evening, munching roast duck by candlelight and attended by a white-aproned waiter in the dining room of the classy Inagh Lodge Hotel, with a peerless view across the wind-ruffled waters of Lough Inagh to another set of lazybed scrapings in the slopes of the Twelve Bens, a picture of the ruins of Letterbreckaun and the desolation of its famine-stricken people came into my mind, perhaps carried there by a chain of unhappy associations. The television news had driven more history lessons home. The violence north of the border was continuing to eat away with ever-increasing appetite at hopes for peace. Loyalists had come across the Donegal border to

Ballyshannon, only a few days after I had stayed the night there, and murdered a local Sinn Fein councillor – the first sectarian blood spilled in the Republic for some years. The IRA had retaliated by killing three soldiers in a mortar-bomb attack. A woman had had her legs blown off while sitting in her car on the driveway of her house – apparently a 'mistake'. And now the latest link in the bitter chain – three IRA members on their way to carry out some other operation had been burned to death in their car as British soldiers riddled it with bullets in a village in County Tyrone.

Meanwhile the protagonists in the Brooke talks were still sulking in their corners, unable to agree on either a venue or a chairman.

Twenty miles more the following day, in the first really hot summer weather of the journey. The naked mountains were soon behind me, stamped in two-dimensional clarity on a sky of unbroken blue. The houses of the hill farms made white specks in the middle of tiny green oases on the brown heathery slopes. I looked forward into a different Connemara, still hard and wild, but rolling now into low-lying bog-land that stretched away to the distant shores of Galway Bay where the sea lay hidden beyond a final rise of ground. The bog was scabbed with shoulders of white rock, glinting like quartzite but chunkier and coarser-grained. This was granite country, tough and unbreakable. I turned off the main highway to walk east along an endless, featureless bog road, and was immediately swallowed up in this rock-strewn, unpeopled landscape. Pools of water glinted here and there among the thousands of acres of peat bog. A step off the potholed road brought a squelch and suck from the waterlogged peat beneath the dry grass, and a quaking tremor under my boots. The sun burned on distant mountain ranges and surrounding bog, masking all intermediate colours. I saw only grey of rock, brown of turf, green of bog and silken blue of water. Robert Lloyd Praeger had eyes more finely tuned when he wrote:

> On a day of bright sky, when the hills are of that intoxicat-
> ing misty blue that belongs especially to the west, the bog-
> land is a lovely, far-reaching expanse of purple and rich
> brown: and the lakelets take on the quite indescribable
> colour that comes from clear sky reflected in bog-water,
> while the sea inlets glow with an intense but rather greener

blue. On such a day the wanderer will thank his lucky star
that it has brought him to Connemara.*

A middle-aged man and his small son were taking a break from
turf-cutting, lying back in the sunshine beside their stack of turf on
the roadside. I stopped to chat, not sorry to get the pack off my
shoulders for a few minutes. The man had a thirty-acre farm a couple
of miles away, but not a farm as an Englishman would understand
the term. 'There's no using farm machinery in these parts,' he told
me. 'That's because of the rocks that are in it. Look there,' and he
indicated the scar of his turf bank, where the dry white granite
gleamed under less than two feet of peat and grass. 'The land has to
be worked by hand, with the spade. So there's not a living to be made
from farming. We go on the dole, and sell a bit of turf; grow our
vegetables and have a few sheep on the hill. There's government
subsidies, too, and that's the only thing that keeps us going. There's
no hope of anything better. The tourists want the landscape to stay
as it is, of course. But I think most of the people in Connemara will
tell you they would rather see some factories here, some employment,
even if it spoils the scenery. It doesn't matter how beautiful the flowers
are – you can't reach out and eat the flowers.'

All along the bog road there were tiny figures in the wide landscape,
bending over their turf banks cutting away, pushing wheelbarrows
piled with turfs over the grass to the roadside and adding another few
sods to their heaps. On the rocks stood their tea flasks and sandwich
boxes. It was a scene of medieval labour, sweat and muscle power,
aching backs and streaming faces under the relentless sunshine. Ten-
year-old boys dug and trundled the turfs far out in the bog, skipping
a day's school to play their part in the family economy. As I walked
the road, I noticed more and more activity among the rocks and pools
of this apparently empty landscape through which I was moving in
idleness, the only unoccupied person there.

Where the road dipped through the granite scabs to the shore of
a deeply indented bay stood a thatched cottage, high on a knoll
overlooking the calm blue waters of Lough Oiriúlach. I paid my
eighty pence and wandered through the little house's couple of bare,
whitewashed rooms; hard wooden beds, a picture or two on the walls.

* *The Way That I Went*

The cottage's interior was a careful reconstruction, for the place had been burned down in 1921. The arsonists had been sanctioned in their work by the British government; they were a detachment of the feared and hated Black and Tans, a paramilitary regiment formed from the toughest available recruits, brought over to Ireland during the 1919–21 War of Independence to mete out summary punishment to the Republican rebels of the IRA. Five or six houses were burned here at Rosmuc in reprisal for a nearby ambush in which British soldiers had been wounded. The Black and Tan raid is still clearly remembered in Rosmuc. As well as burning houses, locals say, they took over the village pub, gorged themselves on free drinks and shot one of the villagers' dogs in the street. Given the Black and Tans' record, the village got off lightly that day. The thatched cottage on the knoll was singled out for destruction for a good reason: it had belonged to Padraic Pearse, the president of the provisional Irish Republican Government, who had proclaimed the infant Republic from the steps of the General Post Office in Dublin on Easter Monday, 1916. Pearse had been dead for five years when the Black and Tans came to Rosmuc, but his cottage was a symbol of resistance too potent to be allowed to stand.

The stirrings of nationalism fired in the aftermath of the Great Famine had spluttered out in one abortive rising after another throughout the nineteenth century, but there was always another group, another individual to blow on the dying torch. In the 1870s and 1880s nationalist fervour had coalesced around the charismatic figure of Charles Stewart Parnell, a Protestant landowner who as a Member of Parliament had championed the Catholic Irish peasants and brought their grievances to the attention of the House of Commons. His constant pressure forced through the 1881 Land Act which gave Irish tenants security of tenure and a fairer system of rents. He enjoyed tremendous support from committed nationalists and ordinary, non-political men and women alike. His attempt in 1885 to introduce a bill that would lead to Home Rule for Ireland failed, but by 1890 it looked as if he had the power base and the swell of opinion behind him to carry it through. But Parnell's sex life was to prove his downfall. He had been conducting an affair with a married woman, Kitty O'Shea, and when her husband filed for divorce in 1890, citing Parnell as co-respondent, the great leader fell from power with a crash. Within two years Parnell was dead. Far from rejecting their

Inishowen landscape: near Malin Head in northernmost Donegal

Ben Wisken raises its pointed head over a boreen in County Sligo

The cool dimness of Hargadon's bar in Sligo town, Holy Grail of Irish drinkers

Tomb of Alexander Black in Skreen churchyard, north-west Sligo: ploughing a furrow in his Sunday best

Right: Michael Monaghan with some of his giant turf-cutting machines, near Bellacorick in the great bog of Mayo

Centre: Modern-day member of the Fianna: Oliver Geraghty stoops for a drink in the wilderness of Mayo's Nephin Beg Mountains

Below: St Patrick blesses the pilgrims at the foot of Croagh Patrick

Left: Didi Korner and Anne Kelly row towards their home on Island More in Clew Bay

Centre: Abandoned farmstead under the quartzite humps of the Twelve Bens in the mountainous heart of Connemara, County Galway

Bottom: Cutting turf in the granite-scabbed bog of southern Connemara, with the Maumturk Mountains in the background

fallen idol, the fervent young Irish nationalists rallied to his cause with even greater passion. The British government, faced with continuing tension in Ireland, finally passed the Home Rule Act in 1914 (with a rider allowing the Six Counties of Ulster to opt out), then suspended it for the duration of the First World War, which broke out soon after. The British Army was a powerful presence in Ireland, but the nationalists were determined to have their way. The long-germinating seeds were about to have a brief and bloody flowering.

The little thatched house in the Connemara bogland was the ground in which many of those seeds grew. When Padraic Pearse built the cottage around the turn of the century, he was a schoolmaster in Dublin, a man in early middle age with a reputation as a poet and writer of short stories. I bought a book of Pearse's stories from the stall in his cottage and read them in bed that night – a boy who flies away with the swallows to the country of eternal summer; an old man who saves his soul by befriending Iosagán, the Holy Child; the Black Chafer witch who curses a family and steals their daughter. Simply written, rooted in the countryside around the cottage, they are based on their author's highly moral, Christian values. Buried in them are allegories of Ireland's sufferings and aspirations. Pearse brought groups of his students to the cottage in Connemara to immerse them in the Irish language and culture, and drew strength and inspiration from these visits. Here he had the time and space to lay the groundwork that would bring his and others' dreams of an independent Irish republic closer to reality.

Along with his literary activity, Pearse was plunging ever deeper into active nationalism. In 1912 he joined the Irish Republican Brotherhood, becoming a member of its Supreme Council in 1915. By Easter 1916, when the IRB had decided to turn the annual 'manoeuvres' of the Irish Volunteers into an armed uprising, Pearse was the key figure in the nationalist movement. Fundamental though it was to the eventual foundation of an independent Ireland, in the short term the Easter Rising was an abysmal failure. Internecine strife, then as now, cut drastically at the roots that should have nourished co-operation among the activists.

The Irish Volunteers and the Irish Republican Brotherhood, though sharing the same ends, could not agree on the means or the timing. The orders issued by the IRB to use the manoeuvres as a springboard for revolution were countermanded on the eve of the

Rising by the commander-in-chief of the Volunteers. By the time the IRB had overruled him and reinstated the go-ahead, most of the potential rebels had abandoned their plans. In the confusion, fewer than two thousand of the intended ten thousand insurgents actually took arms on that Easter Sunday. Around a thousand nationalists, led by Pearse, Tom Clarke, James Connolly and a handful of others, took over several important public buildings in Dublin. On the steps of the G.P.O. Pearse read out the rolling, emotional terms of the proclamation:

> We declare the right of the people of Ireland to the ownership of Ireland, and to the unfettered control of Irish destinies, to be sovereign and indefeasible ... we hereby proclaim the Irish Republic as a Sovereign Independent State and we pledge our lives and the lives of our comrades-in-arms to the cause of its freedom, of its welfare and of its exaltation among the nations.

The rebels pledged their lives, and those pledges were all too soon redeemed. After a week under siege, during which many of the insurgents died and about five hundred British soldiers were killed or injured, the G.P.O. was a smoking ruin and Pearse had no option but to surrender. Within three days of the capitulation he and six other rebel leaders were dead, executed by firing squad in Kilmainham Jail, their bodies reported to have been buried in quicklime to leave no relics or graves for supporters to rally round. Eight more leaders of the Rising were executed over the following months. The 'terrible beauty' of the revolution, in W.B. Yeats's resounding phrase, had been born and done to death in short order. But the long-drawn-out manner in which the executions were carried out began to work against the British. Irish and international opinion, at first against the rebels, swung behind them in sympathy. Now the Sinn Fein ('Ourselves Alone') movement, formed late in the nineteenth century to establish a hand-in-hand government of Ireland by British and Irish, hardened its position and attracted tremendous support for its restatement of the 1916 Proclamation. In 1919, despite having half its seventy-three recently-elected Westminster MPs in jail, it met in the first session of its own Irish Parliament (Dáil Eireann) and demanded the withdrawal from Ireland of all British troops; a demand the British government, committed to the defence of Ulster, was in no position to meet. So began two years of warfare – formal war with organised troops and military hardware on the part of the British, and a scattered affair of ambushes and guerrilla raids by the nationalists, whose squabbling factions of IRB and Irish Volunteers had united under the title of the Irish Republican Army. The British Army and its paramilitary Black and Tans and equally ruthless 'Auxiliaries' (the Police Auxiliary Cadets, set up to inject steel into the Royal Irish Constabulary) outnumbered the IRA by three to one, but they were never able to deal effectively with opponents who could sell them their groceries one day and lie in wait for them by the roadside the next. In July 1921 a truce was declared, followed by the Anglo-Irish Treaty which finally split the Six Counties of Ulster from the Irish Free State, as southern Ireland was now styled.

Padraic Pearse's dream had become reality, but Ireland's nightmare was far from over. The treaty had included among its terms an oath of allegiance to the British sovereign, and the proviso that in time of war or great international upheaval the British armed forces should have the right to base themselves on Irish soil. Hardliners in the IRA, unable to stomach these conditions or to accept that the reunification of the Six Counties of Northern Ireland with the twenty-six of the South was now an irrevocably lost cause, formed themselves into a new Republican movement and bitterly opposed the conciliatory position of the Irish Free State Army, who were prepared to swallow the unpalatable pill for the sake of a peaceful infancy for the newborn country. Opposition in argument soon became opposition in arms, and once again the hills and valleys rang to the sound of gunfire. This time it was Irishman against Irishman, a bloody civil war that raged from June 1922 for almost a year. The Church authorities and most ordinary Irish people were on the side of the Free State Army, having had enough of bloodshed and bitterness, and they were supported by arms, supplies and advice from the British government. When Michael Collins, the charismatic leader of the Free State Army, was killed in an ambush in August 1922 there were more reprisal executions – not by the Black and Tans this time, but by Irish government forces. The Republicans fought on, but the weight of public opinion and the tide of history was against them. In May 1923 the final bullets were fired, the dust began to settle and the Free State – still technically a dominion of the British Empire – riven by civil war, exhausted and shaky to its foundations, emerged into the light of qualified freedom. It would be another twenty-six years before Ireland would officially be declared a republic and sever its ties with the Commonwealth; fifty years before the country of its own free will became part of the European Economic Community and pushed its nose in front of Britain in accepting the political realities of modern Europe. Eire's relations with its self-lacerating neighbour across the border would continue to blow hot and cold. The puzzle is far from complete, even now. But at least some of the pieces – Irish pieces – are in place; and some of these first took their shape in Connemara, in the bare little rooms of the cottage on the knoll.

At six o'clock that evening the road to Rosmuc was suddenly full of youngsters released from summer school and making their noisy way back to their various lodgings. 'Dia dhuit (God be with you),' I hailed them as they passed, using one of the few Irish phrases I had managed to learn. 'Dia agus Mhuire dhuit (God and Mary be with you),' muttered the students in sullen response. I saw that Irish was not the flavour of the day. 'Hello!' I essayed to the next group, a bunch of girls passing a cigarette around between them. 'Oh, hello,' said their spokeswoman brightly in broad Dublin. 'God, it's nice to be speakin' English again!' They walked on, giggling, and I caught a most un-Gaelic phrase floating back to me: 'Oh, feckin' 'ell!'

Somehow I had mistaken the location of Dunmánus, my bed-and-breakfast place. 'Theresa Conroy?' said the woman down at the tip of the Rosmuc peninsula. 'Sure, she lives back there, the way you've come. Five or six miles. Jump in the car and I'll drop you down. No problem.' I squashed in the back seat with her children and we roared back up the long road to the Conroys' house. 'I'll drop you down to Casla,' said Tom Conroy the next morning. 'No, it's no problem. This rain will clear by the evening.' But the rain, which had crept in from the Atlantic overnight, had settled in for the day. That clear blue sky over the Connemara bogland had been streaked with mares'-tails of cloud the previous evening, a weather forecast I should have had the wit to read. I walked five dripping miles south from Casla village, then gave it up as a bad job and caught the bus to the outermost tip of the chain of islands I had been waiting so long to see.

*

At the turn of the century Connemara was one of the neediest recipients of relief from the Congested Districts Board, which had been set up in 1891 to combat some of the problems of overpopulation from which many districts of Ireland, despite the devastation of the Great Famine, were still suffering. The Board paid relief money for road building, pier construction and the establishment of fishing fleets and small industries throughout poverty-stricken rural Ireland, as well as buying up the property of many of the landlords and sharing it out among the people. Here in southern Connemara a series of causeways was built to connect the remote, ragged-edged islands – Lettermore, Gorumna, Lettermullen and several others – that hang down into Galway Bay from the mainland. There was no poorer land in the west of Ireland than these low-lying, rock-strewn scraps of granite and heather, and no population in greater need than their overcrowded inhabitants.

In 1905 the *Manchester Guardian*, a newspaper noted for its championing of the underdog, commissioned two well-known Irishmen to visit the congested districts of Connemara and report on what they found there. John Millington Synge and Jack Butler Yeats were the ideal men for the job. Synge had lived among the Aran Islanders, whose lives he had described in his play *Riders to the Sea*, and he was steeped in the history and lore of the west; while Jack Yeats, brother of the poet W.B. Yeats, had made a name for himself with his paintings and sketches of Connemara. Before setting out on my walk through Ireland I had visited the British Newspaper Library in Colindale, north London and unearthed those yellowing copies of the *Manchester Guardian* for June and July 1905 in which the reports of Synge and Yeats had been published. The articles stood out strikingly from the surrounding copy, a bold pen-and-ink drawing by Yeats forming the centrepiece for a detailed account by Synge of the miseries and desperation witnessed by the two men on their month-long journey.

> At a turning of the road we came in sight of a dozen or more men and women working hurriedly and doggedly improving a further portion of this road, with a ganger swaggering among them and directing their work. Some of the people were cutting out sods from grassy patches near the road, others were carrying down bags of earth in a

slow, inert procession, a few were breaking stones, and three or four women were scraping out a sort of sandpit at a little distance. As we drove quickly by, we could see that every man and woman was working with a sort of hang-dog dejection that would be enough to make any casual passer mistake them for a band of convicts. The wages given on these works are usually a shilling a day, and as a rule one person only, generally the head of the family, is taken from each house. Sometimes the best worker in a family is thus forced away from his ordinary work of farming or fishing or kelp-making for this wretched remuneration at a time when his private industry is most needed. If this system of relief has some things in its favour, it is far from satisfactory in other ways and is not always economical. I have been told of a district not very far from here where there is a ganger, an overseer, an inspector, a paymaster, and an engineer superintending the work of two paupers only. This is possibly an exaggerated account of what is really taking place, yet it probably shows, not too inexactly, a state of things that is not too rare in Ireland.*

Among all the needy districts described in these reports, it was the descriptions and sketches of the chain of islands south of Rosmuc that most moved me as I sat at the microfilm machine in the newspaper library. The typewriter of Synge and the artist's pen of Yeats had both been inspired by this forgotten corner of the west. I had gathered a good idea of the islands from the newspaper accounts – windswept, stony and lonely – but jolting south in that bus, with the schoolchildren of Gorumna shrieking and scuffling in the back seats behind me, I looked out through the rain-streaked windows on a landscape far harsher than my comfortable imaginings.

'Going all the way?' the bus driver had asked incredulously when he picked me up at the roadside. These islands are well off the tourist map, and far removed from the green and smiling image of the Emerald Isle. Their lumpy ground writhes away from rock-studded sea inlets, thickly veined with stone walls so loosely constructed that the sky shows between each piled boulder. The tiny fields, scarcely

* 'Among the Relief Works', *Manchester Guardian*, 17 June 1905

twenty feet square, are half granite lumps and half grass, but what grazing ground exists is so valuable to its owner that the delineating walls are carefully carried on in single lines of stones across the boulders and through the patches of bog. The islands look like a series of green and grey patchwork quilts crumpled up and thrown down in the bay. Like their forefathers, the islanders grow their potatoes in minute squares of lazybeds, tucked in behind rocks and down in clefts, wherever the salty wind (which Synge reported withering the crops of the turn-of-the-century inhabitants) cannot get at them. Houses are built low, on squares of ground levelled off among the hummocks, connected to the winding road by stone-walled boreens with grass growing in their central strips. In the pelting rain it all looked bleak, barren and alien, a landscape with its life and secrets hidden from the stranger.

We drove across the walled causeways which had been built by the islanders in the 1890s to earn the subsidies of the Congested Districts Board. Before their construction, the narrow channels between the islands had been passable only at low tide, or by boat. At the roadside settlement of Tír an Fhia, 'the land of the deer', the riotous school-children got off the bus and chased each other away home down the boreens. The driver sighed with relief, ground his gears and carried me on in company with two or three cloth-capped and headscarved elderly islanders, sitting straight-backed in wordless patience.

Down on the toe of Gorumna I stepped out on to a gleaming wet roadway and knocked at the door of Ost na nOilean. Synge and Yeats had known it as the Hotel of the Isles, a popular place to stay in their day; but on this rainy June evening I was the only guest. There was no knowing if my box-like room had sheltered either of the *Manchester Guardian*'s reporters. The inn has undergone many changes since they came here, descending from classy hotel to youth hostel, then becoming a shady shebeen where the folk of Gorumna and Lettermullen islands could buy health-shaking glasses of the poteen distilled nearby by their fellow islanders. It has come up a long way since then, but not far enough for Bord Fáilte to plant one of their shamrock signs of approval outside. No matter – the welcome was warm, and the view from my bedroom window looked out through a pincer of rocky inlet, draped with ochre-yellow seaweed, to a distant glimpse of the Aran Islands.

Before assaulting my poached salmon I walked out across the

causeways and along the lanes through Lettermullen on to the mile-long Furnace Island. A final burst of rain lashed in from towering Atlantic storm clouds, jumping in silver sparks off the roadway and soaking me to the skin. Then the sun came greasily through and lit up a stupendous double rainbow that arched against the black wall of retreating cloud over the hills of the Connemara mainland. I sang and whistled my way through the puddles to the top of Furnace, where the road faded out into a green path running round the shore to a view over a narrow strait to Dinish Island, the final link in the lonely chain. A couple of houses, deserted for years, occupied the few hundred square yards of Dinish, and the rocky chunk of land lay entirely devoid of sound or movement.

J.M. Synge's article in the *Manchester Guardian* of 21 June 1905, 'The Ferryman of Dinish Island', is illustrated by one of Jack Yeats's most effective drawings. The toothless old ferryman is shown straining at a pair of stout oars, a battered hat on his head, one nailed boot up on the thwart of the boat, his trousers torn into rags. Two feverish points of light glow out of the inky hollows of his eyes.

Synge found out a good deal about the old man during the few hours they spent with him. As he rowed them across to Dinish and walked with them around the island, he spoke movingly of a hard life whose worst years had now come upon him. As a vigorous young sailor of twenty he had gone to America, and worked in New York, Baltimore and New Orleans. He had returned to Europe, plying a coasting trade all round Ireland, Scotland and Wales, moving on to Birkenhead, Manchester and Liverpool. The hard times had begun when his two brothers had emigrated to America, obliging him to come unwillingly back to Dinish Island to take over the family house and scrap of land. From then on it had been an unremitting struggle to feed himself and his family. His wife had died. His potatoes had rotted in the ground. He had gone on the relief works for a shilling a day, but could not make ends meet. For a time the old man had ferried the schoolmistress and ten children across from Lettermullen to Dinish, but the school had closed down. Now he was living on credit from the shop, to be paid back from the few shillings he would make burning kelp to supply the glass-making industry in the summer months. One of his daughters had managed to send him £3 from America, and two other daughters were soon to follow her there.

Perhaps, the old man said, he himself would then be able to escape. He hated Dinish, he told Synge, with a bitter hatred.

'Isn't it a queer thing to be sitting here now thinking on those times, and I after being near twenty years back on this bit of a rock that a dog wouldn't look at, where the pigs die and the spuds die, and even the judges and quality do come out and do lower our rents when they see the wild Atlantic driving in across the accursed stones ... So there I am now with no pigs, and no cows, and a young family running round with no mother to mind them, and what can you do with children that know nothing at all, and will often put down as much in the pot one day as would do three days, and do be wasting the meal, though you can't say a word against them, for it's young and ignor- ant they are? If it wasn't for them, I'd be off this evening, and I'd earn my living easy on the sea, for I'm only fifty- seven years of age, and I have good health, but how can I leave my young children? And I don't know what way I'm to go on living in this place that the Lord created last, I'm thinking, in the end of time, and it's often when I sit down and look around on it I do begin cursing and damning and asking myself how poor people can go on executing their religion at all.'

For a while he said nothing, and we could see tears in his eyes ...

'It's to America we'll all be going, and isn't it a fearful thing to think I'll be kept here another ten years may-be tending the children and striving to keep them alive, when I might be abroad in America living in decency and earning my bread?'

In the bar of Ost na nOilean that night a young man approached me. 'Excuse me for asking,' he said politely, 'but was that you I saw down on the beach on Furnace? You had a book in your hand, I think. I saw you from my house.' It was not a casual sighting, I realised when we had talked a while. The young islander, and probably others like him as well, had been watching me carefully. He was supplementing his dole money with a little business on the side, picking winkles on the shore and selling them, and had been wondering if I might be a 'gauger', an official from the social security office, checking up on these or other clandestine activities.

Reassured by my responses to his few gentle questions, the young man leaped up on to the little stage at the end of the bar and belted out a song in Gaelic. It was Saturday night out at Ost na nOilean, and the two-man band had put the evening on a lively footing. Someone else sang a sentimental ballad in English. A heavy-bellied man shuffled a jig in his fancy shoes. Two couples waltzed. A group of women sat bolt upright in smart hair-dos and party skirts, while two old men in the wrinkled jackets and trousers they had been working in all day joked together in Irish at the next table. A red-headed boy strapped on the bandleader's melodeon and played a few tunes with all the expert's twiddly bits in all the right places. 'All Ireland Under-15 Champion, that boy,' murmured the picker of winkles, replacing fluids lost during his own performance. The lad smiled modestly when I congratulated him on his playing. 'I've a long way to go yet,' he said. The barman served him with a pint of stout for his father and a chocolate bar for himself. All the people in the room stood up, and most of them sang, as the band played the Irish national anthem at the end of the evening.

I slipped outside to cool my head and sniff the rising wind. The sea roared and crashed out in the bay, and fifteen miles across the water there was the palest of glows in the sky behind the long double hump of Inishmore, the largest of the Aran Islands. In thirty-six hours I would be over there myself, in Connemara's remote Atlantic outpost.

In 1898 John Millington Synge had come to live for a while in the Aran Islands, on the recommendation of W.B. Yeats, who recognised in the young writer the ability to describe life as it really was in those remote, still primitive islands. From Synge's book *The Aran Islanders* and his play *Riders to the Sea* I had a picture of rough lives lived at the mercy of the elements, dominated by rock and water and by fear and superstition. The picture had been further coloured by the book I was reading as I walked through Connemara. The Aran Islands' most famous literary son, Liam O'Flaherty, produced a classic island novel in *Skerrett* (1932), a page-turner of high tension and drama, as well as a concentrated dose of turn-of-the-century Aran Island life. O'Flaherty's story was based closely on real events that divided the island community and threw into sharp focus the conflict between tradition and progress that has been intensifying ever since.

The schoolmaster of Inishmore, David O'Callaghan ('David Skerrett' in the novel), developed a bitter hatred of his employer, the parish priest Father Murty Farragher ('Father Moclair'). For several years the two men tried all they could to do the other down. The schoolmaster came to stand for everything proud, independent and traditional in island life; while the priest, with his schemes for material improvement of the islanders' lot and his dominance of their daily lives, both spiritual and economic, represented the new and steadily growing influence of the outside world that was eroding those traditional customs and beliefs. O'Flaherty, who had been a pupil of O'Callaghan's at Oatquarter school on Inishmore, depicts his old teacher as a stubborn, violent man, ruled by his passions but jealously guarding what O'Flaherty himself most valued, while 'Father Moclair' is shown as a clever, greedy fat-cat exploiting the islanders' ignorance and desire for a less limited way of life in order to feather his own nest.

> The new gospel of love for their language and traditional mode of living, together with a longing for national freedom, which [Skerrett] began to preach to them, made no appeal to these peasants, who, like all peasants, were only too eager to sell any birth-right for a mess of pottage. And Father Moclair, the man of progress and materialist, had the pottage . . . it seems a people cannot progress without losing their innocence in the cunning necessary for ambitious commerce; and that avarice brings in its train dissension, strife and manifold corruption.*

The outcome of the strife between teacher and employer was a foregone conclusion. David O'Callaghan ended his thirty-four years' service in Inishmore by being thrown out of school, job and the island itself. Liam O'Flaherty compounds the disaster in his book: Skerrett, having lost his son in an accident and seen his wife removed to an asylum as an insane alcoholic, ends his days on the mainland in the same asylum, while Father Moclair leaves shortly afterwards to

---

* *Skerret* by Liam O'Flaherty, Wolfhound Press, Dublin 1988 (originally published 1932)

become bishop of the diocese. The two combatants have held centre-stage throughout the book, but all the characters are subordinate to the stage itself on which the drama is played out, the intractable, all-devouring island and surrounding sea.

To set against this doom-laden picture of the Aran Islands I had only what my outdated guidebooks could tell me about the island men in their pampooties (shoes of cowhide with the hair turned outside to give a grip on the wet rocks) and their homespun tweed trousers and Aran sweaters, handling their canoe-shaped currachs of wood and canvas with dazzling skill in the surf; the island women in red woollen skirts and shawls; the bare limestone crags in the fields and the wind-scoured cliffs where prehistoric stone forts faced the Atlantic storms. The topography was accurate enough, as I discovered during my visit, but the few currachs on view were lying immobile and upside down on the shore and by the roadside, like sleeping black slugs. The costume of the Inishmore islanders, too, had moved on with the times since those accounts had been penned. The first local man I saw in Kilronan, the main village on Inishmore, wore trainers, jeans and a T-shirt emblazoned 'Official Cannabis Society'. It was the Americans and Japanese among my fellow-passengers aboard *Aran Seabird* who displayed the traditional costume of the tourist community: fluorescent windbreakers and camera cases on body straps. The Dubliners holidaymaking in Connemara wore much the same as the islanders. They dived into the Kilronan pubs to lay into the Guinness until sailing time, while the windbreaker-and-camera crew hired all the bicycles at the pier and pedalled away towards the clifftop fort of Dún Aengus, the main tourist attraction of the Aran Islands. In ten minutes there was hardly a newcomer in sight.

The three limestone islands lie about ten miles south of the upper coast of Galway Bay, eight-mile-long Inishmore to the west with the smaller blobs of Inishmaan and Inisheer in line astern. Inishmore swells gently into two central domes, falling away southward to a breathtaking coast of squared-off cliffs dropping from level platforms of stone sheer into the sea two or three hundred feet below. The fields and their straight lines of stone walls lie mostly north and south, running away in parallel ranks as if streamed across the surface of the island by a square-tipped artist's brush, over the crest and down to the cliff platforms that face the distant coast of County Clare across Galway Bay.

I spent a long day wandering through this formidable, desolate landscape, first climbing up to the ruins of the ancient oratory on the hill above Killeany Bay at the south-east end of Inishmore. The miniature shell of Teampall Bheanáin, 10 feet by 15 feet, perched in a grey wilderness of limestone pavement where lemon-yellow rock roses grew in the cracks between the slabs. A slit of a doorway and a round-arched window were the only chinks in the little grey stone fortress built by St Benignus when he came to Inishmore around the turn of the sixth century AD, one of a host of early Christian hermits whose cells and tiny churches are studded throughout the Aran Islands. What a view the saint commanded up here – the low line of the Burren hinterland of Clare, the entire sweep of Galway Bay and a prospect north over the Connemara bogland to the Maumturks and the Twelve Bens standing proudly on the skyline nearly thirty miles away.

The blocks of limestone pavement wobbled and creaked under my feet as I picked my way down across the stone-littered fields to the cliffs. The Atlantic had been swept into a heavy swell by the winds of the past few days, and its green waves were pounding the cliffs and swirling round the caves it had licked out over the centuries. Walking the cliffs was a tiring business, stepping interminably up and down the limestone ledges. The sea boomed and shuddered, throwing out great white plumes of spray where the incoming waves collided with the outgoing water pouring in thick curtains off the rock ledges. Kittiwakes screamed round the crevices, and herring gulls yakked crossly from their sheltered spots under the walls. Dún Dúchathair, the Black Fort, stood splendidly isolated on its flat headland, a snaking rampart of stone blocks twenty feet high enclosing a strange little labyrinth of low walls in a grassy bay. No one knows when the Black Fort was built, but it was probably before the first century BC. Those ancient islanders must have had good reason to fear attack, for they built four great clifftop strongholds on Inishmore alone. The dark, isolated structure of Dún Dúchathair is thought to be older than the better-preserved Dún Aengus, and in its way is even more impressive. But few tourists take the rocky path here in preference to the motor road that leads to within easy walking distance of Dún Aengus. On this sunny day I had the crumbling stairs and ruined walkways of Dún Dúchathair to myself.

At six o'clock in the evening I came to Dún Aengus to find that mighty fort deserted as well. While I had been bumping on a hired bicycle down the winding boreen that threads the wild southern side of Inishmore, the day visitors had been streaming back in the opposite direction along the tarmac road to the ferry waiting at Kilronan pier. Where the stony roller-coaster of the boreen reached its crest there was a wonderful wide view down over the waist of the island and up again to the semi-circle of Dún Aengus hanging above three hundred feet of sheer cliff-face. In the field below the fort a stout girl sat on a stone stile, cheerfully gossiping with a friend on the mainland by portable phone, with the ageless landscape of Aran stretched out all around her. I picked a careful path through the *chevaux de frise*, a belt of knife-edged blades of stone set upright at the time the fort was built as an outer defence which would slow a charge by attackers to a painful forward stumble, giving the defenders of Dún Aengus time to organise themselves and pick off their enemies one by one. Who those enemies might have been, though – and, for that matter, who the builders and defenders of Dún Aengus were – can only be hazily conjectured. Iron Age farmer-warriors, perhaps? Whereas the door-ways and walls of the Black Fort had been reduced by time and storms to near shapelessness, those of Dún Aengus stood clear-cut and solid in three concentric semi-circles, their outer ends running to the very edge of the cliff.

As I left Dún Aengus I passed two young Americans busy impressing their girlfriends by shying rocks at one of the upright stones in the *chevaux de frise*. They shouted and swore with glee as the chips of stone flew – the only instance of hooligan behaviour I had seen in Ireland. Down on the road I came across three more asses: furry ones with long ears, who came up to nuzzle the bike and block my path. I scratched their ears sentimentally, but the islander who came round the corner in his car to find the road full of donkeys was more practical. He rolled down his window, shouted 'Heh!' and gave the nearest donkey a good thump with his fist, bestowing a scowl on me as he drove away. At Oatquarter, further along the road, I passed the school where Liam O'Flaherty had been thrashed and instructed by the choleric David O'Callaghan – a mere shell now, but with a healthy tree growing out of its ruins, an apt symbol.

My host for the night was Kevin Gill, principal of Inishmore's little secondary school, who had come back to Aran after several years teaching in Africa. Kevin's family goes back at least two hundred years in Inishmore, and we spent many enjoyable hours chatting over island affairs past and present. 'One of our problems,' said Kevin amid the clatter of workmen building an extension to his house, 'is that the bright young people tend to go right through with their education and then leave Inishmore. Then they probably won't come back until they're well into middle age. Mind you, those that stay do well enough with the fishing: many of them could buy up the ones who get jobs away. But it's emigration that's killed us in the past.'

I recounted my walk along the southern edge of the island, commenting on the absence of tourists there. 'Oh, yes,' Kevin said, 'you won't find yourself crowded if you go out to those parts. We get two kinds of tourists; those who stay in the Kilronan pubs and see nothing, and those who are interested in the island and explore it on foot – but there's not so many of those. Inishmore is changing with tourism, of course, and with the influence of the modern world. They wanted to make a film of *Skerrett* recently, but the director couldn't find a location for the village that didn't have telegraph poles sticking up in it. If you want to see a part of Aran that's hardly changed at all, you'd do better to get over to Inishmaan.'

Inishmore is only half an hour's boat ride from Rossaveal on the mainland, and you can reach Inisheer, the smallest of the three Aran islands, from the village of Doolin on the coast of County Clare in the same time. Inishmaan, the potato-shaped island in the middle of the chain, has maintained a much more traditional way of life and an atmosphere far more relaxed and free of the pressures of time and progress, by virtue of its relative inaccessibility. The boats can't get in to the jetty on Inishmaan at certain states of tide, and the little Islander planes of Aer Arann only hop in and out of the Inishmaan airstrip on a few of their flights between the other two islands. A strong wind and misty rain kept the next morning's flight grounded at Galway airport, and I hung around in Inishmore's tiny airstrip building hoping for a break in the weather and talking to the man who does everything from organising flights to making tea for the waiting passengers. He confirmed Kevin Gill's comments about the drift of youngsters away from the island.

'There's about nine hundred people on Inishmore now, whereas a hundred years ago there were 2700. We fed the figures into a computer, and it predicted there would only be about 450 by the turn of the century. Yes, the young people are going, and leaving their father and mother in the house. Then the old people die, and there's an empty house. Incomers would be very glad to buy them, but the people are not inclined to sell. I think myself it will change, though. It's a poor outlook for islands in the future. They'll become havens for drop-outs and misfits, or holiday places for a few rich people. The grants and the dole are certainly keeping people on the islands and in the poor parts just now, but they're ruining us at the same time. The dole is a very short-sighted thing, to my mind. If you really have to work hard for your money, then you earn your own peace of mind, and you also help your community.

'When I was young the people here had their own butter and milk and vegetables, and they grew corn and flax. They were completely self-sufficient. We could go down on the shore on a moonlit night and pick up lobsters, mackerel and herring on the rocks. But not now. All the boats go fishing deep-sea, and that's been bad for the past few years. Of course, we could become a tourist island and nothing else, but we wouldn't want to live that way.'

There were three other passengers for the plane that eventually came buzzing in from Galway. Sister Beánin in the seat beside me crossed herself as we took off and circled over the bay. 'That was built by my patron saint,' she said, looking down at the little dot of Teampall Bheanáin among the rocks on the spine of Inishmore. The flight took seven minutes from airstrip to airstrip, and I made a fool of myself as soon as we had landed on Inishmaan, running across the strip to snap a photograph of the plane taking off with the island houses in the background. Roger Faherty, who had brought his Land-Rover down to collect parcels from the plane, gave me an unsmiling stare as I came back. 'You're not supposed to do that,' he told me severely. 'If it had been any other pilot he would have stopped the plane and shouted at you.'

I felt chastened, particularly as Roger turned out to be the husband of Angela Faherty, who was putting me up for the night. But at Cregmore House there was tea and a kind welcome, and I soon made my peace with Roger.

Things are different on Inishmaan. There are the same stone walls round tiny fields, the same rocky hinterland and wave-beaten coast-line of limestone ledges as on Inishmore. But few tourists come to the middle island, and those that do are keen to walk, to enjoy the wild flowers and all-embracing peace of the place and to disturb nothing and nobody. There are no hotels, no gift shops, nothing that might attract day visitors. I had made a bad start by blundering across one of the few rules of Inishmaan, but within half an hour I had put it behind me and was just another unobtrusively welcome guest. Down at the jetty I leaned against the wall among a group of islanders and watched *Rose of Aran* unloading the big cardboard boxes that held groceries, spare parts of machinery, tools and household goods. Babies asleep in pushchairs were handed across the heaving gap between ship and jetty. Below on the sandy slipway two men in yellow oilskins were pushing a currach out into the waves on their way to check their lobster pots – a currach traditionally built of wooden laths and tarred canvas, but powered by an outboard engine mounted on the stern. In the lane above the jetty a boy on a bicycle stopped me. 'Did you see any kegs coming ashore?' he asked anxiously. The island's pub was running out of Guinness, and with the wind rising no one could be sure when the next shipment of black nectar might arrive.

Inishmaan, like any other small island, relies heavily on its plane and boats for the import of essential goods, but there's an air of self-reliance and independence about both place and people. Most practical aspects of life are arranged by a strong and well supported co-operative, which buys goods in bulk and distributes them evenly. A knitwear factory (run, admittedly, by a Dubliner) employs a good few of Inishmaan's youngsters. There's a tiny school for the island's handful of young children, though at twelve they have to leave and attend boarding schools on the mainland. Inishmaan is a great place to be brought up. The children can wander along the little network of roads in complete safety. There are no child molesters or abductors here, and no dangers from traffic. The island has just one car (belonging to the nurse), three Land-Rovers, a few motorbikes and a small number of tractors. On Inishmaan, feet are still the main means of transport.

The island population of 250 use their light, buoyant currachs to fish for lobster and salmon, and grow their own hay and vegetables and raise their cows and sheep in the diminutive fields on soil laboriously created, now as in times past, by mixing seaweed and sand. Stones cleared by hand from the fields have been built into walls strong enough to withstand all but the most violent gales, with stone-filled gateway gaps that can be unblocked and filled in again in a few

moments when beasts have to be moved from field to field. The walls
are shoulder-high, giving a clear view of anyone in the vicinity. I soon
grew used to the sight of a cloth-capped or shawled head moving
slowly along the line of a wall, thirty feet and three fields away. Many
of the older Inishmaan islanders still wear traditional dress, not for
the benefit of tourist cameras, but because no modern clothing has
its capacity to resist weather and hard wear. Walking round the island
I came across men in thick, homespun cloth trousers and jackets,
squatting in twos and threes out of the wind in the lee of the stone
walls as they smoked and talked. At one point I fell in step behind
an old lady going slowly home with her dog leading the way and her
cat following. She wore a navy-blue wool skirt and knitted sweater,
and had a brightly-coloured shawl in a criss-cross, tartan-like pattern
pulled close over her head. On her feet were what seemed to be shoes
studded with hobnails, their points flashing in the sun with every step.
I quickened my stride and caught up with her as she turned into the
garden gate of her thatched cottage. Tradition, alas, had stopped at
her woollen-stockinged ankles. The shoes were fashionable trainers,
with fluorescent studs winking in their soles.

On the road that ran by Inishmaan's few houses stood a sign
marked 'Teach Synge', pointing to a semi-derelict cottage with grass
and moss sprouting in its thatch. A knock at the neighbouring house
brought a white-haired, bespectacled woman to the door. Dia dhuit.
Could I please look round the old house? Well – it wasn't open to
visitors usually. But if I would like to go with her . . .

She held open the green-painted door of the cottage and I walked
into what had once been the kitchen. The peeling walls were colour-
washed in faded yellow and blue, and a blackened chimney-breast
ran up one wall. Piles of fishing net were heaped all over the floor,
blocking a doorway through which I had a glimpse into a green-walled
bedroom. Here between 1898 and 1902 J.M. Synge had lodged each
year with the McDonagh family while he gathered material for the
articles that would be collected to form *The Aran Islanders*, as well as
inspiration for his plays *Riders to the Sea* and *The Playboy of the Western
World*. 'My room is at one end of the cottage,' he wrote,

> with a boarded floor and ceiling, and two windows opposite
> each other. Then there is the kitchen with earth floor and
> open rafters . . . The kitchen itself, where I will spend

most of my time, is full of beauty and distinction. The red dresses of the women who cluster round the fire on their stools give a glow of almost Eastern richness, and the walls have been toned by the turf smoke to a soft brown that blends with the grey earth-colour of the floor. Many sorts of fishing-tackle, and the nets and oil-skins of the men, are hung upon the walls or among the open rafters; and right overhead, under the thatch, there is a whole cowskin from which they make pampooties.

The fishing nets are still there in the cottage, but the life and colour have long gone from the fireside where the old story-teller of Inishmaan, the bent and rheumatic Pat Dirane, would sit and tell Synge tall stories and legends by the hour. Other well-known Irish writers and activists in the revival of Gaelic culture would lodge with the McDonaghs, among them Padraic Pearse. My guide gradually let drop the information that she was the granddaughter of Synge's landlady. Occasionally a Synge enthusiast would ask to look round the cottage, but it wasn't a great attraction. 'This would be a lovely site if anyone wanted to build a new house,' she said ruminatively as we shut the door of Teach Synge. That remark caused me to wonder how much longer the cottage where so much Irish literary heritage is rooted will continue to stand.

From the end of the tarred road a boreen, scarcely wide enough for one person, ran out to the rock-strewn edge of Creaga Dubha, the Black Cliffs. Synge's Chair still stood there, a little semi-circular stone enclosure in which he used to sit sheltered from the wind, jotting notes and gazing out west across Gregory's Sound towards Inishmore. I squatted inside the walls to jot a few notes of my own, and gasped at the power of the wind whistling across the top of the enclosure. The sea was whitening as the gale rose, but tucked away from the salt spray in the crevices of limestone pavement and behind stone walls grew a brilliant mass of little flowers – tiny white anemones, rock roses, thrift, bright yellow loose-headed clover.

The long southerly snout of Inishmaan dipped gently towards the spouting ledges at the tip, two solid miles of shattered grey limestone that made the southern fields of Inishmore seem like easy terrain by comparison. The back of Inishmaan was plated like the hide of a dinosaur with blocks of the underlying rock, on which lay an impenetrable litter of loose slabs three or four feet thick in places, thrown up in a long collar around the coast by storm waves.

Angela Faherty had graphically described the power of the sea during a terrific gale the previous winter – the worst that the oldest islanders could remember – when walls of white water had come rolling in to tear chunks out of the harbour, drown sheep and throw boulders bigger than a man well inland. Angela hugged herself and shivered as she relived the frightening moments: 'To see that sea between Inishmaan and Inisheer coming towards us like something alive – well, it scared all of us. The sound of the sea as it hit the island was like a bomb going off.' Today's storm was only a vigorous puff in comparison, but the force with which the green Atlantic rollers swept up, crashing in sheets of spray on the rock ledges and hissing over them, made me glad to be walking high up and out of reach on the quaking collar of slabs. On the inner side of the barrier stood a little round stone tower, built by the people of Inishmaan to commemorate an islander who had recently met the death he had hoped for, dying in his own field out here in the wildest corner of his island.

I found a boreen which had once brought kelp-gatherers from the village to these seaweed-strewn shores, and followed it back inland. Towards the humped centre of the island the stones had been cleared as far as possible and built into yet more walls – not the chunky walls of rounded stones that enclosed the more sheltered fields around the village, but thin walls of blade-like stones, a hundred at least to each yard of wall. Little thatched stone barns were scattered in the corners of fields, reached by boreens so narrow as to be indistinguishable from the lines of field walls running parallel to them. The wind blew me along and in through the door of the island's pub, where two or three silent men in thick dark clothes were impassively sitting and watching American children's cartoons on the bar's television set. The young boy who had asked me if the kegs had arrived on *Rose of Aran* stood behind the bar, chirpily serving pints and chaffing the customers.

Later in the evening, restored by Angela Faherty's lamb cutlets and superb, floury potatoes (Inishmaan potatoes should have an epic poem composed in their honour), I walked back to the pub with the two Dubliners who were staying with me at Cregmore. Rita Brennan spent her working life demonstrating manufacturers' goods at exhibitions; Joe Brennan drove a Dublin taxi, a rich mine of human experience which he was exploiting in the writing of a sprawling and perhaps-to-be-finished novel. They had been escaping to Inishmaan for years, driving to Galway airport and flying Aer Arann over to the island – three hours from their home pub to this one, as Joe put it. 'This island is a world on its own,' Rita said at some point in the timeless evening. 'We walk all day, and no one minds us. The people here are very independent, and they don't want to see any more tourism than they're getting at the moment. They organise themselves through the co-operative, so no one's going to spoil things with a hotel or any of that. And there are no day-trippers like on Inishmore and Inisheer, because it's not so easy to get here and back in a day. The visitors who come respect the island and its people. We don't know anywhere else like it at all.'

I walked back down the lanes to Cregmore in a rainstorm, passing little groups of islanders who murmured 'Good night' out of the darkness. My watch told me that midnight had come and gone a long time ago, yet the pub had been full when I left. A funny thing, as that watch was usually so reliable. The sea spray had affected it, no doubt.

'There'll be no boat today,' said Roger Faherty next morning, looking out of the kitchen window at grey waves rolling heavily through the sound. The wind rose in howling bursts, whipping dark sheets of rain across the island and trembling the plants in the walled garden. The currachs were stacked upside down by the pier, with their owners resigned to finding their lobster pots driven ashore some time during the day. Head bent against the weather, I walked up to morning Mass in the church. Next to me a dog lay curled up asleep under the bench where his master knelt in prayer. The elderly women of Inishmaan were out in force in their criss-cross headscarves and blue and red woollen dresses, rosaries softly clicking through their fingers. Among them stood younger women in trousers, heads uncovered.

The service was in Irish, but I followed it well enough, murmuring my English responses in counterpoint to the Gaelic. Afterwards I sat for a long time in the vestry with Father Raymond, bearded and gentle-voiced, a great fiddle-player and singer and a story-teller of renown. Inishmaan's regular priest had been granted a sabbatical year to write a book, and Father Raymond had been standing in for him. Now he was due to leave, sad to say goodbye to the islanders but pleased to be returning to the outside world. 'God bless you, Christopher,' said Father Raymond as he stood in the doorway. 'Always be a bearer of Christ, remember!'

Back at Cregmore, Angela had been on the phone to Aer Arann to book me a seat to Galway that afternoon. The gale was dying down, but the waves were still beating in white spouts on the coast of Inisheer across the sound. When the Inishmaan islanders get the deep-water pier they have long been asking for, there will be few days when the mainland link cannot be maintained. The little Aer Arann planes can only carry eight or nine people, but they have established a service so reliable that only mist and fog can keep them away. Big passenger ferries, of course, can sail through fog protected by their modern navigational aids. With the building of the pier, there will be a way on and off Inishmaan by one route or the other in all but the fiercest storms.

The islanders are only too well aware of the pressure and inducements to cater for the mass tourist market they will have to face when their sea communications improve. Insensitive tour operators could soon be offering them the earth in exchange for permission to build a hotel on Inishmaan and run horse-buggy trips round the lanes, stopping for photo opportunities with the unspoiled locals in their traditional costume. 'We have to wait and see what will happen,' said Roger Faherty as he shook my hand at the airstrip. 'We need the pier badly. I think it will be all right.'

The Islander juddered to the end of the airstrip and turned for take-off. In the seat in front of me an amply-constructed old lady sat squeezed up next to Father Raymond, nervously crossing herself with one hand while gripping the priest's arm with the other for reassurance. Between them they filled the plane wall to wall. Father Raymond produced a bottle of holy water and flicked copious showers over all the passengers, laughing heartily. The youthful pilot revved the engines and we swept up for the bumping ride over the bay to Galway airport. The island tilted and turned under us as we banked towards the north, and I looked down through the rain-streaked windows of the Islander to see Roger Faherty's Land-Rover making its slow way back up the walled lane five hundred feet below.

4

THE BREADTH OF
THE BURREN
Galway City to Limerick

The little mites in grubby tracksuits, smeary-faced travellers' children of hardly more than infant-school age, had the pavements of Eyre Square well parcelled out. They stood at each corner and halfway down each side, the rain darkening their hair into rats' tails, tiny pink palms held out. 'Spare a penny?' they squealed at the hurrying passers-by. Their mothers stood a few yards off, rocking babies in pushchairs, watching the business out of the corners of their eyes. Inscrutable or hangdog, they waited for the coins of embarrassed tourists from dawn to dusk, in drizzle or in sunshine. Across the street on the steps of the opulent Great Southern Hotel the stout doorman, lordly in top hat and brass buttons, held the swing doors open for guests whose nightly bill would have fed the travellers for a month. Thinking back over my time in Galway city, it is those knee-high, sodden little beggars and their frowning mothers, their monumental patience and indifference to rejection, that come to mind. I crossed Eyre Square, the meeting place of Galway's roads, several times a day, and the dourly watchful travellers were always there, a sharp needle in the conscience to set against the bustling prosperity of the lively little city.

Galway is the place to be young: a city jammed with high-spirited boys and girls. Students from the university thronged its narrow streets, packed its dark bars and shrieked with laughter in its doorways. Itinerant musicians dumped themselves down without ceremony on the pavements and under the shop arcades, shoved out their open instrument cases for manna from heaven and thrashed away at country songs, dance tunes and their own howling compositions. Hitchhikers and bus riders with towering backpacks slouched along, thumbs in belt loops, dropping none of their carefully-counted coins into beggars' hands or fiddlers' cases, checking cafés and hostels for the cheapest deal. In the evenings the smartly got-up young bank clerks and shop assistants of Galway sat on high stools in the bars where the musicians didn't go, putting tyrannical bosses to the verbal sword. And in among these constantly swirling, brightly-coloured tides of youth moved the middle-aged and elderly citizens, resignedly smiling and occasionally tut-tutting at the antics and unbridled bad language of the youngsters.

Galway city is used to coping with all manner of strangers. In medieval times Spanish and French wine traders tied up their galleons and merchantmen at the quays and stayed in the city for weeks at a time. Galway merchants were rich and powerful then; they ran the city as a free-trading, independent port, a prosperous Catholic stronghold in many ways more closely linked to the Continent than to the rest of Ireland. These Anglo-Irish descendants of Norman settlers, known as the Tribes of Galway, feared only the O'Flaherty clan whom they had displaced from Galway. 'From the fury of the O'Flahertys good Lord protect us' they inscribed over the western gate in the city walls. But the reckoning was to come to the Tribes of Galway from the east, in the shape of the armies of Oliver Cromwell. Galway was sacked and burned in 1652 after an epic nine-month siege, in retribution for its support of the Catholic King Charles I and its involvement in Catholic unrest and uprisings. The city dived into a trough of depression, not to rise again until twentieth-century tourism and renewed commerce engendered in the west by Ireland's membership of the European Community. Nowadays Galway city flourishes, the west of Ireland's centre for Irish language and culture, ringed by the factories and offices of multinational companies, infused with optimism and loud liveliness.

I idled in Galway for several days, resting my feet and recapturing energy, spending hours propped against bookshop shelves reading Irish history and American trash novels, sleeping, shooting the breeze, daring to blow my harmonica in company with pipers and melodeon players of infinitely greater skill and commendable tolerance. One night, in the middle of a session of breakneck tunes in Taafe's bar, a mild-faced man who had been sitting quietly at a table suddenly threw back his head and carolled a nursery nonsense song with such volume and conviction that the whole room, including the hard-boiled pub musicians, stamped and roared for more. It was the crack in operation. The flaxen-haired Dutch and German tourists, who had been glancing nervously from face to face as they wondered whether to join in or not, relaxed with yells of delight. Only one man sat unsmiling – a bushy-bearded Englishman hunched in a distant corner of the bar with a concertina he hadn't yet nerved himself to play. 'Come on,' urged the guitar player beside me. 'Will you give us a tune, now?' The Englishman blushed as he twiddled his buttons and searched his mind for the opening line of 'The Sweet Nightingale'. Then he sang in a reedy, uncertain voice:

As I went a-roving one morning in May . . .

The accordion player caught the tune after a few bars, and carried it along under the singer's thin melody. The guitarist joined in. A couple of girls in the crowd added harmony. Slowly the old sentimental English air took on a new and forceful Irish life.

... As she sang in the valley below-oh-oh-oh:
As she sang in the valley below!

Fifty voices finished the song in noisy triumph, and the Englishman
sank back in his seat in a sea of applause, dripping with sweat and
wearing the broadest smile in Galway.

One rainy morning I dodged the urchins in Eyre Square for the last
time and struck out southward with recharged batteries and new
springs in my heels. There were fifteen inescapable miles of main
road to cover, and I was thoroughly soaked by rain and lorry-splash
by the time I reached Kinvara village on the south side of Galway
Bay. This summer had been the worst for years, said the farmer at
the bar of the Auld Plaid Shawl, hissing through the four blackened
teeth in his jaws. Sure, it was hard to believe that they'd all been
praying for a drop of rain this time last year. But as I left Kinvara the
grey sky was already patched with blue and enormous, fluffy white
cumulus clouds were rolling across the hills.

'Ireland West – *Slán* ... goodbye ... hope you had a pleasant
stay' said the notice at the edge of the village. I smiled to myself as I
sploshed through the puddles, leafing back through memories of
Sligo, Mayo and Galway – Benbulben and Hargadon's bar; the great
bog and the Nephin Beg adventure; Connemara, the Aran Islands
and Galway city. A pleasant stay, for sure. And now, rising ahead in
pale grey domes and weathered ledges, cloud shadows chasing across
their flanks, the hills of the Burren beckoned me south and west over
the border into County Clare.

The Burren stands alone, a high and wild country that sails like an
alien vessel between the mild green fields of Galway and those of
southern Clare. There are no sharp mountain peaks in these 375
square miles of glacier-scraped, weathered limestone. The Burren
rolls and undulates. Its bare grey hilltops and scrubby valleys make
up a landscape strikingly ambiguous in character, every inch of it open
to view and yet mysterious and secretive. Its borders are clear-cut; at
every part of its perimeter the domed tops of the hills run down
into outward-curving feet planted on a green carpet of seashore or
farmland. You're never in any doubt about whether you're in the
Burren or not. Once there, its unique atmosphere engulfs you com-

pletely. The world beyond its borders might as well not exist. When you leave, it's as if a gate shuts behind you.

Yet it only takes a few hours in the Burren to realise that this is a land you can never fully know. You could take a fifteen-mile round walk south from Ballyvaughan, as I did, passing one superb prehistoric burial chamber after another, and never suspect the existence of the hundreds more scattered across the pathless hillsides within a mile or two of the road, slowly settling back into the stony ground they came from with their secrets still unfathomed. Or you could spend a morning with your nose six inches from the limestone pavements, seeking out the Burren's amazing treasure of wild flowers that hide in the cracks of the limestone, covering perhaps half a mile of ground and finding only a fraction of all there was to find.

There are thousands of settlements from all the ages to be stumbled across in the Burren – stone-walled forts and enclosures, earthen defences, individual stone huts and complete townships – some properly excavated and documented, others seldom visited and never scientifically explored. Ruined medieval churches and crumbling stone crosses stand by the roadside or lie tucked away in lonely valleys where no roads lead. This is a desolate, nearly deserted land, sucked dry of human presence by emigration. There are no towns or villages within the heart of the Burren, scarcely a hamlet of more than two or three houses. Most visitors to the Burren don't walk these wastes, or stray more than a few hundred yards from the road. The Burren's herds of feral goats, its pine martens and badgers, foxes and rabbits have the hills and valleys to themselves.

The village of Ballyvaughan, perched on the northern edge of the Burren looking out into the wide waters of Galway Bay, has one hotel and a handful of shops and pubs, centred round a road junction. There's not much of Ballyvaughan, but what there is serves as the tourist centre of the north Burren. The grey heights enclose the village on three sides, threaded by a couple of motor roads and a number of hill tracks.

My map showed one of these reaching the village by crossing the saddle of ground between the hills of Moneen and Ailwee, but as usual the map turned out to be less than reliable. The lane I was following became a grass-grown boreen, then an indistinct field path that wavered upwards and abruptly stopped where the valley fields met the naked limestone of the hills. Foolishly I took the line of greatest resistance, struggling up over the ledges to land, in a lather of sweat, on the saddle between the hills. As I came level with the ridge a blast of wind knocked me back on my heels and caused the straps of my backpack to flog my cheeks and neck unmercifully. I could only stand there a minute or two, eyes watering and cheeks stinging, blinking at one of the best high-level views in Ireland. Behind me lay the fertile valley from which I had climbed, its farms dotted among fields of pale green where the hay had just been mown. In front the limestone fell away in a series of cliffs and pavements to more green acres, cradling Ballyvaughan on its little scoop of water that widened into twenty or thirty miles of green and blue Galway Bay. Enclosing both valleys, before and behind, rose the bald grey heads of the Burren hills, rolling away to high horizons east, west and south. It was a view to lift the spirits and the feet. I dived down out of the wind, scrambling down the ridged cliffs and teetering across the knobbled wedges of the pavements, making for a boreen I could see four hundred feet below.

In a gateway a young farmer in a blue boilersuit was bent double, throwing small stones from one heap to another two yards away. 'What a beautiful place this is,' I remarked, leaning on the wall of the boreen. 'Yes, I suppose it is,' the farmer said, straightening his back and gazing round the encircling hills as if seeing them for the first time. 'But we never look at it, of course.'

Next morning dawned grey and misty, with ominous dark clouds piling over the hills behind Ballyvaughan. They unleashed milky sheets of rain at ten-minute intervals throughout the day, a gentle downfall that soaked me through. 'A soft sort of day', they call it in County Clare. I set out after a mighty breakfast (porridge, bacon, egg, sausages, tomatoes, black and white puddings, mounds of toast – the usual modest Irish boarding-house morning meal), and walked all day, underground and overground, through the showpiece caves under Ailwee in company with a shuffling group of fellow-tourists, over the limestone pavements in company with the stonechats and the larks, guided by a map a quantum leap from anything the Irish Ordnance Survey has to offer. Somewhere in Connemara or the Burren they should put up a statue to Tim Robinson, originator of the 'Folding Landscape' maps of those regions. Robinson, an Englishman settled in Connemara since the early 1970s, has worked with a depth of understanding and a passion for his chosen areas' history, culture and oral tradition that make his meticulously detailed maps a real joy to have in the hand. The essays, notes and gazetteers that accompany the maps are masterpieces of erudition made accessible to the inexpert traveller. I would cheerfully trust a 'Folding Landscape' to take me to the North Pole and back, let alone to the dolmens and cahers of the Burren. Tim Robinson led me from Ailwee Caves to Glensheen wedge tomb on a path unmarked on the half-inch map. I couldn't find it at first in the limestone wilderness, but that was my fault. Also – frustratingly – he showed me the hundreds of tombs, forts, churches and caves within easy reach of my route that I had no time to explore.

Ailwee Caves, a couple of miles south of Ballyvaughan, were crowded with visitors at half-past ten in the morning, but I was glad to get out of the rain and be part of the human snake that wound after the guide into the tunnel in the hillside. A local farmer, Jacko McGann, had stumbled into the cave system in 1940 while searching for a lost dog. Mr McGann, a brave man if ever there was one, crawled nearly a mile into the hill and discovered one of the Burren's most lucrative tourist attractions. Spotlit and carefully excavated as it is today, the route through the passageways and caverns hollowed out by subterranean rivers still drips and echoes, bringing a primitive chill to the spine. The guide pointed out muddy hollows where brown bears had hibernated in the warming-up period after the last Ice Age, petrified flows of calcite in glistening curtains, a knobby stalagmite that had been growing, drop by drop, for eight thousand years. 'So our life is a drop,' murmured the German visitor next in line to me. Deep inside the hill we skidded down a muddy incline into a pitch-dark cavern filled with the crash of falling water. The guide disappeared into the darkness, gave us a minute's dramatic pause, then flicked a switch. A spotlight in a crevice twenty feet below the walkway shone upwards into a curtain of water gushing from a crack in the roof of the cave, spraying down in a display of silvery sparks. We gasped, and the guide smiled to himself as he perched on the handrail over the chasm, his party piece successfully unveiled for the thousandth time. To him the incandescent waterfall was only a stopping place on a far longer underground journey. He knew what lay beyond the tourist trail, having ventured there himself, crawling on his belly by the light of a helmet lamp: narrow passages worn through the limestone by swirling water, winding for a mile more into the hill to reach the shore of a dark, dead rainwater lake. Divers had explored the depths of the lake, looking for the chamber that experience said must lead out and away from its floor, but to date they had failed to find it. There must be a connecting opening somewhere in the hillside of Ailwee, said the guide, but that, too, had yet to be found. Jacko McGann's discovery was only the threshold of unguessable mysteries beneath the Burren.

Above the cave entrance I scrambled up the little cliffs of limestone, looking for a track marked on Tim Robinson's map. For a long time I searched for that path in vain, but it didn't matter one bit. The couple of hours I spent hopping, skipping and sliding over the rain-greased limestone pavements of Ailwee Mountain took me instead into the absorbing world of clints and grykes.

When the Burren limestones were laid down as sediment under ancient seas, they were more or less flat, a great ragged apron of slowly settling and hardening material in shallowish water. Hoisted high above sea level by subterranean upheavals, the limestone was left exposed, to be gradually weathered into shapes of hill and valley roughly the same as those that stand today. (The retreating glaciers of the Ice Age finished off the job of shaping and smoothing the contemporary landscape of the Burren.) At some time the limestone was plunged beneath the sea again, and overlain with clay sediments that hardened into shale – the southern hills of the Burren still carry their shale coating, which gives them a smoother outline, while weathering has stripped most of their neighbours back to the characteristic cliffs, ledges and domes of the limestone. About 270 million years ago the whole plateau rose again, bulging upwards under enormous pressures from below. The surface of the limestone, hard as it was, cracked across like crocodile skin, as does the smooth, dry surface of a block of dough if bent upwards and inwards into a dome shape. These cracks still line the old whitened face of the Burren, scoring the limestone across and splitting it into innumerable squares and rectangles (clints) separated by deep, narrow fissures (grykes). Botanists from Moose Jaw to Manila come to the Burren to poke their noses and field lenses into the grykes; for in these shady little chambers, in the soil-filled hollows of the clints and in the bogs and wet patches flourishes one of the world's richest and most unusual flora.

No one has properly explained why plants of arctic and alpine origin grow happily in the Burren six inches away from plants that normally thrive in a Mediterranean climate, nor how plants that can only tolerate lime co-exist with those that need neutral or acid soils. It may be the warming and wetting influence of the Gulf Stream, the low incidence of frost, the dropping of strange northern seeds by birds or by the melting glaciers in retreat that had held them in their icy grip since arriving from the north. The limestone makes a warm bed, exposed in nakedness to the sun above and warmed internally by the Gulf Stream waters moving offshore; and enormous amounts of sunlight bounce and reflect from the bare white stone into every gryke and hollow.

There is a notable absence of water in the Burren: the limestone is so riddled with rain-eaten holes and subterranean passages that all its rivers but one (the Caher River in the extreme north-west) flow on the surface for a short distance only – perhaps a couple of miles at best – before vanishing into their underground labyrinths through a swallet hole. These are known locally as 'sluggas', a word intriguingly close to the 'slocker' by which such stream-swallowing holes are known in my native North Somerset. You see very little water above ground in the Burren. When it rains, as it did all through my pavement wanderings, every tiny dimple and niche in the lime-stone collects its share and becomes a potential gathering ground for plant and soil fragments that may ripen a wind-blown seed. Every gryke drips and bubbles, and from three or four feet down poke up the long green spears of harts'-tongue ferns and the pale round leaves and hair-thin black stems of maidenhair fern, greedily seeking the moisture and sunlight.

I was a little too late in the year to find the brilliant blue spring gentians that are one of the Burren's chief delights, but deep mauve bloody cranesbill was everywhere, as were buttery masses of birds'-foot trefoil and a bewildering variety of pink, purple and white orchids. The limestone clints rocked and clicked under my boots as I stepped from one to the next across the grykes, head down, oblivious to rain and wind. This was a flower display in full bloom – creamy yellow mountain avens with little rose-like flowers, each holding its teaspoonful of rainwater; white eyebrights; tiny blue flowers like miniature bluebells, with petals fringed into feathery tips, that I couldn't for the life of me identify. I did at last stumble by chance across the path and had a sense of purpose and direction thrust upon me, but it wasn't what I really wanted.

After the floral pavement show, I have to admit, the stone cahers or forts and the ancient tombs of the Burren held little charm. Dutifully I tramped my fifteen-mile circuit of the roads, ticking off the monuments as they loomed up one by one through the rain. The 4000-year-old Gleninsheen wedge tomb, shaped like a slice cut from a whole round cheese, had a solid capstone sloping gently on great stone slab walls.

A mile along the road a group of Americans filed out of their tour bus and across a stony field to take photographs of Poulnabrone portal dolmen, the best-preserved tomb in the Burren, a mighty piece of architecture that predates the wedge tombs by several hundred years. The capstone was twelve feet long, a jutting porch over the squarish chamber where some chief's bones had once lain. The photographers clicked away, their friends holding umbrellas over them, while other friends climbed the dolmen and draped themselves artistically across the capstone. I had no patience with any of this – my loss, as Poulnabrone was a five-star 'DO NOT MISS' attraction in every guide to the Burren. I trudged on through the pelting rain, round the roads to find the tottering walls of Cahermacnaghten ring fort entirely deserted, the stone blocks of the gateway all but fallen and the circular interior where the O'Davoren clan held their medieval law school a thick morass of cow dung and nettles. The O'Davorens were hereditary lawyers and teachers, a widely respected family to whose school young men from all over the west of Ireland came to be taught the precepts of the ancient Celtic laws known collectively as 'Brehon law'. Cahermacnaghten was a noted centre of learning from early medieval times up until the years of the Cromwellian oppression. There were houses and gardens inside and outside Cahermacnaghten, and a tide of scholars and kinsmen constantly coming and going, when the O'Davorens held sway here. The tombs back along the road, with all their weight of years and their impressive mass, had seemed dead things in contrast with the fluorescent anoraks and bright chatter around them; but this lonely, rainswept circle of stone somehow retained the warmth of its more recent human contact.

Now dry winds began to come in off Galway Bay, streaming soft white clouds across hot blue skies for the next couple of days. The fine weather turned out to be only an interlude; more rainstorms were on their way in from the Atlantic as this wet summer continued its dismal course. I made the most of the sunshine and took to the Burren Way, the first well-signed and waymarked footpath of any length I had followed so far. What a pleasure it was to be striding the green road from one hill crest to the next between the snaking lines of stone walls that dipped and rose for miles ahead, with the sun hot on my face and bare arms and a good strong sea breeze to cool the journey. In the tourist information office in Galway city I had picked up a pamphlet guide to the Burren Way, but once again it was Tim Robinson and his pen-and-ink 'Folding Landscape' map that proved really helpful along the fifteen or so miles between Ballyvaughan and Doolin. The pamphlet's map was based on Robinson's finely detailed work, testimony to his growing reputation in these remoter parts of Ireland still only in the early stages of opening up to tourism.

Leaving Ballyvaughan early in the morning, I passed the drinking fountain put up in 1875 by the Board of Guardians of the Bally- vaughan Union. The Board's chairman at that time was agent to the local landowner, Lord Annaly, who had presented Ballyvaughan with its first public water supply three years before. A third dignitary, Colonel the Hon. Charles White, paid for the connection of fountain to waterworks. Everyone, it seemed, wanted to have their name dis- played in association with this philanthropic act. Local politics had not changed greatly over the intervening century. Regional elections were taking place on the day I walked the Burren Way, and the posters of Fianna Fáil, Fine Gael and the independent candidates were plastered to walls, telegraph poles and hedgerows. The news- papers were forecasting the usual easy victory for the governmental party, Fianna Fáil. The candidates' names stood out from the posters in bold black letters, surnames first: Moran Noel, Killeen Tony and Nagle Jimmy. The transposition made them sound like Chicago gang- sters (Nagle Jimmy will give you plenty of six to five against Killeen Tony); but, like most Irish local politicians, I'm sure they were mild and well-conducted folk.

On the outskirts of the village a stout lady ran down her garden, shrieking at three sheep which were nibbling at her herbaceous border. 'The divils!' she panted furiously, shooing them out of her gate into the road. 'Three times they've got in here and eaten all my plants!' Further along the road I passed another cottage garden where an elderly woman was gently clapping her hands and talking to her plants, softly encouraging them to get on and grow. She looked up furtively as I went by, but I kept a strict eyes-front.

Newtown Castle stood up under Cappanwalla Hill, a stark grey round tower rising five storeys high from triangular buttresses, pierced with crumbling window holes, draped with ivy and crowned with crenellations. The corners of the buttresses, sharp and cleanly cut, were the only part of the structure not eaten ragged by wind and rain. The men working on the nearby farmhouse waved me inside the tower, where a blackened stone stairway spiralled up over gaps and shaky stone steps past cylindrical rooms with domed roofs. In the ancient plasterwork of the ceilings were swirling impressions left by the wicker basket frames that had been pressed up into the wet plaster four hundred years before to hold it in place while it dried. Pieces of twig stuck out of the plaster, dust-dry and brittle. This grim round fortification had been built by sixteenth-century O'Brien chiefs of the area, and had later become the stronghold of the O'Loghlen family, known as 'the Kings of the Burren' in recognition of the influence they, in their turn, wielded locally. At the top I found another round room, its grassy floor thick with buttercups and forget-me-nots. Broken squares of windows – some still retaining their weather-battered stone mullions – looked out north to Ballyvaughan and Galway Bay, east over to grey-domed Ailwee and south along the Burren Way into the heart of the hills.

The shells of ruined churches lay beside the road, their graveyard crosses drowning in rambling roses. The long lane came at last to a fork where the Burren Way turned aside into a steep boreen that forged up the hillside. At the top I looked forward into a new and greener landscape. Elva Mountain stood away in the south, an eleven-hundred-foot whaleback of shale covered in rough grass and plantations of conifers, a dark, softly-rounded bulk behind the outliers of the Burren's terraced limestone hills. Between Elva and where I stood the Caher River had cut down a thousand feet through the limestone, slicing a deep, narrow valley north-westwards to the sea. Into the valley the stone-walled snake of the Burren Way fell in a succession of curves, to cross the river and wriggle again all the way up the far side. It was a stunningly dramatic prospect, matched only by what came suddenly into view once I had gained that opposing ridge. The Aran Islands lay fifteen miles out to sea under blue heat haze, beyond a wide green apron of coastline with a lacy white hem of breaking waves. I could see twenty miles down into the south and west, where the shaly flagstone Cliffs of Moher ran their great square snouts out above collars of foam.

Under a wall a man and his young daughter were sheltering from the wind, opening their lunchtime flask of tea and tin of buttered slices of soda-bread. They had come up the green road to look at their sheep. Would I take a cup of tea? A slice of bread? Sure, go on – we've plenty and to spare. So you're from Bristol, said the man as I drank the hot tea. He had been in Nottingham, working. That would be a few miles from Bristol, so. The neighbours were fine people, he hadn't a doubt, but they wouldn't talk to you. It was just the English way. Have you had enough, now? Well – goodbye!

As soon as I had turned the corner I heard English voices coming up the boreen – the first English walkers I had met since setting out from Malin Head more than two months ago. They passed me with eyes averted, a man and a woman with identical stringy calves and bony bodies, striding with chin-jutting determination. I held back from saying hello, too, as I had not done in all that time. It was just the English way, so.

There was a last dip and rise of the limestone, a series of leg-aching climbs and descents along tarred lanes and a sight of Ballinalacken Castle towering jagged and magnificent out of a dense thicket of trees like the castle of the Sleeping Beauty. Within the hour I was a sleeping beauty myself, knocked out by sunshine and up-and-down walking, slumping flat out and straight into oblivion on my bed at Maeve Fitzgerald's bed-and-breakfast house in Doolin.

Sociologists of the future, seeking an example of a remote community turned on its head by the effects of modern tourism, need look no further than Doolin. This little fishing village at the foot of a green valley on the south-west coast of County Clare had been a favourite place for international glitterati to bathe naked and hold wild parties in the 1920s and 1930s – or so snippets of local gossip led me to deduce – but such goings-on had not been fashionable since the war. Doolin had quickly sunk back into obscurity, overlooked by the outside world until the 1970s. Almost every inhabitant of Doolin was involved one way or another in fishing, making the best living they could. Very few visitors came down the narrow road from the popular spa town of

Lisdoonvarna four miles to the east. Lisdoonvarna had the bed-and-breakfast houses, the hotels, the spa waters and the night life. Doolin lived its own isolated existence, slipping gradually further and further behind the better times that the rest of County Clare was beginning to enjoy as tourists came west for peaceful country holidays. Only the most dedicated enthusiasts of traditional music were aware that Doolin and its surrounding countryside were rich in good musicians, who would gather in the village's three pubs to play with no thought of a fat financial reward or the applause of an audience.

The Holy Grail of the traditional musician is the pub that no one knows, where local musicians play for their own enjoyment in a corner of the bar; the quiet, unmodernised pub where you sit on chipped wooden benches to swap tunes until daybreak; the pub where there are no coachloads of Englishmen and Germans listening in reverent silence, or gangs of swaggering city folk down from Dublin roaring out the corny old drinking songs that bring out the sweat of scorn on a purist's brow. The musicians' Mecca changes every couple of years as the world and his newly-bought bodhrán becomes aware of the current gathering-place. When I walked through the west of Ireland the charm was on Ennistymon, a few miles south of Lisdoonvarna – 'Twenty bloody players in the pub, man, and great crack all night!' For a few years in the early 1970s it had been Doolin, the fishing village in the back of beyond, that held the singers and players of Ireland in a delighted conspiracy. The great young names of Irish music came to Doolin – Christy Moore, Matt Molloy, Sean Cannon – to sit in McGann's, McDermott's and Shannon's pubs, unbothered and unfêted, playing away with the local musicians, incognito and glad to be so. Players keen to learn their art, some destined to win international recognition and others who would never stand on any concert-hall stage, trekked out to Doolin and stayed, sitting at the elbows of the masters in comfortable equality. Doolin was the place to be.

Then, as was bound to happen, the secret leaked out. More and more players arrived, staying for longer and longer. One or two local families went into the bed-and-breakfast business. A popular annual festival of traditional music started up at Lisdoonvarna, and the word went out that the real music was to be heard just down the road in the village at the end of the valley. Curious visitors arrived. The tourist coaches began to squeeze along the lanes, disgorging people in their dozens into the little pubs of Doolin. Big money was coming to the village. More lodging houses opened, along with cheap hostels, seafood restaurants, craft shops and a hotel. Suddenly the place was crowded with foreigners in summer, looking for accommodation, wanting to join in with all the tunes, needing camera film and ice creams. As the local people set themselves, eagerly or reluctantly according to their point of view, to cater for the visitors, many of the musicians who had been in on the Doolin secret picked up their instrument cases and departed, looking for pastures new and unsullied. They left behind them a tourist village in full and flourishing swing.

As I walked into Doolin that afternoon, there was music, music all the way. The Doolin Café had a couple of musicians painted on its signboard. McDermott's pub sported a painting of a harpist on the wall. 'Traditional music nightly' said the notice in the window of McGann's. Jigs and reels were pouring from the loudspeaker under the roof of the music shop on the road to the pier. There were guitar cases in the pub windows, mandolins hanging from the pub ceilings. Doolin knows which side its bread is buttered. But for musicians like Johnny Curtis, the bouzouki player I had met back in Westport, the village is a dead duck. Johnny had lived here, playing all the time, in the great days, and had left when the tourist tide began to run. 'It's not what it was at all,' Johnny had complained over the pints in Hoban's bar. 'The atmosphere's gone. Doolin's finished as a place for music.'

As a place for tourism, though, Doolin is hardly started. Maeve Fitzgerald fired up indignantly when I told her of Johnny's lamentations. 'Sure, you get these people saying "It's not the same as it used to be. Why did you not stick to the thatched cottages instead of building these modern houses?" Lord!' Maeve tossed her head and tapped me crossly on the arm. 'I say to them: "Why did you come to my door asking for en suite rooms? Would you rather go to that old thatched cottage and when you want to go to the toilet you've to go outside and take your pick of forty acres of hillside?" These people want everything to stay just as it was, for their own pleasure. But you can't keep progress out of it! Our school had thirty pupils in those days – now it's eighty-five. Young families are staying in this area, and it's the tourism that gives them jobs and lets them settle. We'd be dead without it. And the atmosphere in the bars – it's just the same as it always was.'

By nine o'clock in the evening McGann's pub by the bridge was full of people. Judging by the accents, nine-tenths of them were far from being Irish. They sat quietly in the dimly-lit bar, respectfully watching two young men getting ready to play. There was certainly an atmosphere of anticipation in the place, the kind of feeling that hangs in a folk club or small theatre before a well-known act gets up to perform. This was an audience, a different animal from the casual gatherings in the Westport pubs who had hardly looked up from their conversations as the players struck up. I heard the subdued murmur of the crowd through the door of the back bar where I sat writing and chatting to Teresa McGann, the wife of the pub's owner. She had little time for the kind of invaders that were packing into Doolin these days. 'Crowds of yuppies come down from Dublin at Bank Holiday weekends, you know, and when they get in the pubs they start singing and shouting their own songs, spoiling it for the musicians and anyone who really enjoys the music. Well, I've turned a stag party of twenty-two men out of here, and you can imagine the money they were spending. I said: "You see the old boy in the corner there with his pint. He's been here every night for years. So he's more important to me than you are, no matter how much you spend." In winter it can still be great – you'll get a knock on the door, and in will come someone with instrument cases in his hand. A session will start up out of nothing; there'll perhaps be just me behind the bar and the musicians up in the corner of the room. The best music often comes out of those sessions that aren't planned, but just happen. We had a marvellous one last summer. They were playing away out the back, and by the bridge – all on stools they'd taken out of the bar – and some more were in here. I was serving pints out of the window till two in the morning, and even the old fellow next door wasn't grumbling about not getting his sleep – he was right there in the thick of it. Now that was great. I thought, "This is it! Doolin like it used to be!"

'But the trouble is that the tourist people want to be in on it. I had a form through the post from Shannon Development, with a whole row of boxes to tick – What time did the music start? What time did it stop? Was it traditional? Folk? They wanted to have it all tied down so that they would know how to publicise it. I said to hell with it, I don't want to know. It just doesn't work like that.

'The problem is the money. There just wasn't any money in the place, and of course once people have seen it they want more and more of it. How do you keep a village like this from being changed and spoiled? The same with all the Burren, for that matter.'

The door to the main bar banged open and a big man in a T-shirt swayed up to the table where we were sitting. His eyes, swollen with drink, wandered over my pens and notebooks. 'Ye're a writer, are ye? Yes? OK! I want to tell ye the plain fuckin' truth about Doolin, man.' Tommy – or some adjacent name – was well gone with the Guinness, but not so far that he didn't know what he had to say. I looked at the muscles bulging under his T-shirt, and wondered whether those big hands would clench into fists if I said the wrong thing. But Tommy wasn't being aggressive. He wasn't interested in hearing anything from me. He was just determined to put his case. Teresa stared coldly at him. She was equally determined to deny him an opening. 'You're barred from every pub around here, Tommy,' she remarked in an even voice. 'So why do you keep coming back here when you know you're not welcome?'

'I just came in for a pint,' Tommy mumbled defensively, 'and to tell this man here about Doolin, that's all.'

'Well,' said Teresa, 'you can walk right out again – the door's through there.'

The bar door slammed behind Tommy's broad back, and Teresa sighed as she got up to see to her customers. Five minutes later, I raised my head from my notepad to see Tommy's red face cautiously peering round the partition, looking for his adversary. He came up and stood over me, staggering slightly: a musician who never made it, a drunk barred from the pubs, but sounding a genuine ring of conviction among the slurred words that spilt out. 'It was us,' he said, quite quietly and sadly, 'us, the fuckin' musicians, that made Doolin. I'm talking about ten, fifteen years ago. This is a famous music pub now – every player comes here – but back then they'd have to send a car twenty miles round about to bring us in. We'd play because we wanted to, and no one took any notice of us at all. Now the publicans and the boarding-house owners is all millionaires, man – and us, the musicians that gave the place its fuckin' name – we become alcoholics and die. Show me a rich musician!'

Tommy leaned down and prodded me hard in the chest, driving

home his point. 'Ye put that in yer book that ye're writing,' he grunted as he turned on his heel and slammed back out through the door.

Another beautiful day, and a walk in prospect along the Cliffs of Moher. I walked down the road through Fisherstreet, the old fishing quarter of the village. Fisherstreet curves prettily from its bridge up along the road to Doolin Pier and the Aran Island ferries. It's as lovely as a Cornish fishing village, and as thoroughly commercialised. I made an inventory of the strip of buildings as I walked up the street:

> The Traditional Music Shop
> Lisa's Kitchen Restaurant and Arts & Crafts Shop
> The Woollen Stores Gift Shop
> Private house
> The Doolin Dinghy Shop
> River View B&B
> Celtic Jewellery and Silversmith
> Gus O'Connor's Pub
> The Piper's Chair General Stores (Purveyors of Art & Artifacts)
> Private house
> Seabird Take-Away Foods (Open All Day)
> St Anthony's B&B
> Sancta Maria B&B

In the yard of the little house behind the Doolin Dinghy Shop a cat lay asleep in a patch of sunlight. A broom swished in the dark interior of the cottage. I knocked, and an old man in cap and shirt-sleeves gave me a pleasant 'Good morning.' I asked him what the street had been like twenty years before.

'Oh, twenty years ago there wasn't a bed-and-breakfast place in it,' he said, smiling. 'There wasn't a tourist. It was all poor fishermen. There was three shops along here, and all of them was doing bad. The pub was Shannon's at that time, and he sold never half a barrel of porter. There was no money in it!'

'So what's brought the changes to Doolin?' I asked.

The old man smiled again, taking up his broom and resuming his sweeping. 'Oh, 'tis all in the good times. In the good times! There'll never be a bad time again that we'll see.'

A green path ran up and along the cliff edge, shiny and spattered with flowers in the strong sunlight. I was balancing on the top bar of a gate, taking a photograph, when a voice below said in good hard Australian, 'Walking along the cliffs? Care for a companion?' It was dark-haired Diane 'from near Melbourne' – a hundred miles near, I discovered as we chattered away – over in Ireland on a longish holiday and game for a good hike. The Twelve Bens and the Maumturk Mountains across the bay lay far off in the sunshine as we climbed the grassy backs of the cliffs through blue patches of scabious where pipits and stonechats were clicking away. The rock outcrops by the path stood dark and solid, hundreds of inch-thick slices of flagstone squeezed together in horizontal layers. The grand heights of the Cliffs of Moher were made of the same stuff, broken and weathered into ledges a foot or so wide where fulmars were nesting on cushion-sized tufts of grass. Just before the 700-foot sheer cliff that marked the summit of the range, the path joined a road, from which an exciting view suddenly lay revealed – an enormous stretch of the Clare coastline, sweeping in long indentations down and down into the southwest to a faint glimpse of the hills of County Kerry. I looked down and away in delight at ten days' worth of my journey spread before me – the link between Clare and the last long stage to the walk's end on Roaringwater Bay. Dark-haired Diane was politely interested, but it was foolish of me to expect her to share my excitement. Perhaps I overdid the exclamations. At all events, she decided she would stop at the tourist centre on the cliffs to write a letter – 'A very long letter, Christopher, so don't you bother to wait for me'.

Sir Cornelius O'Brien, MP for Clare, was either an altruist or a notorious money-grabber, depending on which version you listen to. He was undeniably interested in covering Clare with mighty erections – bridges, schools, columns and towers all went up under his direction in the 1830s and 1840s. 'O'Brien built everything but the cliffs,' said the locals. In 1835 he put up a tower on the crest of the Cliffs of Moher as a viewing point, commanding a gorgeous view down over the long descending curtain of cliffs. On the way up to the tower, I ran a gauntlet of blaring, sentimental Irish ballads pouring from the loudspeakers of tape-sellers. 'Hear the natural unspoiled voice of

Eileen O'Shea!' beseeched their placards. 'Tape includes "Danny Boy", "Molly Malone" and "When Irish Eyes are Smiling"!' Doolin traditionalists would have vomited smartly over the cliffs. I felt like doing the same as I watched a girl in white trousers curling herself up in sex-kitten pose on the very lip of the 700-foot drop as her boyfriend clicked his camera. I swear her buttocks were over the edge. I turned quickly away and looked at the view, hoping not to hear the scream when it came.

Half-past nine on Friday night in McGann's, and a room full of people. Every stool and bench is taken. Francis with his concertina box and John with his fiddle case weave their way between the customers towards the corner by the window where a big notice is propped: 'Reserved for Musicians'. A corn-fed young American couple has occupied the corner seats. Francis bends and speaks a few words to them, lost in the din of chatter – this crowd has been enjoying itself in the sunshine all day and there's not a whiff of holy hush in the place. The American boy and girl slide their drinks and themselves along the bench, and the two musicians settle behind the table with their glasses of Ballygowan mineral water. You can't booze and keep your fingers nimble till midnight, not when you are being paid for your music. One or two customers shift round on their stools in anticipation, but Francis is in the middle of a long and elaborate tall story that has John chuckling. It takes a good quarter of an hour before fiddle and concertina are out of the cases and ready for business.

The first few tunes are tentative, but after a while Francis crosses his legs and John leans back, relaxing into the music. Each tune is followed by a lengthy pause as they talk and joke together. It's a quiet night in McGann's: no one joins in and there are no spontaneous songs from other parts of the bar. Few people are listening to the music. They laugh and chat in cheerful knots around the tables heaped with glasses and overflowing ashtrays – French, German, Dutch, English, American. Scarcely an Irish voice to be heard. Francis and John show complete unconcern for the inattentiveness of the audience. They were playing in Ennistymon last night with a bunch of musicians, fired up to competitive heights by each other's skills. McGann's tonight is just a pleasant transaction of pure business.

As they work their way towards midnight, two pretty, curly-haired Canadian girls from the Rainbow Hostel up the road sit down near them. One is wearing a beautifully embroidered jerkin and multiple strings of beads. John looks across through the diagonal movement of his bow, then winks at Francis. But here come the girls' companions, two tall, blond German youths of heroic build and tan and a dark, intense older man of unguessable nationality. The boys are carrying a crowd of glasses in their brown fists – coffee-coloured cream liqueur, chinking with ice. The smiling group clinks glasses all round. The pretty girl in the beads lets her head fall on the shoulder of one of the German boys, with a sigh of delight. Francis winks back at John and they slip seamlessly from jig to jig. Three tunes more and they can get off to bed.

It was my own incautiousness that landed me headfirst in that ditch halfway between Doolin and Kilfenora. The boreen I was trying to follow had not been used for fifty years, and the night's heavy rain had turned it into a sloppy river of mud. Hoping to spy out my line ahead, I leaped up the bank and grabbed a fence post on the top to heave myself over. The wooden post, rotted through, snapped in half and I fell, pack and all, ten feet into a waterlogged trench. I got out, cursing, with a wrenched shoulder and a jarred knee, soaked from head to foot. In the shelter of an old turf bank I stripped off and got dry clothes out of the pack. The elderly farmer who came by along the bank as I was hopping on one bare leg with my jeans halfway up the other had nothing to say. Neither did I.

I took to the lanes and followed them down to Kilfenora through the rich green Clare countryside. The outlying Burren hills soon sank out of sight behind the folds of grazing ground. Streams trickled in the bottoms of the little valleys round which the walled and hedged lanes curved and wound. Compared to the dry, bare Burren uplands this was lush, well watered country, as quiet as could be. I suddenly realised that I had not heard a single low-flying jet at any stage of the walk. The Irish rambler is spared that thundering bane of the walker in England. Clare was soft and gentle on the eye and ear. This was no landscape to challenge and outface the wanderer, but a green and soothing retreat, a countryside for strolling and sauntering. Only the shapes of the trees up on the rounded ridges told the other, harsher side of the story. They were bent into bushy backs, crouching inland from the winds that come streaming in off the Atlantic in winter.

But this was easy June weather, cloudy and mild. Two teenage boys were driving seven cows along the lane in front of me, the very picture of laziness. The cows strayed off to munch the clover in the verges of the lane, and the boys gently patted them on their bony rumps with the long switches they were twirling idly in their fingers. Their dog trotted quietly along beside the cows, tongue out, not bothering to keep his charges in order. I couldn't have got past them in the narrow lane, even if I had wanted to. But I was quite content to ease the pack on my shoulder, still aching from the tumble, and follow them along the lane into Kilfenora.

The same sleepy air hung over the little grey village that afternoon. The first man I saw set the tone for Kilfenora, yawning hugely as he leaned against a shop doorway watching the world fail to go by. Two lads on tractors did their best to roar life into the place, racing each other along the cratered street, but it was a vain attempt. Above the door of a tiny dark bicycle shop hung an advertisement for Rudge's cycles, 'The Best in Britain'. I don't know when Rudge's stopped making bicycles, but judging by the cobwebs round the notice, it was a very long time ago. A decrepit car, its bonnet tied down with bailer twine, chugged up the street in a cloud of blue exhaust fumes. The driver had his hand pressed firmly to the outside of the car door, perhaps holding that in place as well. 'Kilfenora (Pop. 125) is a thriving market village and the ecclesiastical capital of the diocese of Kilfenora,' my guidebook announced. To back up the claim, tucked away behind the village street was a splendid twelfth-century cathedral, rich in carvings of long-dead bishops but with its chancel roof open to the sky. Scattered in the graveyard and in the field beyond were four magnificent high crosses, their 800-year-old carvings of Christ crucified, of Christ in abbot's hat and habit, of knights on horseback and rich interlacing panels all gently weathering into indecipherability. No other visitor was there to share these medieval masterpieces with me. The village went about its slow business under the grey sky, entirely self-contained.

In Vaughan's pub I asked about a bed for the night. 'Holden's, at the top of the street,' I was told. 'They'll have a bed for you.' They did. Vaughan's had the best music anywhere in County Clare that night. Tommy Peoples, a fiddler famous throughout Ireland, sat with a guitarist and banjo-player in a darkened corner of the bar, delicately

bringing a stream of leaping tunes out of his fiddle while ten customers sat near to listen and forty others chatted away with their
backs to the great man. In nearby Ennistymon a thousand revellers
were whooping it up at the 'fleah', a wild festival of music and dancing,
but here in Kilfenora Tommy wrought his magic for himself and a
small handful of listeners. Sitting beside him and watching his fingers
flickering across the strings, I wondered how long it would be before
Kilfenora became the next well-guarded musicians' secret – and how
long after that before hostels and restaurants began to replace the
dark little shops in the village street.

Kilfenora has one attraction that does bring the tourist coaches in
during the summer season. Near the top of the village the Burren
Display Centre squats low, its modern architecture standing out from
the old houses and shops on each side. The Centre was built in the
1970s in a community effort to halt the decline into which Kilfenora
had slid after bureaucrats decided that its cattle market should be
relocated elsewhere. Interpretive Centres in areas of natural beauty
or scientific importance are all the rage across Europe now, but Kilfenora's co-operatively run centre was the first. Local farmers and
residents were involved as shareholders, thus ensuring their goodwill
and support; local people were recruited as guides round the exhi-
bition. In the afternoon I joined one of the little tours – a short talk
from a young girl, a look at an illuminated relief map of the Burren,
a video narrated by a plummy-voiced Dubliner: 'Even if you're no
entomologist – watch while the spider stings.' The Burren Display
Centre is a brave attempt to head off the potential damage that visitors
could do to the fragile wildlife of the Burren. 'You can't keep tourists
out,' said local people to me. 'Indeed, we need them in an area like
this. But you can try and educate them so they won't destroy the
place entirely.'

When I came to Kilfenora that afternoon in late June, I landed in the
middle of a controversy that had split the community down the middle
and brought the issue of tourism in hitherto unexploited areas into
sharp focus. In the lonely hills of Donegal, in the remote bogs and
mountains of north-west Mayo, the friendly streets of Westport and
the music pubs of Doolin the same questions had nagged away in my
mind. How far can you go with tourism? Where should the line be
drawn, and who should draw it: local people themselves, or concerned

outside experts on their behalf? Does any part of Ireland – or of the world, for that matter – have the right, or the power, to face the incoming visitors and say, 'Leave us alone. Yes, we'd like your money, and your jobs. But we don't want the changes that you'll bring here with you'? And can any small community, having decided to take that stand, gather the influence to persuade governments and tour operators, local politicians and international funding bodies, to drop their plans and save their money?

The Burren is full of special places. Some call them magical or mystical; others see them in terms of their archaeological remains, or their unique geology, or the richness of their flora and fauna. Mullaghmore, ten miles east of Kilfenora, is one such special place. Here the Burren limestone has been twisted up by ancient subterranean movements into fantastic swirls of rock, flowing shapes quite unlike the horizontal ledges seen elsewhere in the region. On yet another rainy morning I stood on the one narrow road that approaches the hill of Mullaghmore, with my mouth hanging open in wonder at the bizarre and beautiful shape of the landscape. The layers of limestone, the weathered cliffs and shattered pavements all swept and curved upwards with a sense of movement as definite as a fairground waltzer, a grey and green scarf of rock thrown over the shoulder of the hill. Two wide turloughs, ponds that fill and empty in response to the level of rainfall, lay at the foot of the hill, unseasonably full of rainwater and alive with duck chatter. The grykes of the rolling limestone pavements were crammed with ferns and flowers, dwarf coniferous shrubs, creeping spikes of stunted holly and fat cushions of twenty different mosses. It took me an hour and a half to climb the hill, picking a path through hidden crevices dense with hazel bushes and sliding over the carpets of broken boulders, scrambling up the steep cliffs by tip of finger and toe of boot, till I stood on the slanted crown of Mullaghmore. From up there the view was just as strange – a petrified whirlpool of limestone printed in the pavement and only discernible from high above, rushing inwards to a calm central ring of grass. This was a primeval landscape of utter silence, open to wind and rain, a spellbinding wilderness, ungrazed and unsown, turning a hard, closed face to the world. If any place should remain difficult of access, dignified in desolation, it is Mullaghmore. Yet as I stood on that hilltop I was aware that within two months, unless the Irish government's Office of Public Works could be persuaded to abandon its plans, the bulldozers and diggers would be at work in the wilderness, clearing the way for the wide new roads, the 1300 square yards of new buildings, the thirty acres of 'landscaped walkways', the sewers and electricity cables and car parks and restaurants of the Mullaghmore Interpretive Centre.

It was European Community development money that paved the way for the bulldozers. Eighteen million pounds of what are called Structural Grants had been made available to build three of these centres in remote areas of Ireland with tourist potential – in the Dingle peninsula in western Kerry, in County Wicklow, and here in County Clare at Mullaghmore. Under the terms of the EC directive the money had to be spent by the summer of 1993, so the sooner construction was under way the better. The Office of Public Works, faced with a delicate public relations exercise in promoting its plans, had made an almighty hash of it. Local feeling in the Burren was that the OPW had sprung the scheme on the area without warning or consultation. It had used a section of the Planning Act that allowed governmental bodies to sidestep normal planning permissions in the case of developments urgently needed by the government. It had failed to carry out the Environmental Impact Assessment that was usually required by the EC for such developments in areas of special scientific interest or outstanding natural beauty. And it had not sought local opinion. The irony was that the OPW itself had a brief to 'conserve the natural and man-made heritage of Ireland for its people'. What it was intending to do at Mullaghmore was the opposite of conservation, in the view of Ireland's people as represented by the Burren's objectors to the scheme. The OPW's tart response to the objections – that everyone knew it had been buying up land in the area since 1974 to create the Burren National Park, and everyone should have realised that an Interpretive Centre would be part of that park – cut little ice. A Burren Action Group was formed soon after the Mullaghmore plans were announced. Their posters, featuring a photograph of the swirling hill and the legend 'No place for tar and cement', fluttered from pub notice boards and were displayed in house windows wherever I went, from Ballyvaughan to Kilfenora.

Tony Holden and Brigid Mullins, with whom I was staying in Kilfenora, were passionate members of the Burren Action Group. I hadn't been in the house ten minutes before the table was covered with information sheets as Brigid put me in the picture. The development had caused terrible ructions in the community. Those who saw money and jobs for a depopulated area in the scheme had branded the objectors 'hippies' and 'élitists', silly outsiders who didn't know what was good for the place. But, said Brigid earnestly, they weren't objecting to a new Interpretive Centre, or better still a refurbishment of the community-run one here in the village. They recognised that the Burren needed the money, and a certain number of tourists. But why put it there at Mullaghmore, in one of the least visited and most unspoiled corners of the Burren? There were a whole string of potential problems – pollution of the complex and unsurveyed underground watercourses by the new sewerage system they'd have to build; a huge increase of traffic on the roads; those walkways and the areas they would intrude on; the effect that the projected sixty thousand extra tourists a year would have on the wildlife of the place. If it was built in one of the existing centres of population, though, where electricity, drains and roads were already laid on, no one would say a word against it.

Behind these concerns lay the worry over what would happen to Kilfenora's own Burren Display Centre. It had looked fairly run-down when I went round with the guide – the illuminated photographs of flowers fading, the model of the Burren dusty and poorly lit, labels fallen to the bottom of showcases. The Centre was badly in need of an injection of funds. And behind that was the indignation over the cavalier behaviour of the Office of Public Works and their lack of any intention to involve the local communities in the scheme; and the feeling that political pressures, big money and unaccountable power were all influencing the course of events in ways that ordinary people were powerless to prevent.

It was summed up for me, forcefully, in Vaughan's pub after Tommy Peoples had packed up his fiddle and gone home. As we sat finishing our drinks and discussing the Mullaghmore business, an Englishman came up and leaned over the table. A Burren resident for a dozen years, an organic horticulturist, bearded, full of fury against the scheme, well-informed, he typified the 'hippy élitist', the 'blow-in' derided by supporters of the Interpretive Centre.

'Listen,' he burst out, 'we have everything here – the flowers, the air, the music, the people. And the madness, which is very necessary. Why spoil it? We don't need that kind of tourism, or any tourism. Mullaghmore will just be a piss-stop on a coach tour; get off, go in the restaurant, look through the window, take a shit – and take a photograph. Always take the photograph! The Burren is one of the few real wildernesses we have left. You can find places like Mullaghmore where you can step on a stone and know that no man has stepped on that stone for generations – perhaps never. So why risk spoiling it? For God's sake, let's just leave it alone.'

The die had almost certainly been cast, however. Eminent botanists, zoologists, environmentalists, geologists, naturalists – every shade of '-ist' – had made their protests to the government, with no measurable effect. Already the verges of the narrow lane to Mullaghmore had been scraped bare of their grass and flowers in preparation for widening. 1 September 1991 was the day appointed for work to begin on the Interpretive Centre. The members of the Burren Action Group were preparing, as a last resort, to lie down in the path of the bulldozers on that day.

Interpretive Centres at tourist honeypots like the Cliffs of Moher probably don't do much damage. Visitors flock there anyway, and an easy-to-grasp explanation of what they are looking at is a useful service. But places like Mullaghmore, remote wildernesses that hold irreplaceable stores of natural treasures, are a different matter. Where will we turn for spiritual refreshment and a proper sense of our insignificance in the natural order of things when they are tamed and ticketed, reached by coach roads and brought under control?

It was hard to turn my back on the Burren, but now my road lay south-eastward again through flat, watery country of sedge and lakelet, full of curlew cries. The dimpled crest of Mullaghmore sank behind me until it was just one flat little hill among the others on the northern skyline. It was Sunday, the day for the farmers of Clare and their families to drive out and visit relations. At midday, with Mass safely over, they began to weave past in rattling old cars, fathers in blue suits at the wheel, mothers in smart dresses beside them, flocks of shiny-haired children in the back. The children waved and pulled faces as they went by. At tea-time strollers appeared in the lanes in ones and twos. A plump boy waited by a garden gate, then grinned with relief as his plump girl banged the front door behind her and vaulted over the wall to link arms and drag him off down the road in a gale of chatter. As I came into Ennis at evening the youngsters of the town were gathering at the corners of the narrow streets, yelling outside the chip shop and revving their motor bikes across the bridge over the River Fergus. They were still at it at two in the morning, when I woke in my bedroom in Queen's Hotel to hear glass breaking and wild laughter as the disco crowd went staggering home.

Ennis is a bustling place, the county town of Clare, full of cramped streets and traffic. I spent a lazy morning wandering around, poking my nose into this and that. Beside the hotel stood the ruins of the thirteenth-century Franciscan friary, a roofless shell with a towering east window. There was a wonderful tomb in the chancel, cobbled together by the Creagh family in the nineteenth century out of two tombs dating back to 1470, with stiff little medieval scenes from Christ's Passion. In the scene in the Garden of Gethsemane, Judas laid a treacherous hand on the shoulder of Jesus, while a helmeted soldier grasped a fistful of His robe. Peter was shown sheathing his sword after striking off the ear of the High Priest's servant, who lay on the ground clasping his head in pain.

Daniel O'Connell stood high above the streets, a statue on a tall column gazing out over the town. 'Swaggering Dan' had led the Irish Catholics in the 1820s in their fight for emancipation. The Penal Laws forbidding Catholics to practise their religion had been relaxed in the last years of the eighteenth century, around the same time as Ireland had been granted a quasi-autonomous parliament. But when direct rule from Westminster was re-imposed after the 1801 Act of Union between Great Britain and Ireland, the Catholics found themselves once again suppressed and denied their rights. O'Connell earned his nickname of 'The Liberator' as he led the long struggle to force a hearing at Westminster for the grievances of the Catholic majority of Irish people. His poorest supporters felt proud to pay the 'Catholic Rent' of a penny a month towards the cause. O'Connell suffered years of powerlessness, but in 1828 a great mass meeting in Ennis swept him to his seat in the House of Commons on the crest of a wave of support too big to be ignored. Even then he had to secure his election, after being excluded from Westminster as a Catholic, by making a stirring speech from the bar of the House. O'Connell finally took his seat in 1829, and the Catholic Emancipation Act soon followed, enshrining the right of any Catholic to sit in Parliament. No wonder Ennis honoured its heroic MP with a heroic statue.

From O'Connell Street I wandered across into Parnell Street, once the main thoroughfare of Ennis, now a run-down road of tottering old shopfronts and tiny, dusty pubs. The old people who had owned them were dying off, and the new generation couldn't be bothered to take on the running of establishments that would hardly pay the rent. The town's council had already begun demolishing the little houses in courtyards behind Parnell Street, and soon the old-fashioned shops and pubs would begin to fall. 'O Tempora O Mores' said a hand-lettered sign in the derelict shopfront window of number 83 above the notice of a clearance sale.

Just up the street I happened on Sean Spellissy's second-hand bookshop, fronted in wood painted red and white, crammed inside with shelves of rare literary treasures and boxes of cheap and cheerful paperbacks in a friendly jumble. Browsers stooped over the boxes, leafing through the dog-eared paperbacks with no intention of buying. Sean himself wasn't in the least bothered. He shoved his hands in his pockets, propped himself behind the counter and gave me half an hour's chapter and verse on the Burren's secret places, the Mullaghmore controversy and much else. He leafed through a greasy old address book, producing the names and telephone numbers of dozens of people who would be able to help and instruct me at every point between the Burren and County Cork. He signed a copy of the book he'd written, *Limerick: The Rich Land*, and presented me with it as I left his shop. I walked out of Ennis on the road to Limerick a more than satisfied customer.

The River Shannon carves in under the bird's beak of the Clare coastline, a great waterway several miles wide that gradually narrows as it winds inland past the city of Limerick and on into the heart of Ireland. South and west of the Shannon one enters tourist country, where the wild mountains and coasts of Kerry and the hills of Cork attract millions of visitors every year. Most of them come to the south-west through Shannon International Airport, a sprawling township of runways and buildings that covers thousands of acres of flat land north of the river. Big planes flew overhead at five-minute intervals as I worked my way along the side lanes towards Limerick. They whistled piercingly as they floated round in circles, wheels down, waiting for clearance to land, or shook both ground and air with thunder as they pointed their round noses at the clouds and climbed away from the airport. Among the green fields beneath the flightpaths I found the noise overwhelming, but the three old men sitting under an apple tree beside the road didn't even raise their heads from their conversation as the white and silver machines filled the sky above them. 'Good afternoon,' I shouted against the din from the skies. 'God save you,' returned one of the old men quietly. 'And a fine afternoon's walk to you.'

I knew I must be properly in tourists' Ireland when the barman in Sixmilebridge twirled his beer spout and drew a shamrock on the head of my glass of Guinness. But that was it as far as Sixmilebridge was concerned. Four miles along the road in Bunratty Castle they were laying the tables and tuning the harps for the first sitting of that night's Medieval Banquet, but Sixmilebridge slumbered in the afternoon sunshine every bit as silently as had Kilfenora. Down by the bridge a father and son were feeding the ducks, and on the parapet a youth sat staring at the hills with an unlit cigarette between his fingers. Five thousand tourists had landed at Shannon Airport while I had been walking from Ennis, and not one had reached this peaceful place. A flake of plaster detached itself from high up on the wall of one of the dilapidated houses in the street and slowly spun down into the gutter, the fastest-moving thing in Sixmilebridge. Sunlight slanted into the roadway and across the river, drawing away what energy I had left until I, too, had abandoned all thoughts of moving any further.

The dinner at Nuala Enright's bed-and-breakfast place that evening was more wholesomely Irish than all the stuffed boars' heads in Bunratty: thick-cut bacon ham, along with a mound of potatoes and cabbage straight out of the garden. There was great traditional entertainment later on, too, in the Gaelic Athletic Association's community hall up the road, where at least four hundred people had gathered by bus and car from all over the district for an evening's bingo. I arrived late, had a book of games and a pen put into my hand and plunged directly into a baffling forest of numbers in which I hacked around uncomprehendingly. The air in the hall was muggy and blue with cigarette smoke. Through the haze I made out the pub keeper who had shamrocked my Guinness standing on the stage at the far end of the room, plucking bouncing coloured balls from a machine and calling their numbers out through a microphone, all-powerful in his role of high priest. His congregation, heads reverently bowed, scanned and ticked their pages in an anticipatory hush. 'On her own – number eight! Downing Street – number ten! Almost there – eighty-nine! Kelly's eye – only one!' chanted the publican. 'All the fours – forty-four! Two and nine – twenty-nine!'

'Check!' cried a woman from the middle of the hall. 'And check-ing!' responded the caller. I glanced at my neighbours, hoping for a clue to the mystery. Nuala Enright beckoned me over. She was playing two games at once, with a dexterity I could only envy. Her pen never ceased flickering up and down the columns as she sorted out my muddles with a few crisp words of explanation. She had already won £10, and was in cracking form. Outside in the corridors and side rooms players were listening to the caller over loudspeakers, shrieking 'Check!' at the tops of their voices to bring the patrolling tellers out to verify their victories. The air grew steadily thicker and bluer. At one point a pair of elaborate silver coffee pots was displayed on the stage, to be whisked away at some other point. I had the impression that no one had come up with the numbers required to win them, but I couldn't be sure. I was still floundering in the number jungle when the games came to an end and we crowded out into the clear night air at half-past ten. 'Did you enjoy it?' asked Nuala as we made our way down the road into a beautiful sunset. 'I wouldn't have missed it,' I told her truthfully.

On the television there was news from north of the border. Unionists and Republicans were at last sitting round a table together at Stor-mont Castle in Belfast, trying to get ahead with Strand One of the Brooke talks. Strand One was to work out what common ground the opposing sides shared. The Unionists had bitterly opposed the sign-ing, in 1985, of the Anglo–Irish agreement, a measure intended to bring the two countries closer together in searching for a solution to the seemingly insoluble problems of the North. Under the Agree-ment, politicians from England and the Republic of Ireland held regular meetings, one of which was scheduled to take place shortly before Strand One of the Brooke talks was due to finish. The Union-ists regarded this clash between the Anglo–Irish Agreement and the Brooke talks as some kind of betrayal or coercion, and were threaten-ing to walk out of the talks. However, the Brooke initiative was for the moment, shakily and haltingly, moving ahead.

Meanwhile, a leading Unionist figure had been buried after being murdered at the weekend by the IRA.

The Troubles had been dwindling as a topic of conversation the further south I went. I had heard nothing of bloodshed, bombs or bitterness for weeks. How strange it seemed, sitting in sleepy Sixmilebridge on the fringe of the tourist board's 'Smiling Ireland', to be hearing of them now. Another piece of the tragic jigsaw of Irish history fell into place the following morning when a resident of Sixmilebridge pulled out a tattered, yellowing newspaper for me to see. This man had inherited the paper from his mother, who had had it pressed under her mattress for decades. We smoothed it out on the table – the *Daily Sketch*, printed in London on the morning of Thursday, 24 August 1922. 'Martyrdom of Michael Collins' announced the banner headline. '"Forgive Them" – His Last Words'. The inside pages of the paper were full of the story: '"Mick" Collins, Fugitive and Favoured Ambassador – Amazing Adventures of the Man Who Played Hide-and-Seek With the Government – Stage Manager of Miraculous Escapes – Brave Heart, Brilliant Brain and Ever-Twinkling Eye'.

Michael Collins had been shot dead by the IRA in an ambush near Bandon in County Cork at about seven o'clock in the evening two days previously, and this was the first edition of the paper to carry the news. A bullet in the head, one of the last shots to be fired in the skirmish, had felled the Commander-in-Chief of the Irish Free State Army, the man on whom both Irish and British governments were pinning their hopes of crushing the Republican rebels of the IRA in the bloody and bitter Civil War then raging throughout Ireland. Collins had been a romantically elusive Scarlet Pimpernel figure in the years after the 1916 Easter Rising when he was the darling of the Republican movement, on the run from the British Army and the Black and Tans. Young, dashing and darkly handsome, he had led the British by the nose in a whole string of wild adventures: dressing as a milkmaid while troops ransacked the village where he was hiding; slipping in disguised as a nun to visit a sick colleague in hospital; escaping from a window wearing only a shirt; hiding in a coffin in a hospital morgue as soldiers searched the wards. He had organised several jailbreaks for Republican prisoners, including that of Éamon de Valera, President of Sinn Fein, who was destined to become both Prime Minister and President of the Republic in the course of his long life.

During Collins's three years as a fugitive he had been protected by 'a personal guard of gunmen, dead shots every one', according to the *Daily Sketch*. But when the Anglo–Irish Treaty was signed in 1921 and Collins ranged himself alongside those who supported it as the best compromise that could be hoped for, he knew that an IRA bullet would almost certainly find him sooner or later. De Valera and the Republicans watched their one-time friend and ally grow in stature, as the newspaper photographs in that old *Daily Sketch* so clearly showed: Collins shaking hands with British ministers; Collins going to meetings in Downing Street with a briefcase in his hand; Collins waving and smiling at waiting journalists. The hunted outlaw had become the darling of the British press, 'fearless and resourceful . . . patriot, loyalist and saviour of his own country'. Now he lay dead, his killing having swept all other news from the papers. Lloyd George, the British Prime Minister, was too upset to comment, but the *Daily Sketch* carried his recent tribute to the 'engaging personality of this gallant young Irishman'.

Michael Collins, I learned from conversations all down the length of Ireland, is still a hero to many people. In 1923 the Free State Army snuffed out the last of the Republican opposition, but Collins had been dead for almost a year by then. His admirers see him as a martyr for the cause of practical politics, the cool-headed road to independence. But cool heads can rapidly heat up when drops of bitter history are added to the present stew of troubles. 'If the British troops were ever pulled out of the North,' I was told during one discussion, 'and the Troubles came south of the border, there's many would remember who was for de Valera and who was for Michael Collins all that time ago. Would they pick up guns to shoot each other? They would. Sure, they would.'

A couple of miles short of Limerick city I sat among suits and ties for the first time in many days, eating a salmon salad in a swish roadhouse. I had a good companion on the other side of the table. Father Michael Liston is the parish priest of Cratloe, a smart little village pulled up from decline by the jobs and money of nearby Shannon Airport. A humorous and quick-minded man, very much involved in youth work and the painful emergence of Ireland's Catholic Church into the modern age, and a great story-teller. Michael has seen the numbers of regular church-goers in steady decline over the past two decades, a turning away from the structures and certainties of the traditional Catholic life of Church and family by young people in the growing towns of Ireland. 'There have been good numbers of young men entering the priesthood,' Michael said, 'but a great drop in applications to religious orders. And hardly any girls wanting to become nuns; that's probably been the biggest change of all. You'd have strong family support a short while ago for anyone who was thinking about joining a religious order, but now the families are tending to put pressure on the other way, to dissuade their young-sters. And the girls, particularly, aren't interested in joining. It's not that they don't want to play their part and be involved, but nowadays they feel a need for personal freedom which was never an issue before.'

There's no question that the Irish are seen – and see themselves – as an exceptionally religious nation. But the Irish Report of the European Values Study which came out in 1984 makes some telling points about the changing face of Catholicism in modern Ireland. Nine out of ten people who responded to the survey said they believed in God; eight out of ten described themselves as practising Catholics. These statistics sound impressive, not greatly different from the figures a similar survey in 1944 or even 1924 might have produced, until one breaks them down a little further. Well over half of the respondents expressed dissatisfaction with the Church, strong desire for the legalisation of divorce and scorn for the doctrine of Papal infallibility. Fewer than half believed that Roman Catholicism was the one and only true faith. One in five saw no comfort or help in prayer or religious faith. It was the under-35s for whom religious values seemed to have least meaning. Half of this group said that they did not believe in Hell or the Devil, that religious principles had nothing to do with their everyday behaviour, and that a Catholic upbringing was not important.

There is plainly a new breed of Catholic coming up fast, one which still feels a need for the old faith as a stabilising influence in an increasingly uncertain world, but which reserves the right to make choices, to reject Church tenets and priestly pronouncements when they seem out of touch with real life. These are largely better-educated Irishmen and Irishwomen, many of them living in the face-less new estates that surround the towns. They are likely to be in technological rather than agricultural jobs, and are sceptical of the Church hierarchy and its judgements, particularly on sexual and edu-cational matters. They listen to their own consciences more and to the pulpit less.

As in every other Western culture, the modern Irish are more self-willed, less obedient to authority than their parents. Since the 1960s their society has become more consumerist, materialistic and dissatisfied. Television, foreign travel, better education and the experiences of returning emigrants have all helped to raise expectations of a better-off, more independent way of life. When the Church seems to be saying nothing relevant to these members of its flock, they simply turn a deaf ear.

Irish Church leaders have made strenuous – if spasmodic – efforts to reclaim centre stage in ordinary people's lives. In the past thirty years they have set up the Council for Social Welfare, the Laity Commission, the Catholic Communications Institute and the Irish Commission for Justice and Peace. The Mass is celebrated in English or Irish these days, with Latin reserved for special or solemn occasions. Priests like Michael Liston spend their energies on the estates and in the inner-city parishes where as few as one adult in ten ever attends Mass.

Yet the sidelining of the Church continues wherever it is felt to be clinging to old, dictatorial, unresponsive attitudes. Its tendency has always been to adapt in the end to changing circumstances and the pressure of events, even if it kicks and grumbles like a cross old dog as it shifts its position. But its erstwhile leading role in shaping those events by direct influence over the participants seems destined more and more to become merely a marginal one.

So the facts and figures indicate, and so people – especially young people – told me whenever the subject of the Catholic faith came up. 'The priests, sure they haven't the power now. We just treat them like anyone else.' Yet hundreds of thousands turned up at Ballybrit racecourse outside Galway city during the visit of Pope John Paul II to Ireland in 1979. They acclaimed him with a barrage of cheers, whistles and yells straight from their communal heart. The Catholic faith was certainly no dead thing to these youngsters; nor to the four teenage girls from Carns on the Sligo/Mayo border to whom a vision of the Virgin Mary appeared in a field on 2 September 1985. Our Lady of Carns presented the Church authorities with a sizeable problem. They weren't prepared to authenticate the site just like that. Yet three thousand ordinary people who had gathered in the field a week after the original apparition were convinced they had seen the Sacred Heart of Jesus shedding drops of blood and an orange star streaking across the sky, in addition to a further vision of the

Virgin. Some had seen a cross and smelled roses, others saw the skies open to reveal a dazzling light. Since then the revelations have continued. No one seems particularly surprised. It's as if the religious life of the Irish people is entirely matter-of-fact, while at the same time so deep-rooted as to be beyond any attempt to structure or control it.

I told Michael Liston about the lunch-hour pilgrims I had seen taking time out to pray at St Bridget's Well up near Ballysodare in County Sligo; the matter-of-fact operation of religion inside the framework of everyday life that was such a striking feature of Ireland. 'Yes,' said Michael, nodding, 'that's what I call the third reality. There's the first reality of organised religion – the Church, the Mass, the hierarchy – and then a second reality of modern, secular life. And in Ireland there's this third reality, a really deep and strong feeling for the Christian religion at a basic level that somehow operates with and yet apart from the other two. I'll give you a good example of this. There's a traditional Irish village, Bunratty Folk Park, for the tourists, just by the Castle. One of the people working there had been badly injured in an accident, and the other people at the Folk Park asked me to celebrate a Mass there for him. Well, I arrived in the middle of a whole crowd of tourists. The girl welcoming them didn't break her speech by one word, but she just nodded me aside to the right door. There was another girl there looking after her group, and when she saw me she pointed a hand outside without dropping a stride of her talk either. So I moved through on these nods and waves, out to the big barn where the Mass was going to be held. It was pretty well empty, but as I was getting ready the colleagues of this man were coming in all the time, and the barn was full up by the time we began the Mass.

'The thing was, you see, that not one of those thousands of tourists in the Folk Park was aware that anything unusual was going on. They never knew that it was just a skeleton staff looking after them, that people were running around covering for other people, and that almost all the man's friends and fellow-workers were there in that barn saying Mass for him.' Michael laughed in high delight. 'All this great tourist system working away, business as usual – and underneath, all unseen, a great tide of faith in action! That was Ireland's third reality, as strong as ever.'

*

Just east of Cratloe I crossed another county border, and said goodbye to Clare. An evening in the traffic-loud streets of Limerick city, a roaring place after the peaceful days in the quiet Clare countryside. A night in a city hotel, as impersonal as an Irish hotel can get. And next day, a newsflash breaking in on the disc-jockey's bright nonsense over the loudspeakers of Limerick Radio. The Brooke talks were over, abandoned without warning. The Northern Ireland Secretary felt that the talks had been constructive, but there was no chance of meeting the Unionists' demand for them to be completed by the date of the forthcoming Anglo–Irish Agreement meeting. The Unionists had accused the British government of 'insensitive and blatant action', and the Irish government of sabotaging the talks. The other side had condemned the whole process as 'futile'. Back to square one again, as the recriminations flew thick and fast.

I caught the plane out of Shannon Airport, one unit among ten thousand. It was time to see the family again, to cast anchor in familiar waters for a few weeks. The tourist season would be at its peak when I came back from England once more for the next long stage of the road to Roaringwater.

5

DOWN WEST TO DINGLE

Tralee to Dingle and Back by the Blasket Islands

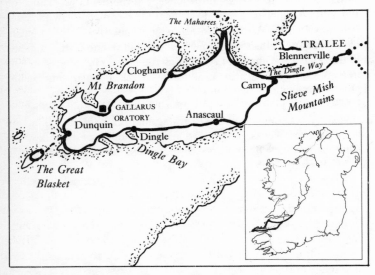

It's never an easy decision to break the chronology of a long journey, as I made up my mind to do when I had come as far south as Limerick city. The settled rhythm of the walk, that steady and purposeful movement south and west through Ireland, had created a flow all of its own that had been sweeping me along on a strong tide of seasonal and geographical change. The primroses and violets of the hills of Donegal and Sligo in springtime had given place to the early-summer mists and rains of the mountains of Mayo and Connemara, the hay-fields of Galway, the rock roses and orchids and bloody cranesbill of the Burren's limestone pavements. The countryside, still only stirring from its winter sleep when I set off from Malin Head in April, had woken up as I was making my way through the Nephin Beg and the Twelve Bens. By the time I reached Galway city the pubs were

bursting with music and the little towns with lively crowds. Summer
– albeit a cool and sunless one – had crept north as I strode south,
and we met up somewhere in Clare. Now my mind was set fifty miles
further along the way, down in the south-west where County Kerry
sticks four peninsulas like four blunt fingers out into the Atlantic.

It was the northernmost of these, the Dingle Peninsula, that tugged
the journey out of shape. Those thirty miles of land with their mountainous backbone of sandstone heights and their fringe of lonely bays
and cliffs had been remote country until recent years. Few casual
visitors came down the bad roads or along the rickety old Tralee &
Dingle Railway line into the Irish-speaking western tip of the peninsula. The old rural lifestyle, its customs, stories and close-knit family
communities, had remained more or less intact as the arrival of the
motor car and the tour coach took the crowds from the lakes of
picturesque Killarney around the mountain views of the much-
vaunted Ring of Kerry in the Iveragh Peninsula on the southern side
of Dingle Bay. Students of Gaelic language and culture had been
coming to Dingle since Victorian days, but modern tourism seemed
largely to have passed the peninsula by.

Recently, however, there had been changes; a tremendous increase
in the number of bed-and-breakfast places; television documentaries
on traditional music and ways of life beginning to feature such
hitherto sleepy towns as Tralee and Dingle; a new pier built in Dingle
for an expected boom in trade. The beautiful and remote Blasket
Islands off the westernmost tip of the peninsula, abandoned by their
tiny population in 1953, had until the 1970s only been reachable via
on-the-spot arrangements with local fishermen. Since then a daily
ferry service had been started. The peninsula was opening up, clearing the way for the tourists and their money. A long-distance footpath,
the Dingle Way, had just been established for thirty miles across the
hills between Tralee and Dingle. West of Dingle it might or might
not exist; no one was quite sure. There seemed to be something
else called the Saints' Road which might provide a way through the
mountains in the loneliest part of the peninsula. Local advice was
cautiously encouraging. By cobbling together these trackways, and
keeping a careful eye on the map, it looked as if I would be able to
tramp the length and breadth of the peninsula in the middle of
August, the height of the tourist season when the Americans, the
Dutch, the French, English and Australians would be flocking down

to Dingle. I would be able to see for myself how the place and the people were coping with the invasion. Would it be like Cornwall at the peak of summer, packed and sweaty, littered and rowdy, with local people nurturing a barely-concealed resentment of the visitors? Or would that relaxed Irish attitude let the Dingle people view the stranger, here as in every other part of the west I'd so far walked through, as a source of interest and pleasure, rather than as a nuisance and a threat?

The Dingle Peninsula stretches out from the flank of western County Kerry, the wildest and remotest county in southern Ireland. Cornwall and County Kerry have a lot in common. Both are peninsular counties in the extreme south-west of their respective countries, both are rugged and weather-beaten, and both have become prime attractions for holidaymakers, Irish and foreign alike. But the foreigner's view of County Kerry is rather different from that of the native Irishman, for whom Kerry has always been something of an affectionate joke, a backwoods place beyond the reach of civilisation. Jokes about the supposed gullibility and innocence of Kerrymen and Kerrywomen are legion. If the English tell tall stories at the expense of the Irish, the Irish pass on the compliment with interest to the long-suffering inhabitants of County Kerry. In a pub in Galway city I had eavesdropped on a circle of students laughing themselves sick over a long and hilarious session of Kerryman jokes. A few samples:

> A Kerryman comes into the house holding something in his hand. 'What's that?' asks his wife. 'Just look what was on the pavement outside,' says the Kerryman. 'By the mercy of God I didn't step in it.'

> A Kerryman went for a walk in the woods and met a girl. 'I'm game,' she says to him. So he shot her.
> Have you heard about the Kerry stuntman? He jumps over twenty motorbikes in a double decker bus.

> CUSTOMS OFFICER: Any pornography in your suitcase, sir?
> KERRYMAN: Sure, what would I be doing with that? I haven't even a pornograph to play it on.

Kerrymen, however, don't suffer in silence. They tell the same jokes about Corkmen. I never did find out at whom Corkmen aim their shafts of wit.

On the August morning I landed at Kerry Airport, ten miles southeast of Tralee, it was the Kerrymen who had the laugh on the Dubliners, though the joke turned out to be on me. The baggage handler whammed one suitcase after another on to the conveyor in the airport building, but my rucksack was not among them. 'It'll most probably be here on the afternoon flight,' soothed the booking girl. 'It's not the first time Dublin's lost a piece of baggage.' I walked out crossly enough, not yet back in tune with Ireland's unflurried tempo. At Farranfore railway station a mile down the road, I contemplated the weed-strewn tracks between the deserted platforms as I paced up and down and waited tensely for the 2.38 to Tralee. At half-past three I ceased to fume and stare up the empty track, sat down on the cracked old seat and began to laugh. It wasn't more than another twenty minutes before a train pulled in to the opposite platform. As it moved off again, something made me call out to the driver, 'Tralee?' He nodded amicably and put on the brakes while I sprinted over the footbridge. 'Not the usual platform, I know. Sorry we're a bit behind time!' he said from his window as I went past. 'Not at all,' I called back, climbing aboard. 'Not at all – it's a pleasure.'

Well and truly wound down, I didn't get away from Tralee until noon the next day. Aer Lingus had fulfilled the booking girl's promise, speeding my rucksack in a taxi to my lodgings in Tralee. 'A busy if unprepossessing town,' commented *Fodor's Ireland*, a judgement only half accurate. Tralee's tight, narrow streets were so crowded that I became used to walking with one foot in the gutter. (Joke: A Garda found a Kerryman walking home in the early hours with one foot on the pavement and one in the gutter. 'Why are you walking with one foot in the gutter?' asked the Garda. 'Oh, thanks be to God, so that's it! I thought I'd gone lame,' said the Kerryman.) The town was gearing up for the Rose of Tralee Festival due to take place the following week, and the streets were hung with bunting and strings of coloured lights. Young women with Irish connections come from all over the world to compete for the title of Rose of Tralee in a final televised throughout Ireland. The winner travels around the world judging other would-be Roses for the following year's contest. 'They share the winners around, of course,' said the barman in Paddy Mac's. 'Last year's Rose was American, as far as I can remember. It's a terrible strain for the girls. The judges are with them, keeping an eye on them, for the whole week, so they have to be on their best behaviour. But you should just see them at the ball after the final – all the Roses going wild, drinking and raving . . . !'

Among rebellious Irish towns Tralee has had a particularly bloody and violent history of reprisal and destruction. The ancient kingdom of Munster incorporated all this south-western part of Ireland, a region that retained a large measure of Celtic independence and culture through invasion and settlement by both Norsemen and Normans. John Fitzthomas Fitzgerald built a castle here in 1243, along with a Dominican abbey, and his descendants – known as the Geraldines – were created Earls of Desmond by the English Crown a century later. But the loyalty of the Munster lords soon turned to rebellion. The Earls of Desmond ran their own autonomous princedom in Kerry, and proved a nest of vipers to the newly-Protestant Tudors during the repressions of the sixteenth century. Resistance to the English throne, fomented by the Desmond rulers, culminated in an attempt to land an international Catholic force on the Dingle Peninsula in the autumn of 1580. Six hundred Spanish and Italian men-at-arms, accompanied by a handful of English and Irish, sailed into Smerwick Bay on the north-western tip of the peninsula at the invitation of the Earl of Desmond. They were soon intercepted. Lord Grey of Wilton, the Viceroy of Ireland, hurried a force of English soldiers down to Smerwick, while ships of the English navy sailed for Smerwick Bay. The invaders, trapped in Dún an Oír (the Fort of Gold), a stronghold built inside an ancient promontory fort, were bombarded from sea and land until they surrendered. Once outside their refuge they were butchered without mercy, except for a few who were kept as hostages. It seems likely that Walter Ralegh was present at the slaughter; he would have been a young captain then, in charge of a small unit of soldiers.

The Catholics of Munster did not learn the intended lesson from the Smerwick débâcle. There were further rebellions and defeats. Tralee was attacked and destroyed in 1583, in the Catholic rebellions of the 1640s and again in the Cromwellian bloodbaths of the following decade. Rebuilt, burned and rebuilt again in war, burned anew in

Aran ancient and modern: portaphone conversation amid the timeless surroundings of stony-backed Inishmore

Above: Launching a currach on Inishmaan, Aran Islands

Right: Clints and grykes – the characteristic limestone pavement of the Burren, County Clare

Young Irish dancers line up in full array on the back of a lorry at the Dingle agricultural show

The abandoned village on Great Blasket Island, looking across Blasket Sound to Slea Head on the mainland

Above: Pól O'Colmáin and Paul Duffy share a non-poetical joke at the summit of Great Blasket Island

Left: Session at Abbeyfeale on the Limerick/Kerry border

Below: The author steps it out across a stream on the old Kenmare road through the Killarney mountains (*photo by Jon Magna*)

Ladies and gentlemen of the Cork Mountaineering Club (*centre l. to r.* Éimer, Frances, Mary, Leonard), flanked on the left by Jon Magna, and on the right by the redoubtable Jack Buckley

Above: Castletownshend waterfront, West Cork: the tower of St Barrahane's Church rises above the castle

Left: Hospitable hosts at the end of the road to Roaringwater: Concubhar and Eleanor O'Driscoll on the jetty at North Harbour on Cape Clear Island

peacetime fires, the old town changed its shape without ever losing its position as the social and financial centre of the region.

There are dignified Georgian buildings in Denny Street leading down to the formal rose gardens of the town park, and a splendid building to house the offices of Kerry County Council, as imposing as any French provincial *mairie*. But the life of the town courses through its crammed shopping streets and ranks of dark pubs. In Paddy Mac's I fell into good company without the least effort, playing and yarning away until midnight with a friendly circle of local musicians in the windowseat of the pub. Flaxen hair and Nordic cheekbones were much in evidence in the crowd, and the roar of conversation above our heads popped and crackled with Swedish and German exclamations. An American couple had their money all ready to drop into the palms of a trio of grubby urchins when the barman spotted what was going on and leaped through the customers to shoo the little beggars out into the street again.

After the Desmond rebellions the area around Tralee was planted with good, reliable Protestant families – Dennys and Blennerhassets. The Blennerhassets took over the little township of Moranstown, a mile out of Tralee on the banks of the River Lee, rebuilding and renaming it Blennerville in their own honour. Blennerville has its own logo these days, a silhouette of its old seven-arched bridge topped by the windmill that stands at the edge of the village. The sails of the mill made a bright white cross against the dark bulk of the Slieve Mish mountains rising to fifteen hundred feet beyond the village. The tourist buses were out in force, swinging wide at the right-angle turn on to the bridge to squeeze over the river with a foot to spare on each side. Blennerville windmill, restored to working condition, had sprouted a ground-level township of its own: craft shops, work-shops, a display centre, a restaurant. Fifty holidaymakers from Llan-gollen were disembarking from their coach as I stood on the bridge, wondering whether to join the queue.

From the other side of the road, behind a group of houses, came muffled hammering and the whine of an electric sander. I followed my ear along a track and came upon a scene of industry. Semi-naked, oil-smeared youths were swarming over four blue and yellow shells of railway carriages, bashing merry hell out of them with an energy and light-heartedness alien to the connoisseur of British steam railway restorers, a dour and lumbering breed. A short length of rusty railway track ran along one side of the yard, while on the other stood an old stone engine shed. I wandered over and peeped through the door. In the shadows lay the bare bones of a locomotive, once the pride of the Tralee & Dingle Light Railway, now stripped down to its frame and wheels. Three silent men lounged beside it, grease cans and spanners in their hands. They stared at me, then glanced sideways at each other.

'Hello,' I ventured. 'How's it going with the engine?' No reply. One man grinned inscrutably; his companions scowled at their boots. 'Are you hoping to get the railway open again?' I hazarded. A grunt from the grinning man was my reward. His ears stuck out from each side of his bony head under a woollen bobble cap. He shifted his spanner from one hand to the other, as if preparing to strike me down for a damned intruder. I braced myself and went in for another round. 'Looks as if you've got a lot of work on hand,' I offered.

One of the scowlers raised his eyes from his boot caps, though not as far as my face. His sulky mouth opened and a few facts came jerking out. 'Been at it three years – get a grant of sorts from Shannon Development – might open a couple of miles of line next year.' His colleagues froze as he was speaking, as if shocked by his garrulity. Abruptly he cut off his trickle of speech, and all three resumed their silent scrutiny of the floor. No British railway buff could have put up a better barrier of surliness. I withdrew and walked away, feeling like an explorer who had disturbed a band of troglodytes in their cave. Outside the youths were still shouting merrily over their sanding and hammering, members of a different tribe.

KERRYMAN IN TRALEE STATION: A return ticket, please.
MAN IN TICKET OFFICE: Certainly, sir. Where to?
KERRYMAN: Back here, in God's name – where else?

The Tralee & Dingle Light Railway managed to stay open from 1891 to 1953, its continued existence a source of wonder and delight to all enthusiasts. The line was notorious for its bad time-keeping, even among Irish railways. Few local people could afford to use it. Its antiquated, almost empty coaches would groan and rattle behind diminutive locomotives up the 1 in 30 incline of the four-mile-long Glennagalt Bank, the appropriately named Glen of the Madmen, round corners that would have been considered far too sharp for any other railway, on rails made slippery by the grass that grew over them, before topping the rise and trundling down to journey's end at Dingle. Towards the end of its life its traffic was reduced to cattle specials, hauled by two locomotives in tandem, their crews (according to local tales) well primed for the fray with stout during the lengthy halt at Castlegregory Junction where Fitzgerald's bar stood conveniently just across the road. The fireman's duties included leaning out to pelt stray sheep on the line with lumps of coal. Ordinary railwaymen would often decline invitations to work their turns over the Tralee & Dingle, so the staff on the line tended to be long-term employees of the company, elderly men who knew just what they were letting themselves in for. The railway ran in its own little world, in its own idiosyncratic way, the butt of a million jokes and the cause of a million missed connections. For most of the twenty-odd miles between Tralee and Dingle it hugged the road, so I became accustomed along the Dingle Way to passing under the rusting girders of its bridges and finding the truncated arches of its viaducts standing over the beds of rivers and side streams.

Beyond Blennerville the Dingle Way, waymarked with a little yellow symbol of a walking man, rose past a tin-roofed farm where sweet-scented peat smoke came drifting from the chimney. Within a mile I was up on the slopes of the Slieve Mish, heading west. The path ran along the flanks of the hills, with an exciting view ahead into the heart of the peninsula where Mount Brandon, twenty-five miles off, stood magnificently at the summit of a jagged ridge with its head in the clouds. A semi-circle of mountains rose at the back of Castlegregory, where the blunt-tipped peninsula of the Maharees ran out in sand dunes towards the coast of North Kerry, with a line of sea horizon beyond. Nearer at hand the sides of the Slieve Mish were split by deep gullies, up which I had stirring views of the great bowls of corries scooped out by Ice Age glaciers. Fionn MacCumhaill's Chair loomed out of the mists, a rounded promontory suitably high and mighty for the posterior of that hero of the quicksilver wits, mighty sinews and unquenchable wrath. The Dingle Way led on, up and down the slopes in deference to local farmers' territorial sensibilities, a bare and open pathway for six or seven miles until it met a surfaced road and wound between the ivy-smothered ruins of the abandoned village of Killelton.

'Cil' signifies a chapel in Gaelic, and the Dingle Peninsula is full of placenames prefixed with 'Kil-'. Early Christian hermits, from the fifth century onward, seeking out the loneliest places to bury themselves in prayer, study, labour and fasting, found what they sought in West Kerry. The ruins of the chapels, little stone clochans (dwelling huts) and souterrains (underground storage chambers) built by themselves and others who came to join them, lie all over the Dingle Peninsula – the greatest concentration of such sites in all Ireland. Just off the path above the shattered shells of Killelton's houses I came across a solid box of stone standing seven feet high, massive walls three feet thick pierced on the west by a narrow doorway and on the east by the stump of an even narrower window. The trees – holly and rowan – pressed round the plain little structure in a green square, with Gearhane Mountain rising 2500 feet overhead. A murmur of cars on the coast road came faintly up on the sea breeze, hardly loud enough to penetrate the leaves. The twentieth century seemed a long way off as I stood there in the ruins of Killelton Church, built thirteen hundred years before by a saint whose name – Elton – is the only thing known about him. Tales of the miracles he worked may have been told in Killelton village before its long, compartmented houses and sloping-roofed sheds were abandoned to the ivy and brambles. The Great Famine put paid to Killelton and its people, I was told by Sean the Scarlet in the bar of Ashe's pub in Camp village that night.

Sean the Scarlet was out to pull this Englishman's leg, but bitter little bursts of history were mixed with the blarney. 'The Famine caused Killelton to die,' he said, his eyes coruscating behind his glasses, 'but ask yourself who caused the Famine. Huh? Eh?' Sean can't have been more than in his middle sixties, but the spirit of 1916 burned brightly in his talk. 'I'm an old card-carrying member of the far left – and I mean *far* left, and I mean *card-carrying*, do you understand what I mean? I'm the man that tipped the winner of the Grand National of 1951 – Russian Hero! Do you know what I'm saying? Eh? Sean the Scarlet – that's what they used to call me.'

In Sean's talk there was no clue as to which of the stories he came out with were grounded in fact. There was the one about the Spanish brigantine that went down laden with treasure in Tralee Bay, and the golden pig that lay buried in a triangular field somewhere nearby; the one about the Armada survivors who came ashore at Dunquin after their ships were wrecked. 'There are girls in Dunquin with hair as black as a pint of Guinness – they're all descendants of those Spaniards. The people welcomed them, of course, because they were enemies of England. Do you understand me? They threw some Frenchmen off the cliffs, thinking they were English, but they looked after the Spanish. Do you know –' Sean leaned closer, an unreadable smile on his face, 'behind the old school house in Dunquin there's a grave, the Prince's Grave they call it. Maybe the locals will show it to you, though they don't really like to talk about it. That prince was the bastard son of King Philip of Spain. He was the admiral of the Spanish fleet. And he's buried there! Please – go and see that grave!' urged Sean the Scarlet with a vehemence half-humorous, half-sinister. 'Please! Go and see it!'

Later, when Sean the Scarlet had gone home, his friend button-holed me. 'I'm afraid he was taking the mickey out of you. I hope you don't mind.' I said I'd taken Sean with a pinch of salt, and the friend grinned in embarrassment, keen to dissociate himself from a display of bad manners to a visitor. At the end of the bar there were other victims listening to blarney of a different sort. A coach party from Tralee had come in to taste some Irish tradition, served unsmilingly to them by a singer and a melodeon player. The visitors sat round the fireplace while the singer gave a performance that included a musical nod to the nationalities he guessed might be represented among his audience – 'Danny Boy', 'The Rose of Tralee', 'Swing Low, Sweet Chariot', 'The Battle Hymn of the Republic' and 'You are My Sunshine'. I gave myself a good mental kick in the backside when I realised how snottily I was turning up my nose, as critical as any Doolin purist. The coach party was still singing along happily as I crept to bed in Maureen O'Shea's bed-and-breakfast place opposite the pub, my path up the stairs lit by a red lamp burning before a picture of the Sacred Heart.

I took it easy all the way from Tralee to Dingle along the Dingle Way: ten miles a day, and plenty of time for idling and eating the breeze. The grassy old tarred road to Anascaul threaded its way up and over the spine of the peninsula, mountains to left and right, hedges dripping blood-red with fuchsia lanterns each side. Caher-conree Mountain turned a steep green face to the path, its long crest hidden in shredding clouds. 'Please climb Caherconree and see the old fort up there. If you want to understand Irish history! Please!'

Sean the Scarlet had urged me with what I now realised had been mock fervour. But the jagged line of the fort was hidden in the clouds, its dark shape emerging for a second or two at intervals. Legend – Irish history of a sort – said that the hero Cuchulainn had raided the fort to win back the beautiful Blathnaid from King Cu Roi MacDaire, who had stolen and married her. Blathnaid gave her lover the signal that the fort was open to attack by pouring milk into the source of the River Finglas to whiten its waters. Cuchulainn launched his attack, killed the king and galloped off in triumph with his lady.

The track ran down through the sprawling turf banks under Knockmore, reaching the southern coast of the peninsula above the great scimitar-shaped three-mile sandspit at Inch. I put the pack in a hedge bottom and sat down to gaze across Dingle Bay at one of the best views of the entire walk. On the east of the sandspit the bay had dried out with the tide's ebb, and lay gleaming in whorls and streaks of subtle blues, greys and pale browns. On the west the waves came seething in to break gently on the beach that ran the length of the spit, their murmur coming up as a soporific whisper to where I sat, half asleep in the cloudy warmth of midday. Across the bay rose the ice-blue shapes of Macgillycuddy's Reeks, proper mountain peaks more challenging than anything Dingle could show, but faded out by the cloud haze into the insubstantial dreaminess of a Japanese painting. Other blue and grey hills, less dramatic than the Reeks but just as compelling, ran down towards the Atlantic tip of the Iveragh Peninsula where they fell away into the sea. Walking on with this tremendous view for company, I watched the cars and coaches far below driving in an unbroken procession down the coast road to Dingle.

In a small garden beside the path a man in a home-knit sweater was harnessing his pony to a scarlet-painted wooden dray. 'Just going down to the shops,' he remarked over the gate. ''Tis handy with the old horse.' We got into desultory conversation, while the patient nag stood head down in the shafts, flicking his ears against the flies.

'There was six of us in a poor family, so I had to emigrate. London, Birmingham, Bristol – I worked in all of them. But I was glad to get back! I'm not one for the city life. I have my health, thank God, and a way to make a living,' – he waved his hand towards the vegetable garden and the round-topped haycocks in his field – 'so it's OK for me. The tourism is growing here now. Dingle town – well, I haven't seen much change in twenty years. But all the tourists go there; why, I don't know. For them 'tis Dingle, Dingle, Dingle and nothing else. So! A good day to you. Enjoy your walk, now.'

So I did, climbing on up the boreen to Maum Pass and another grand view, over Anascaul Lake lying like a dull grey ingot in a bowl of mountain cliffs. From the pass the old road I was on ran like an arrow down the valley and up again, six miles of dead straight drovers' road making unerringly for Dingle. When I turned round halfway down the slope into Anascaul village and looked back, I saw the logic of this directness; the track was aimed exactly at the 1200-foot peak of Brickany Mountain, a marking point visible right across the valley to drovers coming east from Dingle market.

The South Pole Inn, next to the shrine of the Virgin Mary by Anascaul bridge, was closed up tight, with 'For Sale' notices in its windows. But Thomas Crean's name still stood above the door. Crean ran the pub in the early years of this century. He was a famous man, an Antarctic explorer who had been with both Scott and Shackleton on their polar expeditions. As a member of the back-up team on Scott's doomed adventure in 1912 the Irishman had got to within a hundred miles of the South Pole. Had he been picked for the party that made the final attempt, there would have been no tall tales to tell across the bar in Anascaul.

'Money, money, money,' sighed the woman who served me my seafood soup in the newly-opened Clúimín Restaurant. 'That's all they think about in Dingle these days. I was born there, and I can tell you it's changed, all right – and it's in danger of changing too far. Every second shop is a gift shop or craft shop or restaurant, you'll find. Now, twenty years ago people came to Dingle because it was – I don't quite know how to put it – well, it was a relaxed and quiet kind of a place, with very friendly people. Today they see too many tourists and too much money. They'll have to be very careful they don't spoil it altogether – like Killarney. Now that's a place I hate with a passion! Have you been there? No? Well, don't! Horrible! Green, white and gold everywhere – colleens and bawneens, linen and leprechauns! They've destroyed the town entirely for the sake of the Americans. But the Americans love it, so I suppose there must be a call for it. It's funny when you think of it; people get to love a place because it's got a genuine unspoilt atmosphere to it, and then it always changes into the kind of place that no one with any sense would want to go near. Is it the tourists that want these changes, I wonder, or do the locals do it themselves because they think the tourists want it?'

This was the Doolin conundrum all over again; and it set me wondering, as I took to the old drovers' road again next morning, whether I would find a shamrocked hell-hole where Dingle used to be. But it wasn't quite like that.

Dingle Races were just finished, and Dingle Regatta was still a couple of weeks away, but the little town on its beautiful circular bay was completely jam-packed with people. It was one-foot-in-the-gutter time once more, dodging the Scandinavians with their mighty backpacks and the English worrying over menus on the pub walls. The tills rang merrily in craft shops and cafés, all the way up the hill from the harbour where the new pier was well on the way to completion. There were smart boats in the bay, and the smart Hotel Skellig in a squat modern mass on its own green headland. New houses, too, down on the Tralee road and out round the back of the town. Dingle was doing well in this mid-August week, with spitting rain driving people off the streets and into the open arms of the shopkeepers. 'We're sick and tired of them,' muttered one whom I collared for a word in a rare quiet moment. 'Can't wait for October and them to be gone.' But his till was chiming freely enough to belie his words.

A tourist town, then, and an unashamed one, coining it with concentrated energy while the harvest was on. But soon another side of Dingle began to rub through the veneer of money-making. The fishermen on the quay were going about their business, loading, unloading and making ready for sea with never a glance to spare for the pointed cameras above their heads. The small bars in the upper streets of the town, the ones without notices in the windows and with only a plain owner's name over the door, growled low with sporadic conversation in Irish among their blue-jacketed and heavy-booted elderly regulars. A butcher came out of his shop door, wiping his red hands on his apron, to take a string-bound parcel of magazines from a small boy who had run up with it from the corner shop. And I began to notice a movement among the old men in cloth caps and the Dingle mothers with excited children, a general drift down Main Street against the flow of the tourist crowds, round the corner by the bridge and out of sight. I fell in behind a couple of thickset brothers carrying sticks, and followed them away from the ring of the tills and out where the local people were heading.

The beast market stood a little out of town, an ugly grey block looking over a sloping plateau of concrete animal pens to great hills rising all round. Most of the villages in the peninsula must have been empty this afternoon; men, women, children and animals had all come down to Dingle for the agricultural show. A stone catapulted from the seething pavements of Main Street over the house tops could easily have landed in the middle of the show, but as far as I could tell I was just about the only non-peninsular show-goer present. Perhaps the show had not been advertised in the tourist parts of the town, or maybe its attractions were too simple. At all events, I wandered round with a crowd speaking more Irish than English, a crowd whose faces round the sheep and cattle pens and the horse ring were frowning with concentration and critical judgement. Showing the animals, and watching them, was serious business. Elderly farmers from up in the hills climbed out of their mud-spattered old cars and off their outdated tractors, and strolled across to hitch themselves in twos and threes across the railings of the pens, arms along the top rail, one leg up on the bottom rung. A Charolais bull had a small crowd all to itself as it stood like a muscle-bound boxer in defeat, head lowered. 'Will you look at the crubeens on that!' said a farmer admiringly. There was a burst of laughter from his friends. The bull's hooves didn't look all that funny to me.

The widest spread of ages was around the walled, grassy patch of ground at the bottom of the market where men were leading horses round and round in a never-ending circle. The handlers hissed soothingly as they walked, their brown arms straining the short leading reins against the nervous tossing of the horses' heads. A group of young boys perched on the wall, grass blades in their mouths and caps on the backs of their heads, watching the horses unsmilingly, the spit and image of their uncles and grandfathers beside them. The animals drew an intentness from the onlookers that owed nothing to the modern world; motor cars, tractors and lorries were entirely incidental to this scene of quiet concentration, smelling of dung, straw and tobacco smoke, that might easily have belonged to a Dingle show of a hundred years ago.

Up in the market building things were far livelier. Plump ladies were laying out rows of home-made cakes for judging, furtively testing them with little pinches into their mouths. The Farmers' Union had a stall nearby placarded with posters explaining the likely effects of the EC's Common Agricultural Policy – cuts in grants, subsidies for sheep farming – that had the onlookers in heated debate. In a side area the Best Dressed Dogs were crouching miserably in bowler hats and shirts, their owners not in the least shamefaced. I stopped to talk to a little girl cradling a carefully primped and combed cat in her arms. 'Has she won?' I asked. 'Not yet!' chirped the child, stroking away and grinning from ear to ear.

A big lorry stood nearby, one canvas side rolled up to make a stage for the children's Irish dancing competition. The children stood in a nervous group at the back of the trailer, ordered and numbered, not daring to giggle or lark about with their mothers keeping a stern eye on them from below. Some of the little girls wore exquisitely embroidered traditional costumes with stiff skirts that flew high as they kicked up their legs; others stamped out their jigs and reels in the tracksuit tops and woollen trousers they had worn to the show. A woman played the tunes for dancing on a melodeon; another woman, tall and tense – she must have been the dancing teacher – stood at the back of the wagon whispering admonishment or encouragement to her charges. 'Come on, now, Aloysius, don't forget *everything* you've learned,' I heard her hiss at a tiny lad doing his brave but inadequate best all alone on the wide stage. Number 1 had elaborately ringleted hair, a gorgeous dress, and knees scabbed and bloody from some mishap earlier in the day. How her mother must have cursed her – Those photographs! What *will* she look like? But Number 1 came up trumps, winning two trophies thick with glittering chrome which she held stiffly to her chest with a secretive little grin of pure delight.

I had no way of knowing what proportion of the crowd at the show was from the town of Dingle itself. Not more than half, perhaps. But when it came to holding such a show, a purely local and rural affair, Dingle was still the natural venue. That show had not altered itself one inch to please the tourists. It was as its participants wanted, no more and no less – a forum for the sober judging of farm animals and a bit of home-made fun on the side. That strong dose of ordinary local life sounded, for this onlooker, a reassuring note of solidity and continuity to counterbalance the laments for Dingle lost and gone that I'd heard along the road to the town.

Other aspects of Dingle's community life are also unconnected with the tourist trade. The fishing fleet flourishes, as it has always done. Factories set up and stop work one after another, each new venture bringing optimism to the town as it opens, followed by disillusionment as it folds. The fish processing plant on the far side of the pier keeps going, year in, year out. The town's traditional music is strong both in and out of season, much of it based on the fife and drum as a reminder of Dingle's pre-independence days as an English garrison town. In winter the Dingle businesses and the political parties run social clubs whose get-togethers and dances are in practice open to all the townspeople. And then there's the Wren.

The annual Wren was a familiar tradition in many Irish towns up until this century. It's now been revived in nearby Listowel, after decades of disuse. But Dingle can boast an unbroken line of Wrens. The connection between the hunting of unfortunate small songsters on St Stephen's Day, 26 December, and a day of genial riot in the streets and pubs of the town is obscure. Folklorists seem to agree that both are connected with ancient midwinter fertility celebrations. Dingle needs its Wren, a great outburst of crude vigour and jollity at the most depressing time of the year, when life in a small rain-soaked town at the end of a remote peninsula can seem unbearably grim and claustrophobic. The Wren is 'an explosion of light, colour and boisterous exuberance in the midst of winter's gloom. From damp, cold lifelessness the town erupts in a day's release in marching, music, shouting, dance, fooling and drinking' (Steve MacDonogh, *Green and Gold: The Wrenboys of Dingle*). The Wren is a celebration of fertility and earthy hot blood, of life in the face of death. It's based round a hobby horse, a captain, a band of fife-and-drum musicians and a motley crew of followers dressed in suits of straw, in outlandish fancy costume, in masks, false hair, strange hats – anything that will disguise the identity of the reveller.

Each St Stephen's Day different Wren contingents emerge from the pubs where they are based in several areas of Dingle to parade round the town, in and out of the pubs, gathering ever greater numbers of people, shouting, singing and playing tricks on each other under cover of their disguises. It's a chaotic, disorganised day, in which all present are as good as forced to take part. The day runs into night with pubs and streets ever fuller and rowdier. Those with delicate nerves or thin skins stay at home. This is Dingle's day, with no thought for any outsider. Like the Padstow 'Obby 'Oss in Cornwall or Up Helly Aa in Shetland, the Wren is part of the life blood of the town, an insider's thing. It has been through thin times, through spates of disapproval from clergy and moral crusaders, through periods during which some of Dingle's Wren bands have shrunk to shadows, or faded away altogether. But the event itself doesn't die, and is in no danger of doing so -- and this with scarcely a tourist camera clicked all day.

In An Dreolín café in Lower Main Street I sat down at suppertime in front of a small, flat mutton pie in a bowl, a jug of greasy grey liquid and another jug of milk. Have you heard the one about the Englishman who wanted to pour milk on his Dingle Pie? I hope the proprietor of An Dreolín earned a good few pints of Guinness with that non-Kerryman joke. 'No,' he said politely, 'the milk's for your tea. You pour the other jug over the pie – the one with the broth in.' I did so, and had a squishily delicious meal. Then it was down to the Small Bridge pub on the corner for what was advertised in the window as a 'Mighty Session'.

The Small Bridge was crowded beyond the doors and into the street. It was a fire inspector's nightmare. People were squeezed into the corners, jammed against the walls and piled three on a seat. I slipped my harmonica out of my pocket and found a perch on the back of the bench where the musicians were sitting, with a bird's-eye view over the solid, sweat-dripping crowd. Faces were packed in the doorway beside me, and looking around at one point in the evening I saw another row of disembodied heads filling the open tops of the windows, their owners standing tiptoe on the windowsills outside. The journey to the bar and back was a ten-minute annoyance to those along the route – I dealt out jogged elbows, nudged backs and trampled feet by the score. Muiris Ferris, the pub's owner, somehow kept his cool and his smile throughout. Maybe it was the sound of the till, but more likely it was the good crack roaring in his establishment.

There was a fair proportion of Irish people among the foreigners, chiefly students, the men with pony-tails and the women with short-back-and-sides. They had come along to hear Gerry O'Connor play. Gerry, a slim and modest young man with a trail of black hair down his neck, was about the only person in the place with elbow room, and he put it to excellent use with a string of blindingly fast and expert tunes on fiddle and banjo. In my ignorance I had never heard his name before, but it soon became clear that this was one of the young heroes of Irish traditional music. 'So how did the interview in Dublin go?' I heard the accompanying pipe player ask him. 'And the tour – all fixed up?' put in the guitarist from his corner. Youngsters shoved their way to the front of the crowd and shyly put down their money for a tape of Gerry's music from the box open on the table in front of him.

After things had got well under way a handsomely built woman with chestnut-red hair tumbling down her back arrived with two flutes and squeezed in between the mandolin and the bodhrán. Casting an eye over the table top and seeing most glasses were empty, she rose majestically to her feet and gave a great bellow over the noise of the crowd: 'Muiris, are you working the bar at all? Five pints, man, and move it!' This was Dolores Keane, another famous figure in Irish music. For all I knew, every man and woman round that table might have been a living legend to the young aspiring musicians peeping in under one another's armpits.

Suddenly I remembered what I was supposed to be doing: finding out why the foreigners were coming to Dingle. I chose a face at random from the gallery beside me, a young girl with a long nose and dreamy, music-sodden grin. 'Where do you come from?' I shouted in her ear.

'From Chairmany!'

'Why did you come to Dingle?'

'Pecause . . . I like! It's . . . nice fun!'

That seemed to be as good an explanation as I was going to get.

Next morning, on my way out of town, I went down to the pier where shivering families in anoraks were waiting in the wind for the Dolphin Special. There's a strong suspicion in Dingle that Bord Fáilte have got Fungi the bottle-nosed dolphin under contract. Fungi is a film star and has had his biography published. He's been Dingle's little pot of gold ever since arriving in 1984 and settling around the entrance to the bay. Fungi loves publicity and thrives on attention. He'll jump obligingly out of the water for any boatload of tourists, his beaky mouth fixed in a bland smile for the cameras. Everyone loves Fungi. Handicapped children are taken out for therapeutic contact with him. Dingle fishermen – those with boats for hire – think he's a fine fellow.

It's as if Neptune has blessed the town with a minor miracle. Cynical locals speculate on who will win the contract to build a shrine to St Fungi when their finny chum rolls over for the last time.

The man in the shop where I went to buy postcards had more sombre matters on his mind. 'S.O.S.' read the badge on his sweater. '"Save Our Shore", it stands for,' he told me with a preoccupied frown. 'The results of the public inquiry haven't been published yet, but we won't let them get away with it. Not a hope.' The story came out with angry vehemence. A development company had applied to build forty apartment blocks for letting to holidaymakers on the shore near the Hotel Skellig, along with a marina for three hundred boats. Twenty-three acres of shoreline would disappear, a green and peaceful place popular with Dingle folk for strolling and chatting. Potential jobs and money, weighed against the town's own wishes. The shop-keeper had no doubt as to how the balance would come down.

'The people of the town don't want it. They think it's totally unnecessary. And they'll make sure it never happens. If a bulldozer was ever put down there, it wouldn't get back up again.' His eyes flashed furiously. I wouldn't care to be the contractor who starts work on that development.

The clouds were down again, slicing off the hills under the thousand-foot contour. I walked fast along the Dingle Way, round the foot of Caherard and down into Ventry where a long strand of white sand curved for a couple of miles under the 1700-foot Mount Eagle. If there were eagles up there, they were hidden in the murk. A strong wind was blowing in from the Atlantic, driving sand particles into my eyes as I plodded against its force down the beach. Halfway along, a solitary graveyard stood among the dunes, with figures moving slowly among its overgrown headstones – old men in flapping serge suits, old women in black coats, a splash of scarlet and white from the T-shirts of children. 'It's a funeral,' said the wild-haired man leaning with his friend on the graveyard wall. 'Sure, you're welcome and more to join them.'

Perhaps 150 people had gathered around the grave to say their goodbyes to the dead man. He had died at eighty-eight, an inhabitant of the neighbouring hamlet of Caherantrant all his long life. 'We bury them well hereabouts,' whispered the woman beside me. The wind whipped her words away along with those of the priest, whipped at the coats and dresses of the mourners and the heads of the grasses that hid the gravestones. A freckly infant broke away from his mother and went skittering over the graves, oblivious of the solemn faces and folded hands. The pipe of curlews came across the graveyard from the slopes of Mount Eagle. It was not the worst place in the world to be buried, with the mountain behind and the strand stretched out in front, the wind flattening the grasses and the sea sparkling in gleams of sunshine between the headlands of Ventry Bay.

I tramped on through silent lanes that gave way to grassy boreens, winding a slow way round the flanks of Mount Eagle, making for a stream marked 'Glenfahan' on the map. Once across it, the Dingle Way guidebook told me, I would be right in the heart of the richest concentration of clochans, souterrains and stone crosses in the whole of Ireland. I spotted only one souterrain, and not a single cross, but the clochans were everywhere. Here on the slopes of the mountain, where the peninsula curves from west to north at its outermost tip, the wind and foul Atlantic weather come inland with a vigour gathered over three thousand miles. Life for those early Christian hermits must have been almost unbearably hard on the site they chose for themselves, hanging steeply between mountain and sea on a barren and stony hillside right in the teeth of the weather. No wonder they built their hemispherical clochans with walls of closely-knit stones two or three feet thick and narrow doors half the height of a man. I rummaged around among the little structures, finding some like stone doughnuts with their tops crumbled or scavenged away, others complete with caps of wind-blown turf and vegetation. Many of the clochans were still in use as animal pens full of dung and trampled straw or as store houses for heaps of shimmering nylon fishing net. Others held only bracken, along with the sheep that charged out frantically at my approach. The souterrain I happened across stood in the shadow of a clochan, an angle of stone wall buried in a bank that once held whatever produce the saintly owner of the clochan had managed to grow on the bare side of the hill.

I followed the sheep along the green track under the stone walls, wondering how many of those hermits and their acolytes had succumbed during their first winter at the sharp end of the Dingle Peninsula. West coast weather has a way of sorting out the 'blow-ins'. It wasn't the weather, though, but the fatal draining wounds of emigration and economic disadvantage that finally drove the inhabitants of the Great Blasket ashore for ever.

The little line of Blasket Islands – Inishvickillaun, Inishnabro and the Great Blasket – had been slowly swimming into sight one after the other as I rounded Slea Head on the very tip of the peninsula, and standing on the hillside above Coumeenoul beach I looked down across Blasket Sound at their distinctive shapes: Inishvickillaun spread low, Inishnabro humped and rough-backed, and the double hump of the much larger Great Blasket, four miles from the cliffs at the western end to the tiny square of fertile slopes and the curved yellow strand on the landward side. To that slip of land on the eastern extremity of the Great Blasket a community had clung in fair and hard weather, in bad times and good, until in 1953 the remaining elderly islanders decided they had had enough and left the Blasket for softer and more compli-cated lives ashore. Two miles of tide-ripped sound was all the physical barrier between the Blasket and the mainland; but the islanders were men and women apart, in custom, tradition and mode of life. The most westerly people in Europe, they had maintained a purity of Gaelic language that attracted scholars from the mid-nineteenth century onwards to venture the treacherous crossing of the sound by currach and find lodgings with the Blasket Islanders. There were no machines on the Great Blasket then; no electricity, gas, piped water, metalled roads; no church, shop, pub; no doctor or priest; scarcely a horse. Donkeys did the horse's work, carrying creels of turf and other goods. The islanders lived a narrow life in narrow ways, connected only tenuously with the modern world, right up until their evacuation in 1953. Yet the Great Blasket became famous far beyond Ireland for an extraordi-nary literary heritage, a rich harvest out of apparently barren soil.

The oral tradition had persisted in the lonely island even as it began to fade all over mainland Ireland; and Tomás O'Crohan, the first of the islanders to see his work in print, could be said to have been merely the channel through which hundreds of years of Blasket oral tradition were released, a channel unblocked simply by the gift of pens and paper and the encouragement of a student, Brian O'Kelly from Killarney, who wanted to continue his Gaelic studies with O'Crohan by post after leaving the island. But that would be to ignore O'Crohan's own marvellous gift for communication. How I would love to know enough Irish to read *Allagar na hInise* (*Island Cross-Talk*, 1928) and *An tOileanach* (*The Islandman*, 1929) in the original.

O'Crohan wrote as he spoke and heard speak, and relayed his observations, conversations and snippets of island life as if murmuring in the reader's ear at the fireside:

> I turned for home with five or six fish, my first day out fishing this year. I was thankful I was no 'glab', as they always call a fisherman without a catch. Síle was digging potatoes and I asked her if she was pleased with them.
>
> 'I pulled up a stalk with forty potatoes under it and every one of them would go through the eye of a needle,' said she. 'Virgin Mary, isn't it a great wonder that there is no crop and the blue blossoms still on them!'
>
> 'But seeing how your own bloom has faded from you, aren't you glad that the blossom is on your potatoes, Síle?'
>
> 'Holy Mary, my bloom is vanished. Look at my hair today as white as chalk, and not even half of it left, compared to the lovely golden locks I had on me once of a day.'
>
> 'By my baptism,' said she again, 'whatever number of grey hairs I have, they will grow greyer still unless it is God's will to send me a handful of good potatoes, for there is no other pound or sixpence to be earned.'
>
> Up she springs out of the trench, plunges her hand into her pocket, pulls out a match, plunges her hand in again and hauls out a clay pipe as black as coal.
>
> She reddened it.
>
> 'We must make the most of what we have,' said she.
>
> On my reckoning she must have spent fifteen pounds on tobacco for her pipe by this stage of her life.*

This extract in translation, subtly balanced and beautifully observed as it is, is only a pale shadow of the original, according to those Irish-speakers with whom I talked about the Blasket writers. Tomás O'Crohan had only learned to read and write Irish a few years before compiling the diary whose entries were collected and published as *Island Cross-Talk*. Of the world's literature he had read nothing (though he was soon to read and greatly enjoy a volume of the short stories of Maxim Gorky given to him by Brian O'Kelly), and he had

---

* *Island Cross-Talk* (translated by Robin Flower)

never travelled further than the western end of County Kerry.

A second member of the great trio of Blasket authors, Maurice O'Sullivan, had likewise only a smattering of experience as a Garda in Dublin when in 1933 he published his exuberant, dashing and highly poetical account of his boyhood on the island, *Fiche Blian ag Fás* (*Twenty Years A-Growing*), the most 'literary' (though not at all self-consciously so) of the Blasket books. I found this the best read of the lot, a flowing, elegiac tribute to the island and its people, crammed full of sharp observations and funny incidents:

> Some of the curraghs were leaving now, moving out west through the mouth of the Strand. When my father was ready they put me out of the curragh and she moved away. I walked up to the top of the slip. There I met Tomás.
>
> 'Do you know where we will go now?' said he. 'Back to the top of the Strand and we will have a great view of the curraghs fishing.'
>
> There was not an old woman in the village but was already there, sitting on her haunches looking out at the curraghs. The evening was very still. It was a fine sight to look out towards the shore of Yellow Island at the shoals of mackerel, and the curraghs running round on them like big black flies.
>
> There was no understanding the old women now, who were foaming at the mouth with their roaring.
>
> 'Your soul to the devil,' cried one to her husband, 'throw the head of your net behind them!'
>
> 'Musha, my love for ever, Dermod!' cried another when she saw her husband making a fine haul of fish.
>
> One woman, Kate O'Shea, her hair streaming in the wind like a mad woman's, was screaming: 'The devil take you, Tigue, draw in your nets and go west to the south of the Sound where you will get fish for the souls of the dead. Och, my pity to be married to you, you good-for-nothing!'
>
> 'May the yellow devil fly away with you, you have the place destroyed with your noise!' shouted one of the fishermen when he heard the screams ashore.
>
> As for Tomás and me, our hearts were black with laughing at the old women. Their shawls thrown off, waving

their arms at their husbands, they called to them to come here and to come there around the fish, until the fish themselves seemed to be distracted by them.

Peig Sayers, on the other hand, while far and away the best-known islandwoman even while still living there, set foot on the Great Blasket for the first time as the young bride of an islandman. Her books *Peig* (1936) and *Machtnamh Seana-mhná* (*An Old Woman's Reflections*, 1939) pursued the conversational, idiomatic tradition, fleshing out the barer bones of O'Crohan's style:

> Let me tell you what happened to an Islandman on one occasion many years ago. He passed east through Dingle on his way to the pounding-mill with two bags of wool to be carded. There was a crowd of women at the mill before him and the miller told them that they'd have to allow the Islandman to go first because he had travelled such a long journey from home. *Erra*, man dear, when they heard that he was from the Great Blasket Island they were staring at him so intently that you'd think they would eat him up with their eyes. The miller noticed them.
>
> 'The devil fire ye!' he said. 'What staring have ye at that decent man? Can't ye see that he's as gentle, as kind and as capable-looking as any other man? Or is it the way ye think he has horns growing out of his head?'
>
> When they heard this they shrivelled up, and even if he had six horns on his head they wouldn't have dared to look at him any more. That same man was the handsomest and nicest man on the Island, God be good to his soul. The people in this Island are pleasant, honest, generous and hospitable and the stranger can experience friendship and kindness among them. And if he doesn't, it's his own fault!
> (From *Peig*)

It's worth pausing to reflect that the entire population of the Great Blasket was somewhere around 120 at the time Tomás O'Crohan, Maurice O'Sullivan and Peig Sayers were writing their books. Unless literary genius made an unprecedented descent on the island between the two world wars, it's more than likely that at least one such writer

could have been found among the Blasket people – always numbering
fewer than two hundred, and as remote as any community in Ireland
– at almost any time in their history, if a Brian O'Kelly had happened
along to set the bucket under the spring.

I thought of some of this as I sat in a small open boat going out to
the Great Blasket from Dunquin. There was a heavy swell running
in Blasket Sound, a legacy of the night's strong wind. Maurice O'Sullivan, who had been farmed out to a 'stranger woman' in Dingle after
his mother had died while he was still a baby, made his return to the
Blasket at the age of seven on such a day of swell, and tossing in the
light currach had begun 'to feel my guts going in and out of each
other, and as the curragh rose and fell I became seven times
worse . . .'

> 'Put your hand back in your throat,' said my father, 'as far
> back as it will go, and then you will have it.'
> I did as he said, but I did not like it.
> 'Have no fear,' said my father.
> 'But isn't it the way I am worst when I put my hand back
> in my mouth?'
> I tried again and again . . . till at last I felt my belly
> beating against the small of my back. Then up came the
> burden and I threw it out.

Luckily, I had the youthful boatman to chat to by way of distraction.
An Interpretive Centre like the one that was causing all the conster-
nation up at Mullaghmore in the Burren was planned for Dunquin,
the little fishing village on the clifftops opposite the Blaskets. A big
central building was to have other, smaller buildings scattered around
it, to symbolise the relationship of the islands to the mainland, or
perhaps of the smaller islands to the Great Blasket – the boatman
was rather unsure on that point. 'I think it's supposed to be for easy
understanding of the islands, the Centre. It'll go just on that piece of
land there –' he pointed back over the stern of the boat to a low green
saddle of empty ground between the village and the sea. 'There's strong
local feeling about it, for and against. It's the plans, the design that most
people don't like – not the idea of the Centre itself.'

The young man shrugged. 'Personally, I don't get involved or take
any side. But how many visitors will be coming? They say that place

up at Glencolumbkille in Donegal gets a hundred and fifty thousand a year. Anyway,' he smiled, 'it's all been cancelled for the next year, whatever. Lack of money, so they say.'

The boat crept along parallel to the mainland before heading out directly into the blue rollers of the sound. The boatman may have been not much more than a boy, but he handled the little craft and its outboard engine every bit as skilfully as former generations of Dunquin men had handled their currachs. The landing place below the village on the island was guarded by jaws of rock not more than fifteen feet apart, but with a seal watching us from the sound the boatman judged the swell and ran us in safely to the slipway. Above on the Great Blasket's small green apron of habitable land stood the roofless stone shells of more than thirty little houses; one living room and one bedroom separated by the stone breast and gable of the chimney, windows and doors without lintels or frames, nettles and grass on the floors, cracks setting inexorably across weak places. The snaking lines of grass-grown pathways were still clear on the ground, and along towards the west the islanders' fields were still sharply laid out in rectangular order between stone walls. But these fields had been cropless for many years, and of the old houses only one was roofed and in good repair. Tents were pitched in the ruins, and among those wandering through the deserted village I overheard speculations in English, French and German as to which ruins had once housed the Blasket's famous writers.

The Great Blasket is far from unvisited at any time of the year. In the summer the island makes a wonderfully lonely camping ground, and there are day visitors whenever conditions in the sound are right for crossing. Even in the winter the mainland owners of the sheep that dot every slope of the Blasket come across from time to time to check on their animals. It is the sense of a continued community and its traditions that's missing from the place, a poignant absence to anyone who has read those vivid accounts of jokes and squabbles, of marriage-making and egg-gathering, sack-hauling and furze-cutting. I had fully expected to enjoy a long nostalgic mope in the ruins, mooning among the stones that once sheltered Tomás O'Crohan and Peig Sayers. But Peig's house at the top of the village turned out to be in excellent repair, glazed, roofed and furnished, and home to as lively a pair of two-year-old twins as any the old woman can have known.

Caoimhe and Saidhbhe Duffy were toddling in and out of the kitchen, sucking at baby bottles and cheeking their mother. Mary O'Flaherty wasn't at all perturbed to find me knocking on the door. In next to no time I was sitting at the kitchen table, notebook out and a cup of coffee to hand, hearing the tale of how she and her husband Paul Duffy had exchanged the dark streets of Dublin for a wild winter alone with the babies on the Great Blasket. Mary had been working as a hairdresser in the city, Paul in a molasses plant down in the docks. They had come to know and love the island over several years of summer visits, making friends with another couple, Pól and Marie O'Colmáin, who had set up a summertime tea shop and bed-and-breakfast business in the house next door. The winter of 1990–91 had drawn Paul and Mary out to the Great Blasket to try their hand at a whole twelve months on the island. Pól and Marie would be away on the mainland for the winter, and they would be up against the elements on their own.

The adventure had turned out remarkably well. The little girls could not have looked healthier or livelier. Paul and Mary had revelled in the storms, the solitude and the endless hard work – learning to cook and bake everything for themselves, and all vegetarian (no electricity meant no refrigerator to keep meat fresh), hauling coal and gas cylinders up from the slipway by hand, finding out through sheer necessity how to replace slates on a roof torn into holes by the gales. They had walked endlessly, on the high paths along the humped back of the island in the teeth of storms, down on the strand among the winter population of five hundred seals. Mary's worst difficulty, over-all, had been simply the lack of a washing machine. She had been off the island with the children just once during the winter, a terrifying journey over a sound so angry that they had not been able to return for three weeks.

'I was alone on the island for those three weeks,' said Paul, making ready for a walk to the far end. 'I learned a lot about myself in that time, discovered an inner strength I'd never found before.' Nothing in Paul's previous life had prepared him for this. A powerfully-built man of thirty-seven with close-cropped hair and a determined jaw, he was a Dubliner from the poor side of town, a city boy through and through, though with a love of nature born of weekend trips with his parents into the country. He was used to self-discipline, having been captain of Ireland's international karate team. But now he had to do battle with internal forces – fear, loneliness, periodic depression of the kind native islanders know only too well – and he came out of the experience a changed man.

'I used to go down and sit in Tomás O'Crohan's house,' he told me, 'feeling sad and lonely, trying and trying to think myself back into those times. I imagined Hallowe'en – do you remember that description in *Twenty Years A-Growing*? – when all the lower village would be gathered there in O'Crohan's and all the upper village in Peig Sayers's. The talk and laughing, the sense of community and life. In the end I was writing myself, trying out little poems.'

Paul's friend Pól O'Colmáin, a former art teacher and also from Dublin, had himself been writing poems during his years on the Blasket, and the two of them at last found the confidence and scraped together the money to publish a little book together, *Island Thoughts*. Paul was delighted when I told him I would like to buy a copy, and immediately went next door to have it inscribed in Irish by Pól: 'Do Criostóir, an Fánaí' (To Christopher, the Wanderer).

At midday the three of us set off in company with a couple of holidaymaking lads and Pól's son to walk the green road built along the steep slope of the Great Blasket as a relief scheme during the Famine. The sun had emerged from thin clouds to release rich smells from the heather and put a sparkle on the sea a couple of hundred feet beneath us. The stories of the Blasket writers were full of descriptions of expeditions along the narrow roadway in the side of the island – expeditions to cut turf from the hill, to hunt rabbits and seabirds, to scramble down into the almost inaccessible coves by dangerous paths and rock ledges to kill seals for their meat and skins on the beaches. The islanders had not been a fanatically religious community of an orthodox sort, in spite of their constant salting of conversation with 'Mary, Holy Mother!', 'upon my soul', 'by Our Lady' and 'by my baptism'. With neither priest nor church, and having to contend with tides in the sound that often prevented them from attending Mass in Dunquin for months at a time, they would content themselves with saying the Rosary and other prayers, and not be altogether sorry to save time and labour thereby. 'I've come to realise,' said Pól at one point in our walk, stopping to look over the green curves of the island's sides and the distant mountains of Iveragh across Dingle Bay, 'that the Blasket islanders' religion was far more bound up in all this – something much closer to nature. It's been the case with me as well.'

We went on along the path, talking of the writers and their books, of island history and lore. Out in the sea to the west of the Great Blasket rose the cathedral-like spires and pinnacles of the Tearacht Rock. Pól told me a horrifying story about Inishtooskert, the island shaped like a sleeping giant, with craggy face upturned and hands folded on his belly, that came into view as we climbed to the crest of the hill. A woman and her husband, living there in the 1850s in an ancient clochan, had been stormbound for six weeks. At last rescuers managed to get a boat to the island, to find the woman insane in the hut, surrounded by gobbets of flesh. Her husband had died and, unable to drag his body up the steps out of the clochan, she had become so desperate at having to shelter there beside it that she had dismembered him and taken out the portions of the corpse one by one. Since then no one had dared to live on Inishtooskert. I wondered during the telling of this grim tale whether I might be having my leg pulled in proper island style; but later on, reading further into Blasket Island lore, I found out that the story was true.

At the top of the island I left the party to carry on towards the western end and turned down along another path on my own, making a slow and delightful walk of it back to the tea shop above the village where one of Marie's carrot-and-apple scones proved ballast enough for the boat ride back to Dunquin. I would have liked to have spent all day in the company of Paul and Pól, but Seán O'Catháin was waiting to have a word with me. Having more than a word was going to be something of a problem. Seán, at eighty years of age, was not only a touch hard of hearing; his English was not much less sketchy than my Irish. Former Blasket natives like Seán, even after forty years on the mainland, still struggle with a tongue that had been entirely unfamiliar to them during their utterly different lives in that tiny, dying community.

Seán's house stood beside a lane above Dunquin harbour, looking out to the Great Blasket. He came to the door and motioned me to take one of the chairs near the fireplace. Then we sat and smiled into the grate and up at one another, both wondering how to make contact across so many barriers. What had it been like on the Blasket? That was all I could find to ask, first in words and then in mime.

'It was a hard life, that time,' Seán said slowly. He paused to prepare his next sentence, visibly making an effort to get the ideas into English. 'On a fine day like today it is all right. But in winter it is very hard.'

'What was good about the life?'

'Ten children – one room,' Seán brought out, following his thread of thought. 'We were poor – very hard.' He gestured, putting both hands together at his right shoulder. 'Everything is carried on the back. The currach was heavy. Very heavy.'

'Why did the islanders have to leave?'

'I would row thirteen miles to the Tearacht,' Seán said, miming a strong pull on oars. 'And then back again!' A laugh split his bony face, and he leaned forward to tap me on the knee. I stemmed my flow of questions and used my ears instead as the old man went steadily on in his own rhythm and his own good time, sorting over and translating his story in his mind before letting it out in small, pungent particles, eked out with gestures.

'It was very dangerous across the sound. We sold mackerel and lobster in Dingle. For lobster we got nine shillings a dozen. It's five pounds for one now! We ate potatoes and fish, and puffins. Have you not tried a seagull's egg? They're good. Everyone had one cow. We had to put them in the currach to bring them to the bull on the mainland. Their legs were tied. How they used to struggle!

'We had to leave. All the girls went! It's a better life here – you have the dry land, anyway. There are only a few of us left now. And we are all getting old. I don't miss the island at all. It was very, very hard.'

That evening in Kruger's guest house in Dunquin I read through the poems in *Island Thoughts*. It was good to know that words were still being spun on the Great Blasket.

> I lay and tried to force myself
> to relax,
> To be calm,
> but still I tossed and turned
> to lie again with sweating limbs
> tangled in tortured sheets.
>
> It was our first night off the Island.

I lay still and almost drowsed
and then was roused again
by rudely passing car
– were cars always so loud?
The street light outside
ambered the unfamiliar room
and trapped me in its jaundiced glare.

It was our first night off the Island.

Two voices passed by on the road
and seemed to shout right in my ear.
I thought of all the food we'd bought,
the butter tasting like rich cream,
an electric squirting orange
and cheese – oh heaven, bliss!
And yet we couldn't seem to eat,
but picked and pecked
and now with swollen stomach lay
and dreamed of rice and lentil pies . . .

And through the thickly turgid fringe
of sleep I was aware that
on the other mattress on the floor
Marie was turning, twisting too.

It was our first night off the Island.

Pól O'Colmáin

The coalfire burns as gales sing their song of power,
Candle flames flicker, playing tricks with the shadows,
Not for the fickleminded.
Listen! Listen to the sound of the fiddle, as the young
Ones dance a reel,
While children sit hunkered in a corner, a world of
Passing legs, telling ghost stories,
Be-capped old men and black shawled women sit
Pipe faced, gossiping,

Who was at the well today? How many boxes of
Mackerel did you say?
They dance, talk and sing over cups of tea,
Until finally they tread down beaten paths
As the sun's first rays call another dawn.

Paul Duffy

Next night, eight miles and a world away, I caught a whiff of brim-
stone, an unexpected squall in the middle of a flat calm conversation.
Travelling through the Dingle Peninsula I had been reading Frank
O'Connor's *Guests of the Nation*, a collection of evocative short stories
about the War of Independence – scared young men waiting on dark
nights with bombs primed for the Black and Tans, British hostages
shot by their IRA captors with whom they had become friends, hide-
outs in lonely barns and betrayals in the back streets of Cork. A
friendly, elderly couple from Limerick were sitting across the pub
table from me, and we got chatting about O'Connor. Suddenly the
man leaned over the table and drew another veil of Irish history aside.
'I'm an old Republican,' he said softly, glancing around and squaring
his arms in front of him. 'You'll have had it said to you that de Valera's
men shot Michael Collins. That's nonsense. Nonsense! It was the
British shot him, of course, to give the Republicans a bad name.'

He smiled at me across the table. 'My uncle died for Ireland.'
Slowly and emotionally, he laid out the story.

'This was the way of it. He was a captain in the British Army,
wounded in the First World War, and when he came back home he
joined up with the IRA, an experienced man of twenty-eight.

'He went through two ambushes safely, and then came the one
where he met his doom. He was given orders to ambush a lorry-load
of Black and Tans at a certain crossroads. He had seven or eight
amateurs under his command, ordinary boys. They got to the place
and waited. The lorry came up along the road, and he gave the order
to open fire. And at that moment a second lorry came round the
corner.

'The column scattered, and my uncle began to run across a field.
The Black and Tans got down from the lorry and they fired on him.
He was hit twice, in the hand and here in the bladder.' The man put
his hand to his side to show the place where the bullet had struck.
'The Black and Tans saw him fall, and they came into the field fixing

their bayonets to kill him then and there. But their officer stopped them, saying "Let him die a soldier's death." So they went away and left him there.

'He got up and crossed the road and knocked at the door of a farmhouse. There was no one in, so what did he do but go into the shed and collapse in the hay. That's where the old farmer found him. "I'll drive you into the hospital in Mallow," he says to my uncle. So he harnessed up the old pony and trap and they went off along the road. Soon they heard a car coming towards them. The farmer got scared and leaped over the hedge and away with him, leaving my uncle in the trap. Who was it driving the car but another Freedom Fighter, Donncha by name. He'd heard about the fight and the wounded man, and come round to see what could he do to help. "Do you know where there's a wounded soldier hereabouts?" says Donncha. "That wounded soldier is me," says my uncle.

So Donncha lifted him into the car and away with them down to the hospital in Mallow. And my uncle died there at ten o'clock in the evening.'

Ireland's mountain saints must have judged me wanting. Croagh Patrick had wrapped itself in cloud at my long approach through northwest Mayo, and now St Brendan the Navigator was working the same trick with his holy heap in Kerry. Mount Brandon rises well over three thousand feet above Brandon Bay, and all the time I had been travelling west it, too, was hidden, head, shoulders and body. Without this prime focal point in the landscape I set my feet on the Saints' Road with more than usual faith in map and compass. Somewhere up there in the murk, south of the long, rising ridge of crags whose shape was known to me only from photographs on guest-house walls, I hoped to find the pass of Mullachveal where the path slipped over the neck of the peninsula on the way back east towards Tralee. 'High, isolated and potentially hazardous' comments Maurice Sheehy, author of the guidebook that had brought me safely this far along the Dingle Way. On Sunday morning I looked out of the bedroom window at Breda Ferris's in Emlagh, resigned to another view of blotted-out heights and a long detour by road. But the saint had relented. A beautiful clear day lay spread above the hills. An hour later I was giving thanks in the dark little cell of Gallarus Oratory.

Back in England any remnant of pre-Norman architecture is rare enough to bring a thrill of pleasure, almost of disbelief. A round-topped arch, a crude carving, a narrow doorway – these are the most one hopes to find. But here among the quiet hills of the peninsula the oratory stood entire and complete, a shock to the senses in its perfection, an upturned boat of perfectly sloped and shaped stone blocks fitting against each other as sharp and tight as they did when it was built twelve or thirteen hundred years ago. The little stone ark was pierced with two openings: a door five feet high and two feet wide, and a tiny east window perhaps fifteen inches tall. I ducked inside and stood for a long time thinking of the men who had put the stones together. As with the clochans on the slopes of Mount Eagle, the simplicity of the structure only highlighted its perfection and the thousands of hours of labour it must have called for.

The term 'saint' is a misleading one. It conjures up images of watery smiles and meekly bent knees, an other-worldly softness. Standing in Gallarus Oratory I realised dimly what a down-to-earth religion its builders must have practised; the kind of thing Pól O'Colmáin had talked about on our walk over the Great Blasket. These men's days and much of their nights were filled with hard physical toil – the long hours on the stony hillsides labouring to raise a crop to keep body and soul together; the dangerous fishing trips; the evenings spent homespinning their own clothes, mending tools and cooking. Even with a band of willing acolytes to help out, the vast majority of such hermits' prayers must have been said as an accompaniment to work, chanted or muttered rhythmically as the fingers spun, wove, tied, baited, whittled, grasped and pulled. Those early saints would have walked and climbed scores of miles each day; dug and shifted tons of rock, turf and seaweed from one week's end to the next. They must have fallen on to their straw or bracken beds in sheer exhaustion every night. When would they have found the time for the rarefied spiritual voyages I'd always imagined? I ran my hand across the sill of the little window, worn to a hollow by centuries of trickling raindrops, and found those impenetrable lives emerging in sharper focus from the mists.

It's tempting to imagine the architect of Gallarus taking an hour or two off and leaving the lads to get on with the navvying while he strolled over to see how the neighbours were coming along with their buildings a mile across the hillside at Kilmalkedar. There's no trace now of the settlement founded there by Maolcethair, but it would have been built at about the same time as Gallarus. The roofless church that stands just above the road bears witness to the development of the cultural riches that Irish monks brought home with them from their travels to Rome and throughout Europe shortly after those early Christian settlements were established. Kilmalkedar Church dates from the twelfth century, and its Romanesque doorway and arches, its carvings and chevron decorations belong to an architectural tradition in full and widespread flower.

A couple from County Armagh, down in the South for a holiday, were showing their teenage daughters over the ruins. 'An Ogham stone, look,' instructed Father, showing the girls a line of cross-wise scratchings on the edge of a pillar. 'Could be seventh century, maybe, or even earlier. These were a kind of writing.' He consulted his guidebook. 'ANM MAILE-INBIR MACI BROCANN – "the name of Mael Inbir, son of Brocán".' He led the way inside the church, and fingered a round-shaped series of markings on another pillar. 'Now, this is a development from the Ogham script. It's in Irish – see?' The girls bent dutifully to examine the inscription. Father leaned over their shoulders, prompting: 'That must be a P, and there's an M as far as I can tell.' The girls shook their heads. They couldn't read anything in the blurred runes of the stone. They bided their time until Father was down at the other end of the church taking photographs of the doorway, and slipped off to tickle each other with a furry caterpillar they'd spotted on the sill of the east window.

Mother smiled agreeably at me. 'They say if you can get through that window you'll never suffer from a bad back. I did it once, but now . . .' She put her hands to her generous hips.

'Did it work?' I asked her.

She laughed. 'No, it did not! I got arthritis within the month!'

I looked down at my own far from sylph-like shape, and measured the window with my eye. Nine inches wide at the most. I hopped up on the sill. 'Try it sideways,' Mother advised. There was a nasty moment in mid-squeeze, but I discovered a hinge in my ribcage I didn't know I had, and made it to the outside with nothing worse than a slightly strained back.

From Kilmalkedar I climbed up and away through rough fields of sodden bog. The Saints' Road, by the look of it, had seen no pilgrim feet for many a long year. But the route I was following may well never have seen a sanctified sandal. What was adumbrated in my guidebook bore no relation to what I could see on the ground. Looking at that sweat-stained page now, I have a hazy idea of where I went wrong. Searching for waymarkers with a sign of a haloed man, I blundered over the wrong ridge in the wrong place. Those waymarkers had yet to be put in position, I realised later. They might have saved me an awful lot of leg-ache. But I did at least learn how to climb a six-foot Kerry stone wall, and after a while I became quite proficient in that specialised art.

Did St Brendan discover America some time towards the middle of the sixth century AD? There is evidence that he could have done. When Tim Severin made his 3500-mile voyage in 1976–77 from Brandon Creek below Mount Brandon across the Atlantic to Newfoundland, following in the wake of the saint in a lath-and-leather currach that was a faithful replica of St Brendan's own frail craft, he nailed the legend firmly to the known history of the voyage. Brendan's adventure was written up in about AD 800, more than two centuries after his death. *Navitatio Sancti Brendani* is a tale crammed with peril and high drama, sea serpents and icebergs, mingling myth and reality in a heady brew. But Severin found enough hard facts there to make a framework on which he hung his own preparations and planning. Brendan had been a formidable wanderer by sea for many years before the great adventure, starting with a three-month journey in a currach to the Shetland Islands during which he landed at one point on the back of a sleeping whale. He had sailed to Iceland, too. God could not have chosen a better man to experience, on the top of Mount Brandon, a vision of Hy-Brasil, the Island of Paradise that lay out to the west. Or did the Twelve Apostles of Ireland choose Brendan, having seen a flower brought back from the mystic isle? The saint and his companions prayed on the mountain's peak, readied their currach and set sail into the unknown. The *Navitatio* says they were away for seven years. Somewhere out there they set foot on a beach of white sand. Was it Florida? Or Long Island? Or one of the Caribbean islands? At all events, Brendan's hunger for far horizons remained keen even after this stupendous achievement. He made several more voyages before at last dying in Brittany at the ripe age of ninety-three, a wanderer to the last.

Local legend says that it was Brendan himself who laid out the Saints' Road to his tiny oratory on the summit of Mount Brandon.

But the road was almost certainly beaten out by centuries of feet tramping the pilgrimage route to the oratory in the clouds. Nowadays there is no mass pilgrimage, in the manner of Croagh Patrick, to Brendan's mountain on 16 May, his saint's day. It's doubtful if more than a scattering of people turn out. Brandon is a dangerous enough mountain even in clear weather. T.P. O'Connor, who devised the path I was following through the western end of the peninsula, had routed it well clear of the peak itself. But I had great views northwards to Brandon's sharply angled slope during the long day's hike.

From the ridge above Kilmalkedar I made a winding and curse-laden descent. Peninsula farmers don't build their walls to be climbed over, and they don't provide them with gates – not on the slopes above the Milltown River's deep valley, anyway. Once down there, however, it was plain sailing. I climbed for miles up a green road, over the pass of Mullachveal and down again under great dark hanging crags, into the valley of the Owenmore River, where one of the loneliest farms in Ireland lay at the head of a string of lakes. Ravens croaked from ledges in the rock faces that rose fifteen hundred feet over the valley road to the knife-blade ridge of the corries under Brandon Peak. Down the cliffs poured dozens of thread-like waterfalls, falling to the gloomy bowl of a dark lake in a rocky bed. From Kilmalkedar to Cloghane village at the mouth of the Owenmore River is a good ten miles, and I met no one along the way. I was glad to put my feet up in O'Connor's pub at Cloghane that evening. An old man by the bar sang half-forgotten verses of 'The Star of the County Down', and the pub owner leaned puffing his pipe in the open doorway, stars behind him, laughing quietly to himself at some private thought.

Cloghane looks down a rocky little estuary to Brandon Bay. This is one of the back-country corners of the peninsula, where the few visitors are those who happen to be in the know. In the morning, with pelting rain and low cloud once again hiding the hills, I overtook a strange couple striding out along the estuary road. The man was tall and gawky, with a hedge of eyebrow sprouting above his prow of a nose and luxuriant white dundrearies hanging from his jaws. Ancient waterproof trousers flapped round his legs like wet washing on a line. His bespectacled, angelically smiling companion had such short-cropped, no-nonsense hair that I thought it was another man until the creamiest of well-bred English lady's voices enunciated 'Good morning' as I passed. They were getting such pared-back, thoroughly British enjoyment out of their rain-spattered promenade that I didn't stop to chat.

In a gateway further along the road I came across the old man who had been singing in O'Connor's, waiting patiently with the rain bouncing off his greasy old cap for someone to give him a lift.

'You see those two houses up there,' he said, pointing across the field behind him. 'They're both empty. And so is that one over there. These fields here, now – they used to be full of turmumps, potatoes and swedes. But they're all gone wild now – all wild. Do you know the reason for it?'

He took my arm between finger and thumb and squeezed it gently. ''Tis that there's no work for the young people. There's a fright of young people gone from this place. You might walk the roads round here at night and you wouldn't meet a sinner along the way. When I was young there was lads all over.'

The old man let go of my arm and stood looking at the wet roadway. Unsure if the conversation was over, I stood silently beside him. After a minute he said, 'My generation of young men never married, you see. The girls was all gone to England when she opened up in the War – there was plenty work there and in the States. They wouldn't stay here. Some of the lads went too, but some had to stay on to work on their farms. And they couldn't get married, even though they wanted to.'

He said no more, and I started off down the road with a 'Goodbye' over my shoulder. When I was ten yards away the old man called after me, 'There's a lot of bachelor farmers about.' And very faintly, as I drew further away, ''Tis lonely for them.'

I turned round a couple of times on the long, straight road to wave, and saw his arm lift in response. It wasn't until I was too far along the road to go back that I realised which lonely bachelor farmer he had probably been talking about.

Now the coastline of the peninsula ran out into a mini-peninsula of its own, the broad-tipped and slender-waisted sandspit of the Maharees. I walked six miles or so up its edge, on a broad beach of firm sand, with the clouds slowly lifting from the hills and the waves coming in with a vigorous roar from the west. I suddenly realised that I had heard not a word of German, French, Swedish or American since leaving Dunquin two days ago. Wherever the tourists were on this fine day in the middle of August, it wasn't here. At the tip of the sandy tongue I came to Scraggane pier, another relief work initiated by the Congested Districts Board in the 1880s. Two men were busy not working at the seaward end. Piles of green fishing net sparkled in the sun that had finally slipped through between the clouds. In the bay the long black shapes of currachs rode among a handful of modern trawlers. The calm water lapped a stony shore; oystercatchers piped on the tideline. The hills to the east smoked with cloud. In an hour or two I would be walking towards them, away from the Maharees, through Castlegregory and along the last few miles of the Dingle Way back into Tralee. But not just yet awhile.

6

'WE'RE VERY QUIET
AROUND HERE'
Limerick City to Killarney

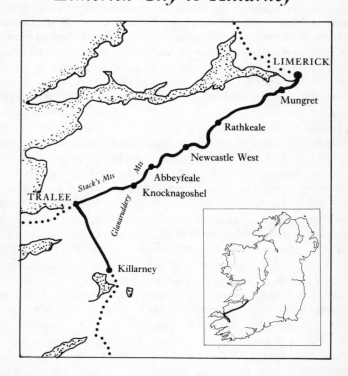

Back in England after the Dingle Peninsula walkabout, I spent the second half of August glooming over reddening bank statements and unmown lawns. Then I girded my loins for the final stage of the road to Roaringwater, kissed the family goodbye, and flew west for the last time in brilliant late-summer sunshine. The allure of Dingle in the dog days had caused me to break the long chain of the journey at

Limerick city back in July, but now as Aer Lingus decanted me at Shannon Airport I was all set to link it up again.

The September sun shone hot on the streets of Limerick, bringing the publicans in shirtsleeves to their doors for a breath of air and putting a rosy glow on the noses of the shopgirls eating their lunch-time sandwiches in the park. The girls munched and chatted as they sat on the grass, their backs to a wildly-painted statue of some Celtic god or other straddling a wheeled chariot, twice life-size, stark naked, a line of silvery flames blazing on his out-thrust arm. Handsomely, even improbably endowed, he made a potent backdrop to the carefree girls and their chummy exchanges. None of them so much as glanced up at his protuberances dangling overhead. Evidently the month or so that had passed since his erection had drawn the sting of contro-versy. Early in his reign some impudent vandal had made off with his wedding tackle – 'STATUE LOSES CROWN JEWELS' trumpeted the headline in the local paper – but now his dignity had been restored. A couple of late-season tourists, strolling past, pointed, snorted and collapsed into laughter, and the shopgirls looked up from their sand-wiches in bafflement. Limerick people can handle these things.

Lines of bunting were strung across the streets, and 'Limerick 300' banners fixed to the lamp posts. The city was in the middle of celebrating the three hundredth anniversary of the signing of the Treaty of Limerick, and doing its best to attract the attention of newcomers fresh off the planes at Shannon Airport. Limerick saw its fair share of fighting and destruction in the dark days of Irish history, but the Treaty of 1691 seemed at the time of its signature to have opened a door of hope to the country's hard-pressed Catholics. In many ways it was a shrewd act of magnanimity on the part of King William III of England, who held his hand at a moment when he could have brought it down with brutal finality on his opponents. He had cause enough to have done so. The deposed King James II, whose vacant throne William had been invited to fill in 1688, had landed in Ireland the following year from France, where he had sought refuge, and mounted what looked like being a serious chal-lenge to his successor, with the backing of the Catholic Irish.

After their crushing defeat at the Battle of the Boyne on 1 July 1690 the rebels fell back on Limerick, there to endure two desperate sieges. The first was lifted after several months of misery, but the second in 1691 brought the Stuart supporters to their knees. The

Treaty of Limerick left them a measure of dignity, allowing them to march out of the beleaguered city in full pomp, their lives secure but their cause dead and buried. King William was inclined to grant the Irish Catholics the rights stipulated in the treaty, but the Irish parliament was dominated by Protestants determined to teach their defeated opponents a lesson they would never forget. Within a short time the Penal Laws had come into operation, squeezing to the marrow those Catholics who remained in Ireland. Many did not – they fled abroad in what came to be known as the 'Flight of the Wild Geese', to fight and prosper or die in the service of Catholic rulers on the Continent. The Treaty of Limerick had brought the fighting in Ireland to an end, but the hopes invested in its terms by the more optimistic Catholics turned out to be wholly illusory.

After the cosy, ramshackle intimacy of those other towns where I had learned to relax and be welcome – Sligo, Westport, Galway, Tralee – I found it hard to come to terms with Limerick. I never found a warm heart to its windy grid of canyon-like streets. Everything in Limerick was laid out in straight lines, every journey mapped out by right-angle turns into yet more long, featureless thoroughfares, more like some metropolis of the American prairies than what I had come to regard as characteristic of Irish towns. There was something cold about Limerick, even in the sunshine of a warm September day, though its people were as cheerful over the Guinness glasses and as helpful on the street corners as any I had met on the journey. They courteously directed me out of town – 'You go down to the traffic lights, turn right, second block along, turn left, go left again by the hotel on the corner, three blocks along you'll see the signpost. Got that, now? Good luck, and enjoy your holiday!' On the interminable trek along drab streets towards a countryside that refused to declare itself, I stopped several passers-by just to hear those softly-accented directions, friendly sparks of human contact among the dingy video shops, the raw grey churches and blank-faced garages.

According to the Irish Ordnance Survey, Limerick city gives way to countryside a mile south-west of its centre, but the builders seemed to have been busy since the map was last revised. It was three long and weary miles to Mungret, and the bungalows and semi-detached houses accompanied me most of the way. At last I came to the round-about that marked the outer edge of the city, and there in the skirts of green fields I found the crumbling remnants of an ecclesiastical community established long before Limerick was even thought of.

Mungret must have been a mighty place indeed when its primitive Christian community was in its first flush of life, a century or more before St Patrick came to Ireland, if tradition has the story right. At one time there were six churches serving the monastery here, and fifteen hundred monks singing, praying and working in this flat green landscape, a buzzing hive of effort and energy. But as Limerick grew under the influence of Norsemen and Normans, so the power of Mungret declined. The monastery was raided, burned, razed, looted and crushed time and again. When its long, narrow abbey was built towards the end of the thirteenth century, the diocese was centred on Limerick and Mungret had been reduced to a secondary role.

At the bend of an unmarked side lane I came across the ruins of the abbey, its thin, gaunt tower standing over the roofless, weed-choked building in a spectacularly overgrown graveyard. I stumbled round among the headstones and tottering stone crosses smothered with blackberries and elderberries, a rich harvest growing unpicked in dead, deserted ground. There were two more ruins not far away, further evidence of the departed glory of Mungret – the shell of the tenth-century church of St Nessan, its entry blocked by a rickety gate tied up with binder twine, and the broken walls of another, even older church.

In medieval times the burgesses of Mungret enjoyed special privileges – they were empowered to hold their own courts, choose their own law-makers and levy fines and penalties on their own terms. Nowadays the little village straggles along its back roads in farming country whose regulation is chiefly in the hands of EC bureaucrats. Mungret might have been deep in the remotest wilds of France, judging by its appearance this hot and sleepy afternoon. The long straight roads were lined with telegraph poles and wires, the tiles and whitewashed walls of the houses baked in the sunshine, and the old men of Mungret leaned gossiping in vests and baggy blue trousers over their fences, turning round to give the stranger a good searching stare before delivering a measured 'Good afternoon. God bless ye!'

I trudged for two days down the hot roads through the flat back country of County Limerick, sweeping the sweat off my face with a handkerchief that soon became sodden, picking dusty blackberries from the hedges and idly kicking stones along the simmering tarmac. The flat pastureland each side of the road looked prosperous enough, but at intervals I found myself passing between fields that were over-run with thistles and ragwort, legacy of the emigration that had left many small farms without a new generation to work them. These pockets of poverty announced themselves among the better-favoured, well-tended farms with unmistakable signals – a smell of turf smoke, a sudden increase in the number of rusting farm implements and ancient car bodies left to rot in the hedges, a ramshackle clutter of scrap and rubbish stacked round the flaking walls of an old house with ragged thatch and weed-strewn front garden. Then a turn of the lane would shut the derelict farmstead away, leaving the Limerick countryside as rich and tidy as ever.

Rich and poor alike, though, this was a corner of Ireland free from any tourist influence. A few miles to the north the cars and lorries were racing up the coast road to Foynes; a few miles to the south they sped down the Killarney road. In between lay a broad triangle of country, left to pursue its peaceful rituals of haymaking and harvest-ing. During those two days of sun-drenched walking I met perhaps half a dozen people on the road, and each encounter involved a lengthy chat in the shade of the hedges. The woman walking her two dogs somewhere near Ballinagarrane had a deal to say about the grim old priest who had flayed his congregation the previous Sunday with a good stiff homily on the subject of folly.

'Most of the priests these days just tend to work in alongside us,' she told me, 'they're just ordinary fellas like everyone else. But Father Murtagh – he's a terror! A very dictatorial old-style priest, you know. He gave us all a hard time on Sunday. He'd decided that folly was the eighth deadly sin! Folly this and folly that. I said, "If folly's a sin, sure we're all for the flames, because we're all fools."'

'And did you say it to Father Murtagh?' I asked her.

'Well . . . I've thought of it. Next time I see him I'll do it, I say to myself!'

A mile along the road I found my throat dry beyond endurance from dust and sour blackberries. A house with a trim garden and neatly hooped rose pergola held promise of a glass of water. 'Oh, come in – you're welcome,' said the woman who came to the door in answer to my knock. 'Would you like a cup of tea?' The living room was full of family – her husband, her daughter and son-in-law, their children, someone else's children. Everyone crowded into the little kitchen, the children staring in fascination as I swung my backpack down beside the table. A stool was dragged out, tea poured, steaming brown bread taken from the oven, cream cake produced and cut. A bottle of beer appeared and was poured enthusiastically into a glass by one of the grandsons till the foam coursed in a cataract over the table top. With complete lack of ceremony I was plied with cake and questions.

'So you've been walking throughout Ireland,' said the man of the house. 'And what do you think of the Irish?'

'They're very hospitable,' I told him, and every face in the kitchen grinned in delight. We got round to the subject of traditional music. 'I used to play the box,' said the grandfather. 'But I gave it up – I wasn't good enough at it.' He went into the next room and came back with a battered old bodhrán, its skin pounded into shiny patches by decades of drumming. 'Have you seen one of these in your travels?'

His wife leaned forward over the table. 'He used to be a great singer. Come on, now – give us a song.' The old man demurred. Only if I would lead off. I found myself launching into 'The Flower Of Magherally' through a mouthful of cake, wondering as I did so where in all of England I could have begged a glass of water and felt myself so instantly at home. When it came to his turn, grandfather became shy. Maybe next year, if I would come back and see them again. 'That'll give you time to think of one,' sighed his wife, to universal laughter.

'There's a lot of Germans around here,' the old man remarked as I was standing up and hoisting my pack. 'The Palatines, as we call them.' A strange little slice of local history was wrapped up in that comment – history personal to me, as I realised later when reading *Limerick: The Rich Land*, the book written by Sean Spellissy of Ennis which he had given me on my visit to his bookshop back in July. As Sean told the story, the Protestant Palatine refugees from the Rhine must have found the people of Ballinagarrane just as hospitable as I did, for they seem to have slid with remarkable smoothness under the skin of Irish life. Not that such harmonious relationships appear to have been the intention of the landlord of Ballinagarrane, Sir Thomas Southwell, when, with gifts of land and housing, he helped them found their settlement on his estate in 1712 or thereabouts.

Southwell, a good and loyal servant of Queen Anne, probably felt that these industrious and God-fearing Rhinelanders, competent farming people driven out of their home territory when Louis XIV annexed the region for France and Catholicism, would exert a stabilising Protestant influence on a region bitterly resentful of the Penal Laws introduced less than two decades before and still inclined to insurrection. The Palatines certainly proved to be hard workers. They soon gained the name of quiet-living, mild-mannered folk, very good at tending their gardens and at bee-keeping. They were practical people, who allowed the geese they kept to flavour themselves on windfall apples while manuring the trees with the apple dung they produced. The German incomers stolidly held to their own language and customs, as John Wesley found when he came to Ballinagarrane to preach to them in June 1756. 'They retain much of the temper and manner of their own country,' Wesley wrote of his potential converts. 'I found much life among this plain, artless serious people.'

There were aspects of the Palatines that Wesley thought unattractive, but his fiery oratory soon brought numbers of them into the Methodist fold. 'Having no minister,' Wesley wrote, 'they became eminent for drunkenness, cursing, swearing and other neglect of religion. But they are washed since they heard and received the truth, which is able to save their souls. An oath is now rarely heard among them, or a drunkard seen in their borders.'

Palatines were formidable carriers of the Word. Some went off to found Methodism in America. Those who stayed seem to have practised their preaching subtly enough to keep on good terms with their Catholic neighbours, though still exercising a prudent restraint in social intercourse. A hundred and thirty years after their arrival, travellers in Limerick reported that the young Palatines were beginning to intermarry with local Irish families, though the old folk still clung to their German speech and habits. By the time of the War of Independence in 1920, many of the Palatines had embraced the Republican cause and were fighting side by side with the Catholic nationalists – hardly an outcome that Sir Thomas Southwell could have foreseen.

Among Sean Spellissy's lists of Palatine families I came across the name of Dolmage. Johann Dolmage had settled on the estate of Sir Thomas back in 1720, founding a large and spreading family. One of the variations that the ensuing couple of centuries wrought on the family name was Delmege. There were Delmeges still living nearby, I learned in conversation along the road. And my own great-grandmother had been a Delmege, of Limerick extraction. Suddenly the unspectacular Limerick countryside became a personal landscape, a landscape in which I had a small but definite stake. I strode the back roads with renewed interest, enquiring in pubs and at house doors whether there were any Delmeges in the vicinity. Perhaps they were passing me on tractors, or brushing my shoulder at shop counters. All at once I knew with a pang of pleasure how those American-Irish visitors must feel, and why they come over the Atlantic to scrabble around in Irish soil for their roots, however distant and tenuous. How I would have loved to have shaken one of my Palatine kinsmen by the hand! But the Delmege clan, wherever they were, never crossed my path in any form substantial enough to grasp and cry 'Cousin!'

At the top of the sleepy main street of Ardagh village I found the green ramparts of Reerasta ring fort. On another September day, back in 1868, a local man by the name of Quinn had gone to Reerasta fort to dig potatoes. What he unearthed there turned out to be one of Ireland's finest hoards of buried treasure. Quinn's spade first brought up the pin of a brooch, then four complete brooches, a wooden cross, a bronze cup (he inadvertently broke this with an over-vigorous thrust) and, the cream of the hoard, a two-handled vessel of gold, silver and bronze seven inches tall, superbly worked and decorated with amber, crystal and enamel. It was a Communion chalice from the eighth century, the most beautiful example ever found in Ireland.

Quinn was more than satisfied with the bargain he struck when he sold his discoveries to Dr Hanlon of Rathkeale town for £50. But the better-informed doctor realised the true worth of what had been lying under Quinn's potatoes. So, belatedly and after her husband had died, did the widow Quinn. After numerous squabbles over ownership and proper compensation, the treasure ended up in 1874 in the National Museum in Dublin. Four years later the Bishop of Limerick received £100 in recognition of his stewardship of the land where the hoard had been found, and confirmed his reputation for fair dealing by giving half his windfall to the widow Quinn.

Strangely enough, it was the humble wooden cross that provided the answer as to how the chalice and the rest of the hoard had come to be buried in the old fort. Quinn made a present of the cross to his parish priest, and on examination the numbers '727' were found inscribed on the back. They probably stood for the date 1727, which suggested that that was when the cross had been made. Local history quickly pieced the rest of the story together.

In 1736 the parish priest, Father Christopher Bermingham, had been at loggerheads with the local landlord, Oliver Stephenson. Stephenson had a reputation as a 'ramping, stamping, tearing, swearing' squire. He had tried to exercise his *droit de seigneur* by attempting to seduce a bride as she and her brand-new husband were on the way home from their marriage service, but Father Bermingham had intervened to save the woman from her fate worse than death. Knowing full well the likely consequences of crossing the hot-blooded squire, the priest had then fled to Limerick. The chances were that he had taken time before his flight to conceal the treasure, which he must have felt lay under his protection, where neither Oliver Stephenson nor anyone else would have a chance of getting hold of it. There, in the seldom-disturbed sanctity of the fort, doubly protected by the fear local people had of the fairies they knew to frequent such places, it stayed hidden until revealed by the spade of the unsuspecting Quinn.

On the third morning out of Limerick I left Newcastle West as the early Mass bell was ringing. Cold trails of mist were swirling through the streets of the little town, refusing to be sucked up by the sun. Westward lay the outlying hills of the Mullaghareirk Mountains, through which County Limerick slips over into County Kerry, and after the long miles through flat pasturelands I had been looking forward to exhilarating views from their tops. But for all the prospect that the enveloping mist allowed, I might as well have been walking in my own back garden.

Ancient and decrepit cars held together by bands of rust came clattering out of the murk to swerve past me on the road, carrying 'mountainy men' and their families from farms up in the hills to Mass in the town. The drivers raised their index fingers off their steering wheels, whether in greeting or admonition I couldn't be sure. I waved back anyway, and trudged on up side lanes where spiders' webs hung in pearly nets across the hedges. I never saw the top of the hill I was climbing. There were signs in what I could make out near at hand, however, to tell me of height being slowly gained – the appearance of bracken in the hedgebanks, tufts of purple heather beginning to show in the ground on each side, a deterioration in the surface of the lane and a growth of grass in a green strip along its centre. The barking of dogs in farmyards far below became hollower and fainter the further I climbed. The mist chilled and thickened, blanking off the crests of Knockanimpaha and Sugar Hill at eleven hundred feet. I came to a junction where six unmarked roads met, and pulled up, soaked in mist and sweat, straining to decipher the minute, spidery lines on the map.

'Like a lift?' called the red-faced farmer as he braked his tractor at the junction. 'I'm going on up myself. Jump on behind – you're welcome.' I scrambled on to the tiny platform at the back of the tractor and clung on as we bucketed and snorted up the mountain road over potholes that made my teeth snap together like a man with a quartern ague. 'I'm going to the bog to bring the winter firing back for my neighbour,' shouted my benefactor over his shoulder. ''Tis a very peaceful place to be, the bog. You can really wind down and be easy there.' We tried to keep up a shouted conversation, but the machine-gun noise of the tractor and the jolting of the potholes soon reduced us to sign language. The farmer held his nose as we passed a herd of wild goats, their leader magnificently equipped with a backward-curving pair of horns three feet long. The sour reek of the animals drifted with the mist across our path. 'In November 'tis the mating season,' roared my friend. 'You wouldn't be able to drive past at all then, with the stink of them!'

At the turn of the lane that led away to the turf banks the farmer put me off with a 'God bless you!', and I walked on across the crest of the hills in a wasteland of bog and heather where plantations of sitka spruce shook their blue needles in a breeze that was springing up. The mist began to shred away and a wan disc of sun looked through the clouds, striking lines of silver out of the hillsides where the narrow bog roads curled. The spruce plantations steamed and glowed blue and green. I shook off my lethargy and walked fast over the high ground, looking down into the valley of the Oolagh River that ran parallel with the road a couple of hundred feet below. The crunch of my boots on the stony surface of the road brought dogs barking to each farmhouse gate I passed. At one farm a small brown and black terrier came scurrying out with a muffled snarl and made for my ankles. I had the Dazer levelled and my finger on the button before I realised that the dog's strangled cries were caused by a leather muzzle wrapped like a tourniquet around its jaws. A stentorian voice roared a volley of curses from the farmhouse, and the terrier slunk back within bounds with disappointment stamped all over the small portion of its face that showed above the straitjacket round its chops. I put the Dazer away without firing a shot and walked down into the sunlit square at Abbeyfeale.

The Sunday peace that lay over the wide, bar-lined streets of the small town lasted maybe half an hour after my arrival. Then a cacophony of car horns broke out, bringing the residents of Abbeyfeale to their doors. They laughed and clapped as the cars drove by, trailing blue-and-white flags out of their windows, braying like tone-deaf donkeys as they headed out of town. It was a great day for Abbeyfeale. Father Casey's Gaelic football team had won through to the final of the county competition, due to be played this afternoon against Galtee Gaels from Limerick city. Tension and expectation ran high. The bars were all but deserted. In front rooms and doorways men and women nibbled their nails nervously over radios as news of the progress of the game came through. They didn't have long to wait. 'Abbey! Abbey's won! Three goals!' shrieked a small boy, haring along the pavement. People shook hands, laughed and jumped up and down with delight. A man in a patterned shirt he must have bought in the 1970s gave me a wide grin. 'There'll be a lot of noise in the town tonight,' he said softly and with emphasis. 'I reckon the pubs won't close till October.'

That evening the streets of Abbeyfeale were lined with townsfolk, cheering themselves hoarse as a hooting cavalcade brought the champions home in triumph. At the head of the procession the team captain perched on the bonnet of a car, brandishing the silver championship cup like a war trophy above his head and grinning like a dog with two tails. Behind him rode the rest of the team. No open-topped coach and mayoral reception for them, but a delirious, swaying circuit of the town standing on the trailer of a lorry, arms round each other's shoulders, roaring out 'Olé-olé-olé-olé!' – the battle chant of the Irish team at the previous year's World Cup football finals. Trailing behind up the street came a motley collection of cars and vans crammed with shouting and whistling supporters, festooned with blue-and-white tokens ranging from official team flags to striped supermarket bags hastily pressed into service. Ecstatic children sat precariously on the windowsills of the cars, their upper bodies leaning out, pounding away on the car roofs and squeaking 'Olé-olé-olé-olé!' like their heroes.

Next morning, wincing out of Abbeyfeale with a head as sore as my feet, I passed the statue of the team's founder in the square. Father William Casey had come to Abbeyfeale as a curate in 1869, taking on the duties of parish priest from 1883 until his death in 1907. The town had always had a reputation as a troublesome place; there were enough cattle-rustlers, robbers and outlaws in the surrounding hills to make Abbeyfeale notorious even before the mysterious and well-marshalled rebels known as the 'Rockites' gave the British soldiers a hard time in the early 1820s. The Rockites, a tough and determined group of insurgents, gained their nickname from the 'Captain Rock' signature on their anti-British proclamations. They were eventually crushed, but the rebellious spirit of Abbeyfeale remained. Father Casey was an ardent supporter of his flock in the land wars of the 1870s when the Irish tenants were struggling to break the power of their landlords and free themselves from the threats of eviction, excessive rent demands and other evils of living on land owned mostly by absentee English and Irishmen. They gained partial redress in 1881 with the introduction of the Land Act, which allowed rents to be assessed impartially and guaranteed security of tenure to the tenants. (Charles Stewart Parnell had made his name and fame in backing these measures and forcing the Westminster parliament to accept them.) In 1903 the British government gave the Irish peasantry the right to buy out their holdings from the landlords, and the bad old system was swept away with a rush. In Abbeyfeale Father William Casey is still well remembered and respected for his part in the early moves towards free ownership of land. 'He found his people struggling in the toils of landlordism,' read the inscription on the plinth under the verdigrised statue in the square. 'He left them owners of the soil and freemen.'

Father Casey fought hard for the rights of his parishioners a century ago, but this morning he seemed to have espoused a new and international cause. His right hand was raised over the sleeping town, apparently clad in a black leather glove, with every appearance of giving a forceful Black Power salute. Closer inspection showed the glove to be a wrapping of shiny masking tape. From his gleaming black fingers dangled a blue-and-white football supporter's flag.

Knotted round his shoulders by the sleeves was a blue-and-white football jersey. He stared across the square at a sagging banner stretched across the street, with 'Good Luck Fr. Casey's' lettered in blue along its white strip. The smallest of smiles lay on Father Casey's green bronze lips.

I crossed the bridge on the outskirts of Abbeyfeale and was in Kerry. Almost immediately, it seemed, the landscape hardened, roughened and steepened. There were blue-ceilinged shrines to the Virgin Mary in the gardens and by the roadside as I climbed the high-banked lanes to Knocknagoshel village, tucked into a lonely crease in the eastern flanks of the Glanaruddery Mountains. The old stone houses and narrow roads of the village were tightly compacted – as tightly-knit as Knocknagoshel's community, I was told later. 'Everyone I've met from up there has been mad,' said a man in Paddy Mac's bar in Tralee that night. 'Mad in a nice way. They have their own way of living, you know. That would have been an interesting place for you to stay.' I had in fact planned to stop in Knocknagoshel and repair some of the damage of Abbeyfeale's football festivities with an afternoon's lazing and nose-poking, followed by an evening's blathering. But there were no bed-and-breakfast places on offer. At eleven o'clock in the morning the three pubs in the main street were shut up tight. The only sound in the place came from the yard of the tiny school, where the twenty or thirty village children were roaring their heads off in their mid-morning break.

In the post office I found the postmistress leaning comfortably on her counter and chuckling over the local newspaper, *Kerry's Eye*. The copy I bought gave me hours of pleasure that evening as I wandered through its maze of petty court cases. *Kerry's Eye* specialised in reports of the '£30 fine' class, each minutely recorded under headlines such as 'Assaulted Doorman', 'Broke Down Door' and 'Put Ashes in Food and Glasses'. Pick of the bunch was the Tralee man who had appeared in court, drunk, to answer a summons.

> Mr O'Brien apologised to the court and pleaded with the Justice to adjourn the case. 'I feel very sick and I'm not able to stand up at present,' said Mr O'Brien. 'I feel like dying. I apologise.'
>
> 'That's because you have drink taken,' said Justice Sullivan, imposing a seven-day sentence.

'Go f... yourself,' said Mr O'Brien, addressing the Justice as he left the courthouse escorted by two gardai.

'That justifies that,' said Justice Sullivan, concluding the case.

The road I was following crawled along the crest of one of the long east–west valleys that cut across the Glanaruddery Mountains. Mountains in name only, they swelled in large, gentle humps of hillside, clothed more and more thickly in bog the further west I walked, flushed pale blue with drifts of scabious and cut into shallow ramparts by centuries of turf excavation. For the past few decades the forests had been slowly advancing across the boglands, crowding the hills with dark blocks of conifers. Some of the emptiness and loneliness of the landscape, along with much of its beauty, had been dissolved as the trees consolidated their grip on the hillsides. But this was still wild country, in the lonely wastes of the Glanaruddery Mountains and on across the road from Listowel to Castleisland where the rolling Kerry country rose again into the higher and even less populated Stack's Mountains. The clouds had lain in an unbroken roof across the sky since I left Abbeyfeale, and now they began to darken, dulling all colours in the landscape to sombre variations on smoky grey and misty blue. There was no one on the road, no one at work on the turf banks. I walked on along the bog road, with a feeling of loneliness sharper than at any time since I had slogged the old drovers' track with Oliver Geraghty through the Nephin Beg in May, far off in north-west Mayo, four months and nearly four hundred miles away.

Somewhere up in the heart of the Stack's Mountains, three or four miles at least from the nearest main road, I stopped to pass the time of day with an elderly man whom I had been watching for a long while making his slow way towards me along the dusty track. His little black dog had been leaping around my legs for ten minutes before he came near enough to return my shout of 'Good afternoon.' His grey pullover was stiff with dark stains, his cap shiny with unguessable years of tugging and resettling above his bat-like ears. He glanced frequently from me to the road and back again as we talked, his sky-blue eyes taking in a snippet of information at a time – pack, boots, map, notebook, stranger, Englishman, a tourist, nosy, harmless. His accent was as strong as turf smoke: so strong that I caught only the drift of what he was saying. My own voice seemed to cut the air between us with an embarrassing clarity, but his frequent 'Eh?' told me that he was struggling for understanding as hard as I was. What did emerge was that he had sold three score acres of his land to the Forestry about twenty years before, and was still smarting over the poor bargain it had turned out to be. If only he had hung on to it, he might have had ten times the price. Then he said, flatly, 'Never been out of Kerry yet.'

'What, not even to Limerick?' I asked incredulously.

'Never! I spent all me days right here,' he said, sweeping his stick over the hills. 'Me brothers and sisters are to the four corners of the world, but I stayed. Never wanted to go, with house and land to work.'

He stumped away down the road, and I watched him for a long time, speculating on the narrow compass of those sixty or seventy years, as isolated and bare as the landscape that had seen every one of them.

The old man who came to the door of his cottage further along the track might also have been rooted to the Stack's Mountains all his life. Over his shoulder I caught a glimpse of a stone-floored scullery, a wood-slatted hallway, a living room with ancient wooden chairs and wallpaper of a floral design that must have been deleted from the pattern books well before the War of Independence, shiny brown with age and turf smoke. A bakelite radio three feet high stood under the dresser. There was nothing to indicate that the past three decades had ever penetrated to this corner of County Kerry. My request for a drink of water was met with a brief smile and a glass of fizzy orange; then the door was closed on the intruder, politely but firmly. I went on, with the strong impression that hereabouts strangers were seldom seen and something less than welcome.

One possible reason for that became clearer when, in idle curiosity, I pushed open the door of an abandoned schoolhouse and began to poke around. The school, its walls scabby with damp, stood in the middle of a grove of untended pine trees. A tiny alcove off the school-room held a double row of sixteen coat pegs. If there were sixteen youngsters still left in these hills, they were hanging their satchels elsewhere these days. But in the classroom there were signs of recent occupation. A couple of wooden benches and a pair of rotting chairs had been drawn up around the cold ashes of a turf fire in the brick grate. On the wall hung a picture of Jesus exposing his Sacred Heart. For a moment I thought the old school must be doing duty as a kind of informal chapel, an impression reinforced by the sight of a whiskey bottle on the windowsill with an inch of colourless liquid in it. Holy water, I thought, stored here by the priest between services. I picked up the bottle and rocked the contents to and fro. The liquid slid up the glass sides in oily smoothness as water never did. I uncorked the bottle and took a sniff. A rank odour of potatoes and lighter fuel filled my nostrils. Holy water indeed, but for internal rather than external application. Holy water distilled very recently, judging by its tear-jerking smell. So one old Irish tradition, at least, was alive and well in the Kerry hills. Standing in the derelict schoolroom with the bottle of poteen in my hand, I thought of the red-haired young man on Gorumna Island and his anxious questions as to what I might be up to; his relief when my inquisitiveness, my map and notebook, turned out to have an innocent explanation. I recorked the bottle, replaced it as exactly as I could in its former position and left the old school-house as unobtrusively as possible.

Did the hills have eyes that afternoon? Certainly I got a couple of hard stares from men who came to their garden edges as I walked by. 'That's a dead end,' shouted a woman from her door, waving both arms in agitation as I hesitated at a fork in the road from which a rutted track ran off into the fastness of the bog. If there was liquid gold in them thar hills, it was not to be stumbled on by any chance prospector.

A thin rain began to fall, and the brown boglands looked barren and inimical. My boots had started to rub. By the time I had limped out of the mountains and down into Tralee, twenty miles and more from Abbeyfeale, I was wishing that I had taken the chance to bless myself with some of that mountainy remedy.

In Bailey's bar two middle-aged men from the hills sat playing fiddles with the regular session musicians. One held his instrument the ortho-dox way, tucked under the chin; the other had it pressed into the crook of his arm. They were playing scratchy little jigs and polkas, tunes that hadn't been heard in Tralee for many years. They rarely came down from their village to the town: this was their first outing for a number of years. On the table in front of them were two glasses of red lemonade, which with cautious sips they spun out over the couple of hours they played.

Before they left the bar, one of them began to play a slow air. The young fiddlers round the table sat still, their eyes fixed on the man from the hills. His old fiddle, shiny and dark with age, trembled with vibrato as the bitter-sweet music floated out into our hushed corner of the pub. By contrast the player's face was wooden, sunk in expressionless contemplation, as hard as his stiff, horny fingers. He might have been doing the milking, or nailing up a shelf. He finished the tune without a flourish, just ceasing to play, letting the bow and fiddle dangle from his hands as he stared at the table, then glanced awkwardly sideways. Blonde-haired Kate, one of the watching fiddle-players, leaned over to me and murmured reverently, 'You'll never hear that air played better, no matter how long you live. You're a lucky man to be here tonight.'

'. . . in North Belfast. The man was married and the father of five children.' The tail-end of a television news bulletin caught my ear as I passed the sitting-room door of the bed-and-breakfast house. No need to ask what the rest of the report had been about.

Next morning the *Irish Times* carried a story with a familiar name in the headline. Peter Brooke, the Secretary of State for Northern Ireland, had come out with an offer to both Unionists and Republicans to restart the talks that had been abandoned back in July. Reaction from both Catholics and Protestants, according to the paper, was 'cautious'.

There was a photograph on another page of the paper of a tractor tipped halfway over in the ruts of a field in County Tyrone. The high-sided farm trailer behind the tractor had lurched askew, throwing its cargo around. The contents of the trailer looked like sacks of animal feed. They were, in fact, the biggest mound of explosives ever assembled in Northern Ireland, with which the IRA had intended to destroy a border post. Houses had been taken over in the area, cars commandeered, everything prepared. Then the tractor driver ran into a ditch.

A couple of miles south of Tralee the old back road to Killarney took a swoop up and over the eastern end of the Slieve Mish Mountains. The sails of the Blennerville windmill made their familiar white cross against the dark wall of hills where the Dingle Way ran off to the very fingertip of the peninsula forty miles away. The clouds that had passed over the Great Blasket two hours before were now rolling in along the Slieve Mish, marching eastwards across County Kerry, rainless clouds heavy with gloom. The Killarney road ran as straight as a die for fifteen miles, a narrow tarmac slash through shallow bowls of pastureland where whitewashed cottages exhaled plumes of turf smoke and men squatted on their hunkers in the middle of the highway to chat with friends. At Ballyfinane crossroads the tiny one-roomed pub was shut, the sole indication of the nature of its business a small metal plate over the door with the legend 'GUINNESS SOLD HERE' whitewashed into near illegibility. 'Yes, 'tis a pub all right,' said the lady in the tin-shack stores by the crossroads, 'but they only open a couple of hours in the evening; and 'tisn't every evening they'd be open. We're very quiet around here.'

Killarney appeared from the slope of the road as a tall church spire rising from a wooded, water-streaked valley under tumbled, humpbacked mountains that revealed themselves modestly, from the ankles upwards, as the low clouds lifted towards evening. All the guidebooks tell you what a disappointment the town of Killarney is, by comparison with the magnificence of its situation at the entrance to 'Ireland's Switzerland', the hills and waters of the Irish Lake District. The trouble is that you can't see the lakes from Killarney, which lies in a hollow. There are splendours enough to be seen from the town in the heaped-up shapes of Macgillycuddy's Reeks immediately to the west, but the charming combination of water and mountain, praised by travellers from the eighteenth century onwards, can only be appreciated by going out of the town.

'It is but a poor place, and commands no view of the lakes,' wrote the author R.M. Ballantyne in 1869. 'It is a poor town, and has a worn and withered look . . . a wretchedly dilapidated aspect,' was the haughty verdict of Mr and Mrs S.C. Hall twenty years earlier in their book *A Week at Killarney*. 'Most of the thoroughfares are narrow and unattractive,' warned the *Ward Lock Guide* for 1932. And opinions of Killarney town have not improved since then. Nowadays it's the rampant commercialism of the place that attracts unfavourable comment in modern guidebooks: 'brash and ugly . . . a conveyor-belt to speed the tourist on his spending way . . . dedicated to making money'.

You do see an awful lot of leprechauns in Killarney, along with a vast deal of shamrock-patterned crockery, lurid green headgear and evil-faced homunculi fashioned out of 'Genuine Irish Bog Oak'. In the main streets of the town the ordinary workaday ironmongers' and grocers' shops were hard to spot among the eateries and gift shops, and the pavements undoubtedly held more Americans than Irish, to judge by the accents. The jaunting cars with smartly trotting horses and smoothly pattering 'jarveys' or coachmen were sweeping the visitors away to the lakes and foothills from early morning onwards. There was a sense of continuing tradition about the town, of providing efficiently and at once what the visitors had come to find, from a quick hamburger and a midnight huddle over guitars on the pavement all the way up to a candle-lit dinner and an expensively guided tour of the local beauty spots.

In a few days I planned to be up among those beautiful mountains myself, taking the old high path from Killarney over to Kenmare on the final stage of the road to Roaringwater. Before that closing act, however, there was one last interval to be enjoyed. Next afternoon I bought the fattest book I could find – Tim Pat Coogan's recently published biography of Michael Collins – and settled myself aboard the bus for the five-hour drive north that would reintroduce me to the quietly-spoken courtesies of County Clare.

'September's the month to visit Lisdoonvarna,' people had told me throughout my wanderings in County Clare. It was good advice. Lisdoonvarna's claim to be Ireland's foremost spa resort has never been seriously challenged since its sulphur, magnesium and iron springs were first discovered and exploited back in the eighteenth and early nineteenth centuries, when spas were all the rage. The fashionable lords and ladies might descend on Cheltenham and Baden-Baden, but the land-owning farmers and small businessmen of Ireland came to Lisdoonvarna, four miles up the road from Doolin, to ease their aches and pains with the mineral waters and to enjoy a week or two of dancing and socialising. The little town prospered, sprouting hotels along its cross-shaped arrangement of streets and putting up an elegant pump room and bath house on the outskirts near the source of the waters. Lisdoonvarna was an all-year-round resort, but September became the favourite month to visit the spa.

Harvest would be over, and the farming families more inclined to relax and celebrate.

It wasn't just the healing waters they came for. Deals of one sort or another, at country fairs and markets, were the stuff of life to the kind of client who patronised Lisdoonvarna, and the marriage deal was one of the most important. Land, prestige and hard cash were in the balance. In a country where families were large and land was subdivided down the generations, it was a difficult matter to get sons and daughters fixed up with suitable partners, especially in the days when the choice was severely limited by the bad roads and shortage of public transport that confined most people to their own immediate districts. But at Lisdoonvarna the 'tanglers' could be relied upon to help things along.

Tanglers were middlemen whose job was to introduce prospective participants in business to each other. In the ordinary way such deals would probably involve the sale and purchase of livestock, land, farm produce and so on. At Lisdoonvarna, however, they would use their wide acquaintance and knowledge of the circumstances of a large number of families to bring together, at the bidding of parents, boys and girls whom they felt might suit each other. This matchmaking became one of the features of the post-harvest season in Lisdoon-varna, and the custom endured until the 1960s, when jets began to take the better-off country people away to package holidays in the sun of Spain and Greece. Young people had started fixing themselves up with partners, too, with less regard for the wishes of their parents than hitherto. Matchmaking in Lisdoonvarna grew to seem a poor and outmoded affair. But recently there had been a revival of the custom, enhanced by the publicity given to it by delighted coverage in newspapers, radio and television. There had been talk of shenanigans in Lisdoonvarna; of planeloads of oil-rich Texan widows swooping off with strapping Catholic farmers clutched in their bejewelled claws. The little spa had never known the like.

It was a stroke of luck to happen on the names of John and Anne Sims of Island View when I was looking for a bed-and-breakfast place in Lisdoonvarna. I'd be surprised if there is a more obliging or a friendlier host and hostess anywhere in Ireland. How the Simses manage to accommodate the demands of a teaching job, family life with three children and enthusiastic involvement in local affairs with the ability to drive their guests back from a dance at one in the morning and be up shortly after dawn to serve them pancakes and fresh fruit, is known only to themselves and the Lord. But they do, with consummate good humour. An hour after I set foot in Island View, halfway between Lisdoonvarna and Doolin, John was placing a steak smothered in a garlic-laden sauce in front of me; an hour later we were standing together admiring the quicksilver manoeuvres of the dancers in the Kincora Hotel.

The matchmaking month at Lisdoonvarna revolves around dancing. Not frenetic, body-flaunting disco dancing, but staid circling with a succession of partners in 'ballrooms of romance', as they were described to me. Whatever spark of romance may touch the couples at these events is only fanned to a roaring furnace after much formality, and observance of the unspoken rules of Lisdoonvarna courtship. The dancers at the Kincora, however, were not courting couples. They were well known to each other, if not actually married. These were expert set dancers, out to show their mettle. They stamped their polished shoes on the wooden dance floor until it shook. They whirled round in tightly-bound 'baskets' of four and flicked their toes and heels in and out like lightning while keeping their arms and upper bodies rigid. The dances were short enough – four or five minutes at the most – but they came in sets of eight at a time, and there was no falling out between them. At the end of each set the dancers reeled away exhausted into the corners of the room and on to chairs, laughing in triumph and relief while they mopped up the sweat with handkerchiefs and shirt sleeves.

Next day in Lisdoonvarna, it was time for the amateurs to take the floor. 'Dancing here! Dancing from 2.00 to 5.00! Dancing all day and all night!' proclaimed the billboards outside the Savoy, the Imperial and the Ritz. From midday onwards every other doorway framed a shuffling group of dancers revolving to the thump of snare drums and the crooning of ballad singers. In the foyer of the Imperial Hotel the uncrowned Matchmaking King of Lisdoonvarna, Jim White, spoke lengthily on the phone while I waited to have a word with him. A busy man, Jim, especially in September. Several thousand people were expected in town tonight, and as the prime mover behind the revival of the matchmaking and owner of several of the hotels that would entertain them, as well as being one of Lisdoonvarna's two official matchmakers, he was at full stretch. 'I'll be with you in ten minutes,' he mouthed at me, receiver to ear. A couple of hours went by. 'Oh, Jaysus, I forgot all about you,' he groaned, clutching his head, when he next caught sight of me. 'A couple of minutes, now.' Half an hour later he threw himself down on the sofa beside me, drew a deep breath and plunged into an explanation of the way things worked during matchmaking.

'It's mostly older people who come – over thirty, let's say, and most of them a bit older than that. Now, what they *don't* do is come for a quick affair and then out and away. The media made a whole meal out of that planeload of fifty American women a few years ago, but let me tell you that at least half of them were married already! As soon as I saw them getting off the tour bus I said to myself, "We won't be fixing many of *that* lot up this week!" But there were five marriages came out of it at the finish.

'What a visit to Lisdoonvarna means to most people is an opportunity to get to know others, make friends and have a good time in a social atmosphere. That's why the whole thing is run round the dances. What they'll do is go down about midday to the wells to drink the water, maybe have a bathe or a sauna, and then have a little dance. Then in the afternoon they'll go out to the dance at Ballinalacken Castle, and maybe they'll see someone they met at the wells. Then in town that night there'll be dancing in all the hotels from early evening onwards, so again there's the chance to get to know that person a bit better. Often things don't happen during their visit here – they'll meet up somewhere else in Ireland or in another country and say, "Oh, weren't you at Lisdoonvarna?" It's amazing how often that happens. And then things will perhaps go on from there. But there's no kind of idea of a quick fling in it at all.'

The day of the tanglers and their business-like marriage arrangements has long gone, but in his role as matchmaker Jim White has often brought lonely hearts together in a more informal way.

'I've tried computer dating, and I do have forms that people fill in, telling a bit about themselves. But what will usually happen is that I'll have in mind a couple of girls that'll be staying at the hotel, and if I see a couple of unattached men I might say to them, "Why don't you give these ladies a lift out to the Kincora?" So that will give them a start if they're a bit shy. And there are results. I'd say that maybe a quarter of all the married couples around here first met at a dance in Lisdoonvarna.'

There's little or no rowdy drunkenness during matchmaking, very few fights or disturbances. Almost all the townspeople take part themselves, and they all benefit from the prosperity the event brings to Lisdoonvarna. Few that I talked to begrudged Jim – a 'blow-in' from County Donegal – the success of his spruce and well-run chain of hotels. Investing in a rural area of Ireland, employing Irish people (though it has to be said that most of the hotel employees had more than a whiff of Donegal in their speech) and bringing in tourist revenue, he's in many ways a shining example of the kind of businessman the west of Ireland is so keen to attract and hold. But when he began to describe his future plans to join up with Shannon Development in replacing the outmoded spa buildings with a modern complex, for cleaning up Lisdoonvarna and 'making it a town with every facility that modern tourists want', my heart sank. Lisdoonvarna, for all its plethora of hotels, is still a town where cars wander like cattle up the middle of unevenly surfaced streets; where shopkeepers engage you in ten minutes of chat before selling you a cheap shirt from the front counter, a toy tractor from somewhere at the side or a tin kettle from unfathomable recesses in the shadows at the back. Notwithstanding, or perhaps on account of, the town's long exposure to visitors in their tens of thousands, its heart beats with a steady and idiosyncratic life of its own. Could it stand up to the advent of thoroughly advertised, utterly 'facilitated' tourism? Jim White took me up, politely but sharply, when I declared an élitist streak and said I thought it would be a shame to change the place.

'No, I can't agree with you there at all. It's easy enough for strangers to take that view, but it's a very different matter for anyone who lives here. Now, I was in politics, in the government, for years before I did this – I represented South-West Donegal in the Dáil. And what took me into politics in the first place was seeing two good friends of mine off from Cork when they had to emigrate to the United States. I never expected to see them again. And they certainly never expected to see their own mothers and fathers again. That made a big impression on me at the age of twenty-one, especially coming from Donegal where so many youngsters had no jobs and were forced to emigrate. And I went into politics a few years later absolutely determined to get something done that would help our young people live and work in their own land.'

Jim's easy smile had cooled by several degrees. This was a subject near his heart. He leaned forward and tapped a finger on the Michael Collins biography I had been reading and had put down on the table top. 'If you've been reading about that fella you'll know all about the problems Ireland has had. We need the jobs to keep the people in areas like Clare. It's all very well to talk about keeping places such as Lisdoonvarna or the Burren for what you describe as "élitists" to come and admire as "unspoiled". We'd try to be careful of the environment whatever development we did. But when it comes to local people and can they live in the place they belong – then you have to make some choices. And I'm on the side of tourism and jobs.'

Noon at the spa wells, a green hollow of grassy banks and trees on the edge of Lisdoonvarna. Zig-zag paths led down to the old-fashioned pump room and bath house buildings under the trees. A crowd of people was already in occupation, walking slowly arm in arm along the paths or standing outside the pump room sipping at glasses of spa water. The pump room girl squirted me a glassful from a samovar-shaped machine. The water was cold, clear and flavoured lightly with a sulphurous tang of hard-boiled eggs. I got it down, exchanging grimaces with a pair of old ladies doing the same thing nearby.

The first-floor ballroom in its modern building across the lawn was full of middle-aged and elderly couples. There must have been close on two hundred people going round the floor, with the same number watching and making comments from chairs around the walls. At the organ was Donie, thumping out hits of the forties and fifties. Absolute decorum reigned. Donie's little wisecracks between songs – 'Hold up now! You can manage another!' – were the only manifestation of liveliness in the place. That was my first impression, anyway, as I sat down to watch the dancers. A dashing old chap in a flaring yellow polo-neck shirt scooted past with a stout partner in a floral poncho, both dancers staring fixedly over each other's shoulders. A very old, white-faced gentleman in full suit-and-tie order hobbled along with a young girl in jeans clamped inside the stiffly bent angle of his arm, their bodies at least two feet apart, their faces masked in concentration. On the chairs, groups of bachelors in twos and threes sat staring, like me, at the dancers, with the same respectful fixity of expression.

> Please help me, I'm falling,
> But that would be sin;
> Close the door to temptation,
> Don't let me walk in

sang Donie in a quavering falsetto from his podium. All doors to temptation seemed fairly watertight. But as I watched the waltzing cavalcade I began to see one or two animated expressions, a head thrown back in laughter, a pair of lips murmuring. The demands of the dancing, the necessity of concentrating on one's partner's feet and on neighbouring elbows, were getting people over those awkward silences and giving them conversational straws to grasp at. Later that afternoon, out at the dance at Ballinalacken Castle or down in the cramped little ballroom bar of the Savoy, some of them might begin building on these tentatively dug foundations.

It's hard to pinpoint exactly when a long-term passion first takes root, but I think my own love affair with Celtic traditional music received a significant push in the right direction the night in 1979 that I heard Cathal McConnell sing 'Raglan Road'. Cathal is a County Fermanagh man, a flute-player and singer of great renown in the traditional music world. It was in the unlikely surroundings of the elegant lounge bar of a businessman's hotel in Redditch New Town that at two o'clock in the morning Cathal put down his glass and began:

> On Raglan Road on an August day
> I saw her first and knew
> That her dark hair might weave a snare
> That I would one day rue . . .

Short of stature and thick of spectacle lens, Cathal simply tilted his head back and let the song out like a bird from a cage. I'd never heard anything so haunting and beautiful. 'Ah, do you like that one?' said Cathal. Half an hour later his hand in its baggy blue jacket sleeve appeared over my shoulder, holding two pieces of paper covered in scratchy writing. Unknown to me, he had asked the barmaid for pen and paper, and had sat down in the midst of the uproarious businessmen to write out the whole song for me.

The introduction of Cathal McConnell's name had broken the ice for me at many a session in the west of Ireland. One morning of my stay in Lisdoonvarna I set off armed with it to pay a call on the Russell brothers of Doolin. 'Say hello to Micho Russell for me, will you?' Cathal had requested before I left England. 'He's one of the real old country musicians and singers.'

As it turned out, Micho had just left the house when I located it on the hillside above the village. But I found Gussie Russell in the stone shed beside the house, fumbling with the chain of a motor bike. Gussie stood up slowly, unfolding a lanky six-foot frame as he wiped the oil from his palms before shaking hands. 'Cathal!' he said, smiling with pleasure. 'And so he sends his best wishes. Well, now, you're very welcome.' Gussie must have been well into his seventies. His brown face under its cap broke into a web of lines as he let out another of his sudden smiles. He moved shyly in front of me towards the house, making a sweeping movement with his hand beside his worn corduroy trousers as if encouraging a recalcitrant sheepdog along. 'We'll go into the house, where Micho is,' he murmured. But a search of the rooms failed to unearth his brother. Gussie stood in thought in the middle of the kitchen floor. 'Well, I'd like to play a tune for you,' he said, rummaging in the pocket of a jacket hung up on a hook. Out came a tin whistle in its leather case. Gussie walked around the room, considering. Finally he settled himself across the door frame, crossed his ankles and nodded. 'Will you tell Cathal I played you "The Five Mile Chase"?' said Gussie as he raised the whistle to his lips. The tune fluttered out, full of squeaks and little musical exclamations.

There was another meditative pause. I wanted to reciprocate in kind, but which of my slender store of harmonica tunes could I manage to play without too many mistakes? 'This is called "The Oyster Girl",' I said, plunging in, and ploughed through from end to end without mishap. 'Keep going,' muttered Gussie from the door-way, fingering his whistle. The second time through he had it nailed. We honked and whistled merrily to a concluding flourish. 'A pretty tune,' commented Gussie. 'Will you write down the name of it for me?' I did so, along the crease of a newspaper, while Gussie spoke of the sociable kind of music the Russells had always played.

'My brothers and myself, we used to play at many a dance all night, with plenty of porter. There was never any kind of a silence while we were playing. I think 'tis better to have the ould chat going when you are playing. But others, they want the hush. I remember one man –

he sang a song, and all the people were talking so loud he couldn't be heard at all. He never said a thing then. But when a woman started to sing, suddenly your man roars out, "Will ye all be quiet and listen to the good woman's song, for the Lord's sake?" He meant, "Why the divil couldn't ye all have listened to me when I was singing?" Yes, there's a deal of sideways talk in Ireland. You let people know what you mean without saying it straight out.'

Perhaps this train of thought was linked with Gussie's following observation: 'Lisdoonvarna, that's the place for matchmaking. Now there might be four women there, and yourself, and they might be laughing at you. Letting you know that they're there. Now that's a kind of laughing I don't care for. I wonder what would you call that style of laughing?'

'Inviting laughing?' I suggested.

Gussie nodded thoughtfully. 'That's the very word for it, now.'

I spent three days in and around Lisdoonvarna, dipping into this and that activity. On Saturday ten thousand pleasure-seekers converged on the town, cramming every pavement, pub and ballroom. I plucked up my courage and waltzed round the Savoy's springy dance floor, grinding sexagenarian toes under my feet and smiling till my cheeks ached. I walked down into Doolin and found twenty over-refreshed Dubliners in O'Connor's pub yelling 'Ring-a-ring-a-Rosie' at the tops of their combined voices, impervious to the disapproving silence of the purist musicians waiting to play in the same room, rocking hilariously in their seats as a scarlet-faced fat man conducted them with a Guinness bottle. I went into McGann's to shake hands with Teresa McGann, and came out twelve hours later having written two thousand words, broken three reeds in my harmonica and dared at last to sing 'Raglan Road' in public. I ate greasy chips out of someone else's paper bag in the back seat of a car at half-past two in the morning, travelling in what turned out to be the opposite direction to Island View. And as I climbed wearily aboard the bus in Lisdoonvarna on Sunday morning and set what remained of my mind back south towards Killarney and the end of my long road, I caught sight of a sticker in the back window of a car. It read: 'Lisdoonvarna – For the Crack'.

7

TO THE END OF THE ROAD
Killarney to Cape Clear Island

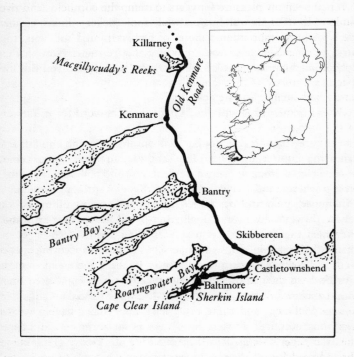

Another shift in the seasons: a touch of frost on the ground at night, an autumnal nip to the air in the mornings. The purple of heather on the hills began to blaze with fiery orange in patches, and the early sun drew up a smoke of mist from streams and rivers. Summer was having its final bright fling, the outlines of the Killarney mountains sharpened and clarified against an ice-blue sky. The late-season tourists in the jaunting cars clutched heavy coats round themselves as the jarveys trotted them out to the lakes. The horses' breath steamed, and their shoes clattered and echoed on the roads in the cold air. A change in the weather was overdue.

Out in the Atlantic equinoctial storms were building in a series of deepening depressions, curving in, one behind another, towards the west coast of Ireland. I hung around Killarney for a couple of days, keeping an eye on the mountains, trusting the weather to hold while I waited for Jon Magna to arrive.

It had been my pleasure for years to tramp the cornfields and river banks of East Anglia with Jon, erstwhile apple picker, window cleaner, tile baker, mineral bottler, restorer of timber-framed buildings, rock band tour manager and founder of a wholefood co-operative: a philosopher, and a handy man with both story and song. Jon likes to gather together threads of his tangled family history, and had recently unravelled a line leading to John Magner, his great-great-great-grandfather, who came over to England from Ireland around the turn of the nineteenth century to join the 17th Lancers. That faint lead, and the prospect of a day or two in the mountains, had combined to bring Jon into Cork on the overnight ferry. I was looking forward immensely to his company in the hills south of Killarney, rough terrain where a good companion would lighten the lonely miles.

It rained, blew and chilled throughout most of Jon's few days in the south-west of Ireland. Those autumn gales came sweeping ashore even as his ferry was docking in Cork, driving a belt of rain before them and dragging more in their skirts. The Killarney mountains wept and roared. But within an hour of Jon stepping down from the Cork bus we were striding in among them during a miraculous break in the storms. A steely silence had settled over sky and land, an ominous stillness falling suddenly at midday and due to be swept away that evening. 'Tomorrow: severe gales, heavy rain,' predicted the local paper's soothsayer. Jon and I rode our luck and passed over the old road from Killarney to Kenmare in what was to be the only lull in a spell of miserable weather.

In the wild tract of land between Killarney and Kenmare stand not only the tallest mountains in Ireland, but some of the remotest of its high country – plateaux of bog, forgotten droving tracks, passes where only the red deer and the most intrepid of mountain walkers go, craggy ridges above seldom-seen lakelets and waterfalls. The old Kenmare road climbs away from tourist's Killarney, the beautifully wooded shores of Lough Leane (Lower Lake), where you pay dearly to have yourself landed on islands once inhabited by monks and chieftains. With sweet chestnut and monkey-puzzle trees, rhododendrons and pine groves, the Victorian landowners improved upon nature. Where the Torc Cascade tumbled down a rocky staircase in the toehills of the Mangerton mountain range on the southern shore of Lough Leane they built a stepped pathway so that ladies and gentlemen could ascend to view the falls with the minimum of exertion before rowing beneath Eagle's Nest hill from Lower to Upper Lake for a sylvan picnic. Later generations of visitors basked equally ecstatically in the romantic glow of the Killarney scenery – a glow made more tender by contrast with the rude realities of the bleak lands above and beyond, as Mary Gorges gushed in 1912 in her book *Killarney*:

> The Mecca of every pilgrim in search of the sublime and beautiful in Nature – the mountain paradise of the west. Yet if the magical softness of the shimmering wave and wooded isle, the glory of their colouring, the ineffable peace which broods over hill and vale, tempt the summer visitor to think that Paradise could not be fairer, there are dark glens, frowning mountains and sombre passes, which but too vividly remind the beholder that on earth must the shadow always follow the sunshine, the minor note of sadness be heard . . .

The brooding peace and frowning mountains can continue to brood and frown undisturbed hereabouts, thanks to the foresight of successive Irish governments. When the American philanthropists and Killarney landowners Mr and Mrs William Bowers Bourn and their son-in-law Senator Arthur Vincent gave ten thousand acres of the Muckross Estate around Lough Leane to the Irish nation in 1932, they established the heart of Ireland's showpiece National Park. As land around what was then called the Bourn Vincent Memorial Park became available, the government bought it up to stave off any threat of development. Looking at the unrestrainedly out-of-keeping development which is beginning to rear its head in and around so many of the towns in the west of Ireland – long strips of hacienda bungalows, ugly concrete car parks, exuberantly designed hotels – one can only be thankful for the safeguarding of the Killarney lakes and hills, such tempting targets for would-be builders of holiday villages or hotel complexes. These decades of land purchase, added to other gifts of property, have more than doubled the area of the original Bourn Vincent gift, putting a ring fence around the town and neighbouring lakes of Killarney itself as well as a good chunk of the mountainous country to the south.

Jon and I scrambled and slithered up and over these protected miles of bare rock, bog and icy water, ducking through groves of dwarfish oaks and ancient hollies, threading in and out of the miniature gorge of Esknamucky Glen, following the sometimes stony and sometimes peat-soft line of the old and now entirely abandoned high road to Kenmare. Jon's clumping pair of black army boots, borrowed from an obliging captain in the Sappers just before setting off for the ferry, rubbed steadily at his as yet untoughened ankles, and my fingers were nipped by a cold they had not felt since the springtime chill of the Ox Mountains. But we still managed to enjoy ourselves. I doubt if Shaking Rock and Peakeen Mountain had echoed to the music-hall strains of 'It's a Great Big Shame' and 'I Can't Do My Bally Bottom Button Up' since intrepid Victorian walking parties made merry along the Kenmare road. Now they did, and with a vengeance.

Scattered along the side of the track were the familiar ruins of long-deserted houses and sedge-choked fields. How did communities like the one under Windy Gap manage to survive in such isolation? The screen of pines and oaks that had sheltered the little huddle of houses from the south-west winds had grown and tangled into a dark thicket, in whose shadow the angles of stone walls, the broken chimneys and sagging slates crouched like beaten animals waiting for a final blow. The settlement's spring ran unchecked between the houses, and the sunken green channels of boreens led into jungles of bushes. A couple of roof timbers shaggy with moss lay embedded in the ground. Eviction? Famine? Emigration? Isolation? The tumbledown houses held fast to the secret of their ruin. During the Great Famine the Kenmare road had been shut to traffic by the landowner, Lord Lansdowne. The local interpretation of this act was that by cutting the lifeline of the tenants, he would force them off land that he wanted to turn into a deer forest. If so, he succeeded. Red deer now graze the empty fields of Esknamucky Glen and Windy Gap.

There was a chill south-west wind blowing over Windy Gap, and rain was beginning to spatter out of a greasy grey sky as we came down into the darkening streets of Kenmare. We weren't expecting anything more in the way of music than we had already howled out across the empty uplands, but I had forgotten that Kenmare was home to Christy O'Leary, colleague of Cathal McConnell and piper with the Boys of the Lough. Christy was standing behind the counter of the Green Note music shop when we looked in, minding the shop for the owner, relaxing on home territory after a hectic tour of the States. I'd only met Christy a couple of times previously, but his warm handshake and invitation to join the session later on in the pub across the street were right in the Irish tradition. At half-past ten that rainy night, sore feet stuck far out under the table, a crowded room and a pint of Guinness in front of him, Jon sang 'Hares on the Mountain', entirely at home after some fifteen hours in Ireland.

On Saturday morning I drew back the curtains at Keal na Gower House to see the Roughty River swollen and racing under lashing rain, carrying a coat of leaves stripped from the trees by the gale. A heron stood knee-deep in the water of a side channel below my window, head and neck tucked into a double bend, picking grubs from the ripples with lightning-quick darts of his beak. As I watched, the mud between his toes crumbled and was washed away. He toppled sideways, recovered himself with a furious flap of his umbrella-like wings, and moved with stiff dignity to a more secure foothold. But the channel was far too agitated and stained with mud for serious fishing. By the time I looked out again the water had risen to brush the dangling leaves of the bushes along the bank, and the heron had gone.

It rained all day, sending the shoppers scurrying for shelter and filling the bars and restaurants. Cycling cape sales boomed. The clouds raced in over the mountains. The trees of Kenmare sighed and dripped, releasing their yellowing leaves in solid drifts. I sat and wrote, dreamily and continuously, while the children of the house squabbled amicably on the far side of the kitchen door. Meanwhile Jon chuckled by the fire over a book on the Rolling Stones. We were content to laze, gathering our forces for combat with the Cork Mountaineering Club the following day.

It won't be Jack Buckley's fault if hill walking fails to get a proper grip on Irish affections. You'd need a pretty stout shackle and chain to keep Jack off the hill paths and mountain roads that he explores with unquenchable enthusiasm. By all reasonable reckoning his autumn years should be fully upon him, but Jack tackles the hills around his native city of Cork – and much further afield – with energy enough to put people half his age to shame. A couple of phone calls on my part had set him scurrying around for weeks, trying to whip up enough members of the Cork Mountaineering Club to march Jon and me over the western flanks of the Shehy Mountains to Bantry in suitable style. Jack was full of apologies when we met him on Sunday morning outside the Youth Hostel in Kenmare. He had mustered a party of five, and was worried at the thinness of the turn-out. But it proved to be a perfect day, both in weather and company. Harnessed to the clinking pace set by Éimer and Leonard, Frances, Mary and Jack himself, we marched up hill and down dale for twenty miles under a cold, clouding sky, tarmac and stones spurned beneath our pounding boots, chattering like seven magpies.

'. . . walked from Cork to Limerick – that's sixty miles,' recounted Jack, pumping his arms to keep up a steady four miles an hour as we climbed uphill. 'So we did a walk of thirty-eight miles to prepare for it. Your man turned up late, and we didn't get away till half-past six in the morning. I'd phoned ahead to a pub on the way to have a meal waiting on the table for us, the way we wouldn't waste any time, but didn't the waitress come round with: "And what would you like to eat?" God save us! "Jakers!" says I, "Sure, we'll never get away!" We came in past midnight, but at least we'd done it under the twenty-four hours, all right.'

These were heroics that Jon and I could only envy. I slipped my friend a glucose energy tablet and tried to steady my breathing. On the soles of Jon's feet was a crop of squashily painful blisters, garnered on the old Kenmare road two days before. On our own, the two of us would have limped those hills in wincing discomfort. But the stories and relentless pace carried us on in spite of ourselves, by Coolnacoppagh, Curragrainue and Drehideighteragh, trumpet-calls of names for pipsqueaks of places. At Coolnacoppagh we found a green road marked on the map as an indistinct straggle of microscopic dots, and following its sodden ruts we came upon an abandoned settlement of houses sinking back into the ground. A flame-red Virginia creeper, sole remnant of some bygone farmhouse, ran riot over the thorn bushes. We sprawled out on a square sward of grass and munched our sandwiches in honeyed sunlight, with bare crags at our backs and a wide valley spread in front beyond the overgrown trees of the hamlet. 'The best picnic spot I've ever found,' sighed Mary.

On the way up to the wild pass the map named as 'Priest's Leap', we got into conversation with an old woman who had come out to her farm gate to quell her furious dogs, and heard the story from her.

'It was passed down to me by generations,' she said, glancing from face to face of her audience. 'Well, the priest was up there above under the rock, saying Mass, and didn't they come for to catch him.'

'That was in the days of the Penal Laws,' amplified Jack. The old lady glared, but not at the interruption. Mention of bad times past had stirred bygone indignations. 'Yes, and didn't they kill another priest below there when they caught him! Anyway, this man ran out and away with him to the top of the road, with the Host in his pocket and the soldiers behind. There was a horse waiting up there. "Get up, Father," said the people. "Up, now!" And so he jumped up on the horse and he lepped out off the rock, and the horse landed in Bantry ten miles away!'

She grinned with pleasure at the thought of the miraculous escape. 'Well, when the horse landed he left the marks of his hooves in the rock. You can see them there today, just beside the road on the side. They were tarring that road a while since, and they covered up the marks. But when they came back in the morning, the tar had turned aside and the marks were there as clear as ever!'

During the story the woman's husband had come over and settled himself against the wall of the lane. 'That must have been a good horse,' he murmured, smiling round at us. His wife puckered her brows, digging back into her memory. 'I used to know the song that was made about the Priest's Lep,' she said diffidently, 'but the old brains are going and maybe I haven't it now.'

Encouraged by the expectant silence, she began to string together words and lines as they came to mind – a fragment about the priest and his faithful flock under the rock, a phrase or two describing his flight to the top of the hill, a complete verse depicting the mighty 'lep' from the pass. 'You should sing that song for the local radio people,' said Jack as she came to a standstill. 'They'd love it.'

'I thought you might have one of those recording things about you,' said the old woman shyly. 'Sure you looked as if you might!'

Up at the pass we found an iron cross planted on the site of the 'lep', standing over a sweeping prospect from Kerry into West Cork, a view that fell away fifteen hundred feet through a rocky valley to the bulk of Whiddy Island down in Bantry Bay. On the long, snaking descent Jack kept us going with an account of the terrific explosion a few years before that had wrecked the oil storage depot on the island and claimed many lives. The supertanker *Betelgeuse* had gone up like an almighty firework, with a roar that had been heard fifteen miles off, devastating the terminal built on Whiddy by the Gulf Oil Corporation. There had been other accidents on the rocks around the long, pincer-shaped bay: collisions that had torn holes in tankers and released hundreds of thousands of gallons of crude oil to smear the shoreline and smother the wildlife. Present prosperity set against potential calamity; the juggling act which remote places like West Cork, stricken by poverty and emigration, have willingly or unwillingly to perform.

I tried to think back to Mullaghmore and Dunquin, to draw parallels and make comparisons. But my heart wasn't really in it. There was rapidly mounting, sharply focused excitement in me. Ahead lay spread out the start of the final stage in the long walk from northernmost Donegal. Just beyond those blue ridges at the far side of Bantry Bay, two days' march away and for the moment out of sight, journey's end was beckoning. Roaringwater Bay stood clear in my imagination, already visible on the lowest section of the last map I would need to carry in the holder round my neck. Forty miles to go.

South of Bantry, the mountains smooth gradually out into the characteristic rounded small hills and steep little valleys of south-west Cork. The sea cuts deeply into the foot of Ireland here. The long, slender toes of the Sheep's Head and Mizen peninsulas run with a southwesterly slant for fifteen miles out into the Atlantic, separated by the narrow inlet of Dunmanus Bay. Mizen Head, a sandstone nose of blunt cliffs on the tip of the peninsula, is the most southerly point of mainland Ireland. 'Malin to Mizen!' is the battle-cry of long-distance road walkers laden with sponsorships, footslogging for charity the length of Ireland. Cold logic would have had me shaping my own course the same way at the finish of my journey. But to hell with logic. Roaringwater Bay, a ragged incursion of the sea to the south and east of the Mizen Peninsula, had 127 rocks, blobs, islets and full-blown islands scattered across its treacherous waters – and the outermost of these, Cape Clear Island, stood a mile or so south of Mizen Head. Islands, and everything to do with them, had held me in thrall for many years. Standing at the lowest tip of Cape Clear, I would have got as far south as I could possibly get from Malin Head, and I'd have the added pleasure of ending the mighty trek on one of those lonely little worlds in the water that I loved.

There was another attraction, too, one even less susceptible to logic. Who could resist the ferocious and elemental name of Roaringwater Bay?

From Killarney south by way of Kenmare, Bantry and Skibbereen I walked through a land tortured more than any other part of Ireland during the Great Famine. Remote and wild, devoid of proper roads, dotted with communities many miles from the nearest hospital, public works scheme or workhouse, southern Kerry and south-west Cork had bowed before the agonies of disease, starvation and death in abject misery. The sufferings of most of the rural settlements out in the lonely valleys and hills went unrecorded. Their story is to be read in lazybed outlines and mossy heaps of stones.

But in the towns it was a different matter. Great Britain across the water was entering on the pomp and pride of the golden era of Queen Victoria's reign, with most of her citizens only dimly aware, if at all, of the true extent of Ireland's catastrophe. Mr and Mrs S.C. Hall could write of the Irish beggars in *A Week at Killarney*, published only a year after the end of the Famine, as if those desperate people were putting on a music-hall turn for their benefit:

> Every town is full of objects who parade their afflictions with ostentation, or exhibit their half-naked children, as so many claims to alms as a right. Age, decrepitude, imbecility, and disease surround the car the moment it stops. They have not yet learned to consider state provisions as a right – a right that has been earned by labour and contributions to state wealth, and we believe they will long continue to prefer the miserable hovels in which they dwell, and the wretched fare upon which they subsist, to the comforts of the workhouse.

The downcast beggars of south-west Ireland were contrasted unfavourably with those in other parts of the country, whom the Halls found 'merry and good-humoured, though most provokingly clamorous'.

Other accounts of the hellish conditions in the towns of Kerry and Cork, however, had been compiled by those who were there on the spot – priests, Quaker missionaries, officials of the Irish Board of Health. What they witnessed came pouring in anger and frustration out of their pens in images that are hard to take in even today, 150 years after the event. In Kenmare, for example, the civilised little town where Jon Magna and I had spent such a pleasant couple of days, the local practice of subdividing land among members of the same family had left most of the people without even the half-acre of ground they needed to grow sufficient food to keep themselves alive. In February 1847 the parish priest reported finding a man lying in bed in his cabin, barely living, his dead wife and two dead children beside him. The third child, also dead, was being eaten by the cat. Over the mountains at Bantry, at the same time, the fever hospital was crammed full of sufferers from typhus and relapsing fever, the living and dead laid out naked side by side on heaps of straw. There was no medicine to be had, no fire in the freezing winter, nothing to eat or drink. The doctor was himself ill, and the only attendant was a pauper nurse without any medical skill. 'Language would fail to give an adequate idea of its state,' commented the inspector of the Board of Health in his report on the hospital. 'It was appalling, awful, heartsickening.' One can see that shocked man reaching for phrases to convey an impression of what he had seen, in the full knowledge of failure even as he wrote them down.

Further south at Skibbereen, things were even worse. In that terrible winter, diarrhoea ran like a plague through the emaciated bodies of the children admitted to the workhouse, killing more than half of them. Those who could not get a place in the workhouse stood even less chance of survival. There was no relief money from the government, as in the chaotic conditions no relief committee had been formed in the area. Local landowners had failed to subscribe, and wages on the relief works were at the starvation rate of eightpence a day. The agonised reports of priests and Board of Health inspectors told of corpses eaten by rats, families too weak from fever and malnourishment to bury their dead, women begging with their dead babies in their arms.

In the midst of all this suffering, Skibbereen market continued to offer bread, meat, fish and corn meal. But the starving people, even if they had had the energy to drag themselves there, had no money to buy the food.

Jack Buckley and company landed us in Vickery's Hotel in Bantry, rinsed the dust from their throats and departed for the drive back to Cork city with what Mr and Mrs S.C. Hall would undoubtedly have termed 'mutual protestations of goodwill'. I had the feeling that Jack would cheerfully have walked home, had he been on his own. It was all Jon and I could do to drag ourselves from bar to bed. Jon's blisters now had blisters of their own, but he limped manfully downstairs to see me off at eight o'clock the following morning. For him there would be a day's thumbing in the direction of Cork city, to burrow for Magnas and Magners in the records office there before catching the evening ferry back to England: for me, twenty-three miles of back-country roads to reach the coast beyond Skibbereen.

Short of standing fully-clothed in the shower with the taps hard on, I couldn't have got more comprehensively soaked that day. 'A soft morning, so it is,' said Mrs Crowley in the bar at Cullomane cross-roads, five sodden miles out of Bantry, where I skulked for an hour in vain hopes that the rain would ease off. The air was seething with gently falling moisture too fine to be called rain, but with all of rain's pervasive powers. The tent-like yellow cycling cape I'd bought in Kenmare as an insurance against the long-range weather forecast was no help in this water-laden atmosphere. Neither was the sou'wester that came with the cape. It funnelled a slow but steady stream of water down my neck with depressing accuracy. I saw almost nothing of West Cork as I splashed up the hills and down into the valleys. The clouds had fitted themselves like caps over the hills, and drifts of rain swirled over field and forest, blotting out all far views. The trees steamed. The hedges dripped. It rained and rained and rained. At the roadside shrine to Our Lady of Tralibawn, the marble statue of the Virgin raised her eyes to the clouds as the rain streamed down her white, impassive face. Somewhere out there in one of those grey valleys I passed a farmhouse where an elderly farmer perched on a ladder against the roof of his barn, nailing up a gushing gutter pipe that had sagged loose. A gigantic sow was rooting in the puddled muck of the farmyard, her teats swinging below her pink belly with every thrust of her snout. As the rainwater sluiced over his knees, the old man waved his hammer in my direction, part benediction on the traveller, part curse on the day. I squelched down into the narrow streets of Skibbereen resolved to find a tolerant hotel, strip off every stitch of clammy clothing and punish the tea pot. But the coast lay only five miles ahead. I couldn't get any wetter, no matter what. The internal engine was still ticking over, quietly delivering energy to the system, fuelling my hunger for the end of the journey. Push on, then.

If I had stayed in Skibbereen, the Jehovah's Witness from Middlesex would have had a barren afternoon. He passed me in the lane beyond the town on his old black boneshaker of a bicycle with no more than a friendly 'Hello there!' Five minutes later I heard his tyres swishing behind me, and saw the rickety bicycle draw level. His lean, burning face looked earnestly into mine. 'Hi there. I saw you a while back. I was wondering if you would be interested in having a look at the *Watch Tower*.' He indicated a dripping package tied to the bicycle. Oh, no! I thought as he dismounted and fell uninvited into step beside me. Not a bloody Jehovah's Witness, here of all places! No front door to close firmly against his budget of Good News. How can I get rid of him? But something in his rain-washed humility made me ashamed of the thought. Didn't I think, he was saying, that the world was going wrong? Especially hereabouts?

'It's rather a sad area, yes,' I responded cautiously. Maybe I could stave off the invitation to join the Saved by out-talking him. 'Not surprising, when you look at its history. The Great Famine . . . emigration . . . unemployment . . .'

'I haven't read much history,' he murmured. 'But it's terrible what's happening up in the North. Religion has been responsible for so many terrible things. Now, if you think about what God really intended for his family of humans –'

His wet hands clenched white on the handlebars. The mild voice quivered, poised to jump into its predetermined groove. Desperately I caught the ball and patted it back.

'Family, yes. Have you got a family?'

He swallowed and blinked, arrested in mid-leap. 'Uh . . . yes . . . a brother . . . he's . . . he's handicapped. My mother and father . . . a hard time . . . moved over here from Middlesex five years ago . . .' The holy spark faded from his eyes. He lifted the rain-blotched leg of his sensible trousers over the crossbar of the bicycle, gripped my hand and pumped it up and down, fumbling for the prescribed formula at parting. 'I hope you'll think over what I've been saying. I'm sure you will,' he said brightly, and pedalled off down a side turning, sitting ramrod straight on the saddle. I walked on, unsure if I had made or spoiled his day, descending through the misty valleys, spiralling down the twisty lanes into Castletownshend and Somerville territory.

Walking through Ireland for the best part of half a year, I learned many things. Chief among them, perhaps, was my own shocking ignorance of the country, its people and its history when I set out from Malin Head that windy April morning. It seems incredible now that I knew scarcely anything of Oliver Cromwell's devastating influence on Ireland, and nothing at all of the rebellions and suppressions of Tudor times and during the nineteenth century. The root causes of the Easter Rising, the War of Independence, the Civil War – and the story of these events themselves – were blank pages in my mind. The waves of emigration generated before and during the Great Famine, and still surging outwards from the country; the slowly and painfully changing face of the Catholic Church in Ireland; the tenacious survival of the Celtic culture in language, music, talk and hospitality – these had yet to be pencilled in on my imagination. In common, I suspect, with most Englishmen setting foot in Ireland for the first time, I was appalled by what had been going on north of the border, groundlessly apprehensive of what my own reception in the Republic might be, knowing almost nothing of what lay behind that relentlessly terrible string of atrocities. Now, after six months and more than seven hundred miles of walking, talking, singing, playing, reading and listening, of visits researched and planned, of conversations unexpected and unprepared for, I had an inkling; vague and shadowy, superficial perhaps, but a framework substantial enough to hang some understanding on.

That shaky structure had assembled itself from many separate parts. The unrolling, gradually shifting landscape was printed with a social and economic history I had learned to read in half-obliterated lazybed strips on the Mayo hillsides, the barren and changeless rock sheets of the Aran Islands, conifers marching to conquer the boglands of the Stack's Mountains, a spanking new hacienda-style bungalow on a Limerick back road with the blank-faced ruins of an abandoned stone cabin in its garden. No journey by car, bus, train or even bicycle could have opened this particular book to me. It was the step by step, hour by hour, snail's pace of walking the tarmac, the stony tracks, the bog and heather, with the long stretches of reflection that walking enforces when the mind chews independently on subconscious fodder, the times of energy and exhilaration, and the other times of exhaustion and despondency, of which the lone long-distance walker is both victim and beneficiary, that brought the lessons home. They had been given a human face whenever I stumbled or found myself eased into conversation across farm gates, at the roadside, in midday kitchens and midnight bars. Turf-cutters, priests, drunks, shopkeepers, children, bed-and-breakfast landladies, local historians, story tellers and tall-tale peddlers: almost any fragment of chat and passing of the time of day had contained a nugget of insight. I had found the confidence, too, to risk a few halting phrases in those wordless but intimate conversations conducted on the wooden window seats of smoky bars with fiddle, melodeon, bodhrán, guitar and whistle – conversations in which all barriers of nationality, experience and culture crumbled under the burning necessity not to be caught napping when jig suddenly swerved into reel in a moment of collective understanding.

All this had been splendid, enriching and enlightening. But something, all the same, had been missing – a feeling of personal attachment. Those American O'Sullivans and Dohertys, those Australian Kavanaghs and O'Neills touching down in Shannon and Dublin had their place to claim, their family links with Ireland to glorify, mythologise and rejoice in. So far I could only point to the Palatine connection, the Protestant refugee Delmeges of County Limerick whom I had failed to meet when passing through their stamping grounds. But here at Castletownshend in West Cork, almost at the end of the road to Roaringwater, I found my own name rooted at last in Irish soil.

'Somerville?' people had been saying from Letterkenny to Bantry Bay. 'So you're a Somerville. Somerville and Ross – *The Irish RM*! Jesus, I laughed at that one!'

It's wonderful what television can do. A long-neglected book, condemned for years to a publisher's backlist or even out of print altogether, can become an overnight bestseller if a producer decides to unearth it and groom it for living-room stardom. So it had recently been with *The Experiences of an Irish RM*. This classic of Anglo-Irish humour – a clutch of short stories published around the turn of the century in two volumes (*Some Experiences of an Irish RM* in 1899 and *Further Experiences of an Irish RM* in 1908) and describing the trials and tribulations of Major Sinclair Yeates, an Englishman appointed to serve as Resident Magistrate in West Cork – had become a runaway success when serialised on television. Sales of the book, until then sluggish, had soared. A new omnibus edition had just been printed, and was selling at bookstalls and in newsagents all over Ireland. And interest had been revived, to a startling degree, in its co-authors Edith Œnone Somerville of Castletownshend and her cousin Violet Martin ('Martin Ross' to the reading public) of Ross Castle, County Galway.

The cousins first met in January 1886, when Violet came on a visit to Castletownshend with her mother and sister. She was twenty-four, Edith twenty-eight. The Martins had been landowners in Galway for many years, an enlightened Ascendancy family who had all but ruined themselves helping their tenants during the Famine. The Somervilles had been in Ireland since 1690, when William Somerville, a Scottish minister, had come across from south-west Scotland in flight from religious persecution. My own branch of the family had been off-shoots of these Scottish Somervilles, Episcopalians at a time when Presbyterian zealots were hunting establishment churchmen out of house and living. William Somerville had made a hair's-breadth escape with his family, fleeing his house at Leswalt near Stranraer a few hours before the Covenanting bully-boys came knocking at the door for him, and crossing the twenty miles or so to Ulster in an open boat. He died three years afterwards in County Down, a broken-hearted exile. His son, Thomas, moved south, becoming Rector of Castlehaven on the West Cork coast in 1732, and from there the family had shifted to nearby Castletownshend.

The village became the hub around which revolved the closely interwoven and intermarried lives of a handful of Protestant Ascendancy families. The Somervilles lived at Drishane, a handsome (though cold, damp and rat-infested) slate-hung house at the top of the steep street that sloped down to the sea. The Coghills inhabited Glenbarrahane, just below Drishane, while in the castle at the foot of the hill lived the Townshends. In such a remote area these Anglo-Irish families naturally clung together, hunting and socialising, teasing, courting and marrying each other, in a pleasant intimacy that the passing of time scarcely ruffled. Before Violet Martin's first visit to Drishane, her cousin Edith had been best friends with Ethel Coghill of Glenbarrahane. But Ethel had recently got married, and Edith, a horsy outdoor person with a great love of dogs and hunting, found herself in something of an emotional vacuum. Violet was tailor-made to fill the gap, a sensitive and warm-hearted girl with the attractive habit of going off into explosive fits of giggles at the slightest excuse. She, too, adored hunting. Soon the budding friendship had ripened into a mutual love that lasted up to and beyond Violet's death in 1915.

A hunting-and-horses woman Edith Somerville may have been, but she was also a gifted artist and possessed of a markedly anarchic sense of humour, delighting in harvesting and retelling funny incidents and in noting the idiosyncrasies of West Cork Irish/English speech. When the two cousins got together to jot down their ideas and observations, flint met tinder. 'Our work was done conversationally,' Edith wrote later. 'One or other – not infrequently both simultaneously – would state a proposition. This would be argued, combated perhaps, approved or modified; it would then be written down by the (wholly fortuitous) holder of the pen, would be scratched out, scribbled in again.'

This apparently haphazard method of working produced remarkably smooth and stylish writing, making the most of Edith's irreverent eye for oddities of habit and ear for peculiarities of speech, and Violet's bubbling sense of the ridiculous and real talent for composition. When Edith overheard conversations in broad West Cork dialect containing such phrases as 'Whiskey as pliable as new milk', or 'Is it some way wake in the legs y'are?', she would note them down for future use. After a slow start, the cousins managed to get their first book, *An Irish Cousin*, published in 1889 by Richard Bentley & Son (London), and scored a low-key hit which encouraged them to continue. In 1894 they produced *The Real Charlotte*, a novel now regarded as a classic and comparable to Balzac, but which at the time had a mixed reception (the Castletownshend cousinship detested it, according to Edith). Five years later, *Some Experiences of an Irish RM* appeared in print and made the names of Somerville and Ross.

There had been a battered Everyman copy of *The Irish RM* in a faded red cover on my bookshelf for years, but after trying and failing to get to grips with it at the age of fifteen, I had forgotten all about Somerville and Ross. Now, with Castletownshend on the immediate horizon, I had bought the omnibus volume at Dublin Airport and found it, to my surprise and delight, one of the funniest books I had ever read. Somehow the cousins managed to make Major Sinclair Yeates both humourless and hilarious, the eternal fall-guy who engages your sympathy even as you laugh at him. It's Yeates who is surprised by fellow members of the hunt in a compromising situation with a beautiful young Diana; Yeates who is discovered by the imperious Mrs Knox of Aussolas Castle hiding in a gorse patch beside her stolen horse; Yeates (in what is, for my money, the funniest story of the lot, 'The Man that Came to Buy Apples') who somehow finds himself, along with a heap of poached rabbits, trapped in a runaway carriage in the wake of a stampeding herd of cattle. The cast of characters runs riot in caricature – old Mrs Knox, the crazy but canny Anglo-Irish aristocrat; her likeable ne'er-do-well nephew Flurry, whose pack of hounds features throughout in a series of undisciplined escapades; Slipper, the sly poacher; Mrs Cadogan, the stout and hysterical housekeeper; Leigh Kelway, the stiff-necked, fastidious Englishman who ends up discovered by his appalled employer Lord Waterbury in the wreckage of an upset outside-car, 'hatless, muddy and gasping, with (blind-drunk) Driscoll hanging on by his neck, still singing the "Wearing of the Green"'. The originals of some of these characters (despite the denials of Somerville and Ross), and much of the landscape of the book, were recognisable to those who knew West Cork and its Anglo-Irish community.

This wild humour made the book's popularity, but it's the wit of the writing that raises it above the level of slapstick. Major Yeates's staid horse, The Quaker, goes while hunting 'at the equable gallop of a horse in the Bayeux Tapestry'. In old Mrs Knox's handwriting 'no individual word was decipherable, but, with a bold reader, groups could be made to conform to a scheme based on probabilities'. Music at a dance is 'supplied by the organist of the church, who played with religious unction and at the pace of a processional hymn'. And one can imagine the snorts of laughter echoing round the room as the cousins got into their stride describing the participants at that dance:

> Mrs Bennett wore an apple-green satin dress and filled it tightly; wisely mistrusting the hotel supper, she had imported sandwiches and cake in a pocket-handkerchief, and, warmed by two glasses of sherry, she made me the recipient of the remarkable confidence that she had but two back teeth in her head, but, thank God, they met.

Edith had been running the household at Drishane since her father's death in 1898, and in 1903 she became Master of the West Carbery Hunt. For many years she rode sidesaddle to hounds. She was an indomitable woman, somehow keeping hunt and house together even when times got tough and money became scarce. She broke and bred hunters and sold them in America to help get over financial difficulties.

Spiritualism, a lifelong fascination for Edith, helped her cope with the loss of her soulmate when Violet died of a brain tumour on 21 December 1915, aged fifty-three. Edith was convinced that Violet lived on, helping and encouraging her through contact maintained at séances. She made another close friend, the composer Dame Ethel Smyth, but there were complications to this relationship. Ethel Smyth was a practising bisexual, which baffled and worried Edith. She withdrew into heightened spiritual closeness to her dead *alter ego*, and into the writing in which she was sure they were still equally involved. *Further Experiences of an Irish RM* had been succeeded by a couple of animal books and by the third in the Irish RM series, *In Mr Knox's Country*, published shortly before Violet died. Edith continued to write under the name 'Somerville and Ross', producing a dozen novels and books of stories and essays, none of which captured the public's imagination as had the Irish RM's glorious romp through Ascendancy customs and foibles. Edith Somerville died on 8 October 1949, aged ninety-one, and lies buried next to Violet Martin in St Barrahane's churchyard at the lower end of Castletownshend's steep village street.

I limped into Castletownshend at evening like a half-drowned dog, sore and sodden from the long, rainy miles. But next day dawned bright and breezy. In the churchyard the sun struck down through the trees, lighting up the jagged chunk of sandstone that stands for a headstone over Edith Somerville's grave. A gale earlier in the year had toppled and shattered the cross marking Violet's grave alongside, and her little leaf-smothered plot lay bare. All over the graveyard the Protestant families had their memorials – Coghills, Somervilles and Townshends. Inside the church, the long tale of intermarriage and intermixing of these Ascendancy dynasties was written in brass and marble. Townshend Somerville, FitzJohn Townshend, Coghill Somerville – colonels, major-generals, rectors, admirals – long lives of public service ('John FitzHenry Townshend, for twenty-five years

Judge of the High Court of Admiralty in Ireland') and short lives sacrificed ('Lieut. Nevill J.A. Coghill, V.C., 24th Regt., born 25th January 1852, killed in action while saving the colours of his Regt. at Isandhlwana, South Africa, 22nd January 1879'). The church is scrupulously cleaned and kept by the parishioners of Castletownshend. 'Be sure to close the door behind you; otherwise the birds and animals will get in,' I had been warned by St Barrahane's hard-working churchwarden, Rose-Marie Salter-Townshend, at breakfast in her castle earlier in the day.

A fair number of tourists come to Castletownshend each year, braving the dead-end road from Skibbereen to come upon the picturesque double row of cottages sloping down to the quay on the cliff-bound inlet. There were two or three bed-and-breakfast places to choose from, but I struck lucky in settling on the castle. What Rose-Marie Salter-Townshend doesn't know about the history of Castletownshend isn't worth knowing. There wasn't even a village here when her ancestor Colonel Richard Townshend retired to West Cork and built his fortified house on the shore of the bay. He had been in Ireland with Cromwell's army in 1647, commanding the force which left more than three thousand Irish dead at the Battle of Knockineass, and towards the end of his life he withstood a siege at Castletownshend, in the Jacobite rebellion of 1690 during which five hundred supporters of James II under an O'Driscoll chief failed to get the better of the aged colonel and his thirty-five retainers.

Something of that steely determination has been passed down to Rose-Marie, though there could hardly be less of the *grande dame* about her. In her magnificently dark, cluttered and creaking castle, under flaking portraits of dark-browed Townshends in military uniforms, she dispenses hospitality to overnight guests who would have got no nearer than the castle gate when she was a girl. Not in the least disconcerted to find me dripping on her carpet, she soon had my waterlogged clothes hanging from the ceiling on the drying rack in the back passage. 'Oh, heaps of hot water,' she said, showing me a bath big enough to sleep three.

In the morning we ate together in the dining room, I at my table by the window and Rose-Marie at hers across the room, while June Murphy from a neighbouring village waited behind her employer's chair to bring forward the bacon and eggs. After breakfast Rose-

Marie rummaged out books of Somerville history for me, one of them inscribed by Edith Somerville. 'The Townshends were here a good hundred years before the Somervilles,' she told me with quiet satisfaction. 'And the Coghills came *much* later than either, of course. The Chavasses, too – they were French Huguenots, vineyard owners, escaping persecution by the Catholics after the massacre of St Bartholomew's Eve. My husband's family, the Salters and Jagos – Spanish Reformed Church, very unpopular in Spain a couple of hundred years ago when they fled to West Cork. I suppose Castletownshend was as far away as all of them could get from their persecutors. It became a haven from bigotry for those Protestant families. That's why we never had any of those troubles between Catholics and Protestants round here. The Castletownshend families had seen quite enough of it for themselves.'

At the end of a side road below the village street a drive leads from stout wooden gates to The Point, a handsome big house among trees. I wandered down from the castle and stood for a long time by the gates, looking at the house and reflecting on Rose-Marie Salter-Townshend's remark. Mutual tolerance may have been the norm between the Protestants and Catholics of Castletownshend, but when politics were slipped into the balance the scales were always likely to dip one way or the other. It could have happened – but it did not – at any time during the hot tensions of the War of Independence. The irony of the murder of Vice-Admiral Boyle Somerville in the hallway of The Point in 1936 was that it took place at a time when the old antagonisms seemed to have been well and truly buried.

During the War of Independence and the Civil War that followed, West Cork was strongly Republican. The IRA were a formidable power in the area. They took over parts of Castletownshend at one stage of the Civil War, and the Protestant families had to walk a tightrope between the opposing interests, keeping on good terms with both sides in order to avoid having their houses burned, as was happening to other such families all over Ireland. Their previous friendly relations with their Catholic neighbours stood them in good stead, however. The Republicans stole a horse from the Somervilles, and smashed up the Coghills' furniture when they were away from Glenbarrahane, but the Castletownshend Protestants' lives were never seriously threatened. The members of the IRA's local cell all knew them personally, and were equally well known to them. An understanding was reached, and maintained.

In the case of the Somerville family there was a direct, personal reason for this. During the Fenian risings of the 1860s a local man had been sought by the British soldiers. As an act of neighbourly mercy the Somervilles had hidden him away in Drishane House. The fugitive's family had continued to be hot Republicans, and during the Troubles had become the insurgents' chief supporters in Castletownshend. But they had never forgotten what the Somervilles had done for them, and stayed their hands and those of their confederates accordingly.

Edith Somerville herself, while not openly supportive of the rebels, had grown to be sympathetic to the cause of Home Rule, and after the Treaty of 1921 felt that the Irish people should accept the Dominion status offered by the British government. She admired Michael Collins, and when he made his last, fatal trip to West Cork in August 1922, she went with her brother Cameron to Skibbereen to complain to the great man about the IRA detachment that was occupying part of Castletownshend. The date was 22 August. Collins apologised for being unable to spare any troops, then set off back towards Bandon and a sniper's bullet.

Boyle Townshend Somerville was another of Edith's brothers, a Navy man who had risen to the rank of Vice-Admiral. A few years after the end of the Civil War he retired with his family to The Point, where he lived quietly and on good terms with everyone. Among the various duties he undertook during his retirement was giving advice to local young men who were thinking of joining the British Navy. They would come to The Point to have a chat with the Admiral, who from his knowledge of their circumstances and aptitudes could give them a fair idea whether they would be likely to succeed in their applications. A harmless and useful way of contributing to the welfare of the community, it seemed at the time.

His son, Michael, was sixteen when Boyle Somerville came back to Castletownshend. I'd got in touch with Michael, now living in England, before I returned to Ireland for the last stage of the walk, hoping to learn some more Somerville history. We met for lunch in an Oxfordshire pub, and there, sitting at a table in the shadows of the bar, I heard the story of Boyle Somerville's death. As Michael Somerville, now eighty-three years old, relived the events of that night

in March 1936, memories of another story of violent death told to
me in another bar rose in my mind. I saw again the elderly man from
Limerick in the pub at Emlagh on the Dingle Peninsula, leaning
across the table, speaking quietly of Black and Tans fixing their
bayonets in a field in County Cork to finish off his wounded uncle;
an English Army officer ordering them to let him die 'a soldier's
death'; a farm cart jolting towards Mallow hospital with the dying
Republican.

'It was 24 March, 1936. My mother and father were at dinner, alone
in the house. They had a couple of servants, as everyone did in those
days, but they had gone out to a party in Castletownshend village hall.

'Around nine o'clock in the evening there was a knock at the front
door. The young men my father had been interviewing used to turn
up at the house at all hours of the day and night, and my father –
who wore a dinner jacket and a boiled shirt every night of his life –
said to my mother, "Oh, that'll be one of my boys."

'When he opened the door there were two men standing outside.
One of them said, "Are you Admiral Somerville?" "Yes," my father
said, and they shot him. He fell down across his own doorstep. Then
they shot out all the lights in the hall – we had oil lamps in those
days, no electricity – and threw in a note saying "Admiral Somerville
has been sending Irish boys to serve the British Empire, but he will
send no more." Then they ran off, just as my mother came on the
scene: she had heard the shots. The two men were actually stopped
nearby by the Gardai – for having no driving licence. They questioned
them, and then let them go. They weren't local men.

'The whole village turned out for the funeral. They carried my
father's coffin all the way from the house down to the church, with
people kneeling in the street. Everyone in Castletownshend loved
him.'

Slowly but surely, the old threads that bound the Protestant families
to each other and to Castletownshend are working loose. Somervilles
no longer live at The Point. Glenbarrahane has been demolished,
and there are no Coghills in the village nowadays. The castle still has
its Townshends, however, and Rocket House its Chavasses. And up
at the top of the village, in slate-hung Drishane, where Edith Somerville and Violet Martin brought Major Sinclair Yeates and his cronies

to life, Somervilles live on. I would have liked to have roamed around that house, to have stood in the dining room thinking of the cousins giggling over an outrageous passage as they worked there together. But Edith's great-nephew was not at home.

Thick mist cloaked my last day's march, but I had two good reasons not to mind. One was internal and personal: the hunger for the end of the road. Quite frankly, I could have been walking blindfold for all the attention I paid to what little I saw each side of those mazy lanes. They were leading me south and west for the last time. All I wanted to do was to gobble them up as quickly as possible.

The other reason came on four stumpy legs and wholly unbidden: a tiny, sharp-nosed, wire-haired brown imp of a dog, who led me a merry dance over the hills. He threw in his lot with me halfway between Castletownshend and Baltimore, and frisked in front like an amiable, hyperactive sprite. Perhaps that's what he was. At each side turning and crossroads I found him waiting, head alertly cocked, trembling with impatience. He dived between the bars of garden gates, leaped up on to the stone walls and burrowed in the banks. I have never seen so much vitality in so small a frame. When I got to the main road a mile from Baltimore, he simply vanished.

Baltimore harbour looks out to the low back of Sherkin Island, lying in a ragged lump across the entrance to Roaringwater Bay. No one would come to the village of Baltimore for a rowdy seaside holiday. There are more trawlers than cars on the waterfront down here, where West Cork fragments into its component parts of cliff, headland, island and sea. Baltimore has a wild enough history, however: there was a time when Algerian pirates would cruise this coast, looking for pickings. On 19 June 1631, piloted through the obstacle course of rocks and islets in the bay by a local fisherman, they landed in Baltimore in search of human plunder. The pirates wreaked havoc in the village in the few hours they were ashore, and sailed away with scores of people – many of them English settlers – to sell into slavery along the Barbary coast. On my way down the street I passed a pub named 'The Algerian' in memory of that catastrophic raid. In McCarthy's bar on the quay I subsided into a seat and waited for the boat to Cape Clear Island.

'You'll see my husband Concubhar on the boat,' Eleanor O'Driscoll had told me on the phone, 'and I'll be waiting at the jetty for you.' I didn't meet Concubhar O'Driscoll on the hour-long passage out to Cape Clear Island – he was busy in the wheelhouse of *Naomh Ciarán II*, the island's green-and-white painted ferry. A handful of people were on the boat, along with a crate of stores, some barrels of beer and bundles and boxes of this and that. Five or six blue-uniformed schoolchildren larked around the deck, teasing each other: 'I saw you down behind the gym there, smoking away!' These were Cape Clear's teenagers, on their way home from school. The island's population has been steadily in decline, as the old folk die off and the younger ones leave for mainland jobs and bright lights. But the impression I got from out on the rolling swell of Roaringwater Bay was of an island full of houses. They lay scattered over the northern slopes among their small fields, sprinkled in tiny cubes of white and grey above the cliffs and coves. The domed back of the island rose to touch the dark clouds. On the summit of Cape Clear two wind generators faced seaward, whirling their blades round like thin men doing arm exercises.

A good number of the island's 140 people were gathered on the jetty as the ferry slid in between the rocky arms of the North Harbour. Two bird-watchers humped their packs and walked eagerly away down the quay, heading for their windy lookouts on the hill. Cape Clear is famous for rare migrating birds blown in by the autumn gales, and now that the tourists' season had all but finished the bird-watchers had taken their place. There would be few visitors now until spring. More Irish than English would be spoken in the pubs and houses until the outside world intruded once more. Wind and weather were closing in on Cape Clear, drawing a curtain of isolation across the eight miles of sea between island and mainland.

I threw my pack into the boot of Eleanor O'Driscoll's rattletrap car and we chugged and spluttered along the narrow lanes, stopping to leave a parcel from the boat at a neighbour's house, climbing up An Gleann to where the O'Driscolls' bungalow looked out across the mouth of South Harbour. Concubhar would follow once he had seen to the boat, bringing his daughters Aisling ('a dream come true') and Croiona ('the beloved'). Unknown to me, they had been among the perky crowd of children aboard *Naomh Ciarán II*. Later that evening I would get to know them and their younger sister Verona and little brother Concubhar Og. We would sit round a candle-lit table while wind and rain battered the windows, raising a glass of wine to the end of my journey. There would be hot whiskey toddies, warm words of congratulation, kisses and hugs for the stranger. All the hospitality of Ireland would seem to gather in that little house on the hill. But before relaxing into celebration, there was one more step for me to take.

The tiny plastic doll's shoe had slid down to the remotest corner of the inside pocket of my anorak. On the wind-whipped headland that marked the southernmost point of Ireland, I sat down on the grass and drew the shoe out between finger and thumb from the place where it had been lying since that April morning when I had picked it up on Banba's Crown in far-off Donegal. The seven hundred miles from Malin Head had stained it with mud and ink, filled it with fluff and worn its edges smooth and shiny. I held it in my palm and gazed out at the rain-shrouded Atlantic, thinking of many things. Irish folklore says that shoes bring good luck to the traveller, and this shoe had done that.

Beside me on the hillside a blade of grey stone stuck out of the grass. I prised it out, slipped the little shoe into the hole and pushed the stone back in place. Let some future traveller find it there. In the meantime, let the good luck rest at the end of the road to Roaringwater.

INDEX

One Summer's Grace
A Family Voyage Round Britain

Libby Purves

In the summer of 1988 Libby Purves and her husband Paul Heiney set sail in their cutter *Grace O'Malley* with their children Nicholas, aged five, and Rose, three. They sailed the 1,700 miles around Britain, from the offshore labyrinths of the sandy south-east to the towering stacks of Cape Wrath and back home through the North Sea. Her account of the voyage is a new classic of the sea.

'It is that rarest of all books on the yachting shelf – a work of acerbic realism. Libby Purves is wonderfully sharp on the woes of containing a marriage and a family inside their pressure-cooker of a small boat. Her portrait of coastal Britain in the 1980s is wise, affectionate and sceptical; her pleasure in our scary seas rings true because there is not a word of cant or overstatement in her story. This is how it is – and Miss Purves tells it beautifully'

Jonathan Raban

'A delightful book, warm, wise and candid'　　*Sunday Telegraph*

Coleridge Walks the Fells
A Lakeland Journey Retraced

Alan Hankinson
Foreword by Melvyn Bragg

In August 1802, Samuel Taylor Coleridge set out on a nine-day walk around the Lake District. Struggling against opium addiction and marital problems, he climbed among the Lake District's highest mountains, visited most of its lakes, and sat down on the summit of Scafell to write a letter to the woman he was in love with, Sara Hutchinson.

Alan Hankinson, well-known author, broadcaster and resident of Cumbria, has retraced Coleridge's steps in circumstances as close as possible to the original walk. His book is at once a vivid recreation of Coleridge's walk; a compelling record of Hankinson's present-day impressions; and an account of the complex journey made by the Lake District itself in almost two centuries.

'For anyone seeking an escape from the pressures of life this book provides a valuable inspiration.'   *Lancashire Evening Post*

'Rich in literary interest . . . and a pungent and thoughtful commentary on everything from hill farming and rock climbing to the utter devastation of Wordsworth's holy village of Hawkshead.'
                                        William Scammel, *Spectator*

ISBN 0 00 637854 4

HarperCollins Paperbacks – Non-Fiction

HarperCollins is a leading publisher of paperback non-fiction. Below are some recent titles.

- ☐ STORM COMMAND Peter De La Billiere £5.99
- ☐ THE NEW EMPERORS Harrison Salisbury £8.99
- ☐ HAROLD WILSON Ben Pimlott £9.99
- ☐ AN AGENDA FOR BRITAIN Frank Field £6.99
- ☐ JUDY GARLAND David Shipman £6.99
- ☐ MARLENE DIETRICH Stephen Bach £7.99
- ☐ THE HONOURABLE COMPANY John Keay £8.99
- ☐ BRAVER MEN WALK AWAY Peter Gurney £5.99
- ☐ THIS IS ORSON WELLES Ed. Peter Bogdanovich £6.99

You can buy HarperCollins Paperbacks at your local bookshops or newsagents. Or you can order them from HarperCollins Paperbacks, Cash Sales Department, Box 29, Douglas, Isle of Man. Please send a cheque, postal or money order (not currency) worth the price plus 24p per book for postage (maximum postage required is £3.00 for orders within the UK).

NAME (Block letters)_____

ADDRESS_____

_____

While every effort is made to keep prices low, it is sometimes necessary to increase them at short notice. HarperCollins Paperbacks reserve the right to show new retail prices on covers which may differ from those previously advertised in the text or elsewhere.